Camillus

Camillus

A Study of Indo-European
Religion as Roman History

by

Georges Dumézil

Edited, with an Introduction, by

Udo Strutynski

Translations by
Annette Aronowicz
and
Josette Bryson

UNIVERSITY OF CALIFORNIA PRESS
Berkeley   Los Angeles   London

University of California Press
Berkeley and Los Angeles, California

University of California Press, Ltd.
London, England

Library of Congress Cataloging in Publication Data

Dumézil, Georges, 1898–
    Camillus: a study of Indo-European religion as
Roman history.

    Translation of portions of Mythe et épopée (v. 3)
and Fêtes romaines d'été et d'automne suivi de Dix
questions romaines.
    Includes bibliographical references and index.
    1. Mythology, Roman.   2. Mythology, Indo-
European.   3. Camillus, Marcus Furius, d. B.C. 365.
4. Rome—History—to 510 B.C.   I. Strutynski, Udo.
II. Title.
BL805.D77   292'.07   80-36771
ISBN 0-520-02841-4

Printed in the United States of America

1 2 3 4 5 6 7 8 9

Editor's Dedication

In memoriam

GEOFFREY ASHTON

sunt lacrimae rerum et mentem mortalia tangunt

Contents

Contents

Contents

Editor's Preface

Many hands worked to make this translation a reality. The honor of receiving first mention belongs to Annette Aronowicz, whose initial draft set the standards of precision that all subsequent versions were to follow. Unhappily, the urgency of other commitments kept her from seeing the project through to its completion.

The present text is essentially the work of Josette Bryson and three members of a translation workshop that she directed at UCLA: Patricia Barlow, Patricia Dowling, and James Needham. For over a year they labored unstintingly to render Professor Dumézil's elegant and often difficult French into accurate and readable English.

Professor Jaan Puhvel was kind enough to scrutinize the results, and the suggestions he offered markedly improved the text. Final revisions then were made by the editor, who accepts full responsibility for any infelicities that remain.

Two further points should be noted. First, the English text incorporates twelve small but crucial modifications that the author made specifically for this translation. Second, in the present edition, citations from classical authors and other religious and historical documents have been taken from the following English translations: John Dryden's translation, revised by Arthur H. Clough, for Plutarch's *Lives of the Noble Grecians and Romans* (New York, 1932); H. J. Rose, *The Roman Questions of Plutarch: A New*

Translation with Introductory Essays and a Running Commentary (New York, 1974); and Philomen Holland, trans., *"Of Brotherly Love or Amity" in Plutarch's 'Moralia': Twenty Essays* (New York, 1911). For Livy and Ovid, B. O. Foster, trans., *Livy* (London, 1919–1959), and Sir James George Frazer, trans., *Ovid's Fasti* (London, 1931), were the editions consulted. English citations from the Rig Veda were taken from H. H. Wilson, trans., *Rig-Veda-Sanhita*, 4 vols. (London, 1850–1866). Occasionally, a word or two has been quietly altered for the purpose of achieving greater accuracy or consistency in rendering the technical terms. Unless indicated otherwise in a footnote, all other citations have been freshly translated for this edition by taking into account not only the original but also the French translation cited by Dumézil, and by consulting a variety of printed English versions. This was done principally to keep the English reader as close as possible to the precise language of the texts on which Dumézil based his analysis.

Introduction

It is particularly apposite that Georges Dumézil should have chosen to study the career of Marcus Furius Camillus for each, in his way, is a second Adam. Camillus is the putative second founder of Rome, who retook the city in a characteristically stunning attack at daybreak after it had fallen to the Gauls, while Dumézil is recognized as the father of the "new comparative mythology,"[1] a discipline whose older versions had collapsed from the weight of their own errors. Both, too, had their difficulties. The Roman citizenry repaid Camillus for the victories he brought them by exiling him for supposed impiety, while Dumézil—*pace* Pound[2]—had to strive for forty years, out of key with the specialists and structuralists of his time, to resuscitate the consciousness of a dead civilization, to regain "the truth" in the old sense. Each was eventually vindicated: Camillus was entrusted with dictatorial powers an unprecedented five times, straddling his exile; Dumézil was finally honored in October 1978 with an invitation to complete the ranks of the "forty immortals" of the Académie Française, an election that caused *Le Monde* to comment wryly, "On rend quelquefois justice bien tard."[3]

[1] The phrase was coined by C. Scott Littleton. See his *The New Comparative Mythology: An Anthropological Assessment of the Theories of Georges Dumézil*, 2d ed. (Berkeley and Los Angeles, 1973).

[2] See Ezra Pound, "E. P. Ode Pour L'Election de Son Sepulchre I" from "Hugh Selwyn Mauberley (Life and Contacts)."

[3] *Le Monde* (Paris), 28 Oct. 1978, p. 29.

1

From another point of view, it appears unthinkable that Dumézil should have tackled the problem of Camillus, for the interpretation he gives of the protagonist, as protégé of the dawn goddess Mater Matuta, is redolent of the solar mythology that was discredited at the beginning of this century. No one who is in the least familiar with the work of Dumézil could take the possibility of such a regression seriously; but Dumézil's debt to the solar mythologists is greater here than one might think, so it might well be profitable to glance backward at the history of scholarship in order to appreciate more fully the subtlety and splendor of Dumézil's insights and to situate the chronicle of Camillus within the interpretative context to which it properly belongs.

The great system-builders of the past centuries were all universalists of a sort. Unfortunately, most of them were far better collectors than thinkers. Like the pre-Socratics, they approached their data with the naive assumption that it could be reduced to a central principle explicable in terms of a basal, controlling metaphor.[4] Just as Thales had posited that everything is somehow composed of water, while Anaximenes preferred to think in terms of air and Heraclitus saw varying disguises of fire, so Tylor translated religious phenomena into the metaphor of the soul and Müller and his school into metaphors of the sun, storms, or wild beasts, while Frazer saw dying gods, and Jung posited archetypes or neo-Augustinian *rationes seminales* that belie the doctrine of the mind as *tabula rasa*.[5]

---

[4] An excellent treatment of metaphor can be found in Philip Wheelwright, "The Semantic Approach to Myth," in Thomas A. Sebeok, ed., *Myth: A Symposium* (Bloomington, 1968), pp. 154–168. See also Adolf E. Jensen, *Myth and Cult Among Primitive Peoples*, trans. Marianna Tax Choldin and Wolfgang Weissleder (Chicago and London, 1963) for a discussion of the intellectual sophistication of "primitive" peoples, a view confirmed from another angle by Claude Lévi-Strauss in *The Savage Mind* (Chicago, 1966).

[5] Recommended reference works dealing with the history of scholarship in myth and religion are: Jan de Vries, *Forschungsgeschichte der Mythologie* (Freiburg and Munich, 1961); idem, *Perspectives in the History of Religions*, trans. Kees W.

The influences on Dumézil that managed to stick involve metaphors of greater sophistication and abstraction. They comprise, on the one hand, society, and on the other, language. The first tended toward theory; the second depended on data. In time, Dumézil was to modify both in order to forge from them a new entelechy. Their importance as influences requires that one pay closer attention to their complexities.

The roots of the sociological approach—to which Dumézil was exposed in its Durkheimian form through the agency of two Marcels, Mauss and Granet—can be reached by a commodius vicus of recirculation. The *Scienza nuova*[6] that Giambattista Vico developed in the first half of the eighteenth century proceeds from the principle that the human mind cannot fathom anything except what it itself has made. Thus, God and nature are beyond comprehension, and the only study proper to mankind is its works and days. Specifically, its object is the myriad types of human collectivity formed in the matrix of history. This view enabled Vico to succeed better than anyone else of his day at grasping the complexity of myth. In tabulating the ingredients of mythogenesis, Vico listed four elements: creative imagination, religious inspiration, natural phenomena, and the structural organization of society. The fourth of these was adapted by Durkheim to become one of his most important axioms: significant social and cultural realities are "collectively represented" by supernatural beings and concepts.[7] Vico's genius lay in preserving the importance of the other three, but it was Durkheim's thought that gave impetus to Dumézil, at least in the early stages.

Bolle (Berkeley and Los Angeles, 1977); Burton Feldman and Robert D. Richardson, eds., *The Rise of Modern Mythology 1680–1860* (Bloomington and London, 1972); and William A. Lessa and Evon Z. Vogt, eds., *Reader in Comparative Religion: An Anthropological Approach*, 2d ed. (New York, Evanston, and London, 1965).

[6] Thomas Goddard Bergin and Max Harold Fisch, trans., *The New Science of Giambattista Vico* (New York, 1961). See also Giorgio Tagliacozzo and Hayden V. White, eds., *Giambattista Vico: An International Symposium* (Baltimore, 1969).

[7] Cf. Émile Durkheim, *The Elementary Forms of the Religious Life* (London, 1915).

The kind of comparativism that served as Dumézil's other major source began as philology with the recognition that a dominant number of language families ranging over an area from Iceland to India must all have sprung from a common source. The people who spoke this hypothetical mother tongue have been called variously "Indo-Aryan," "Indo-Germanic," and "Indo-European." Sometime between the third and second millennia B.C., they began to disperse in waves, moving in all directions away from their trans-Caspian homeland. Their progress was swift, for they had domesticated the horse and this gave them a distinct advantage in overrunning the populations they encountered en route. Eventually the waves crashed into each other—Celts fighting Romans, Germans driving out Celts, Dorian Greeks slaughtering Mycenaean Greeks—without any of the parties recognizing that their origin and heritage were shared with their opponents. Of course, virtually all that these migrators had in common were bloodlines and linguistic correspondences, both of which were attenuated over time and space and through contact with other peoples. The task the early philologists set themselves was to reconstruct, from the evidence of scattered dialects, a proto-Indo-European language that might have been spoken at the exact moment of dispersion. Another group of early researchers found it profitable to focus less on the forms, as such, of these daughter languages and more on the cultural attitudes that the languages transmitted. And with this new emphasis, comparative mythology was born.

Its principal exponent was Max Müller. Like the philologists, he wanted to get to the very beginnings of things, so he took as his starting point the intuition that, just as the daughter languages are corruptions of the "Aryan" mother tongue, so the later myths of Greece and elsewhere are paraphrases and narrative elaborations arising from a misunderstanding of an original—and literal—concern with sunrises and sunsets. "Aryan" is the mother tongue of the human race, he opined, "a living language spoken in Asia by a small tribe, nay, originally by a small family living under one and the same roof." By hypothesizing that this early language was incapable of abstraction, Müller was able to concoct a scenario of how the all-important solar imagery of its original speakers came to be distorted into *Gelehrtenmärchen* among daughter cultures whose languages had developed abstraction: "When we speak of the sun following the dawn, the ancient poets could only speak and think of the Sun loving and embracing the dawn. What is with us a sunset, was to them the Sun growing old, decaying, or dying. Our sunrise was to them the Night giving birth to a brilliant child."[8]

Owing for the most part to a tenacious lack of flexibility in the exposition of his argument, Müller and his school were eventually discredited by the efforts of Andrew Lang.[9] For, while the solar element is central to many a myth—including that of Camillus— none of them quite fits the a priori mold that Müller had prepared for it. And most myths were patently concerned with other matters, so that Müller's reductive efforts created a yawning gap between text and interpretation. But it would be a mistake to sell Müller short altogether. He correctly assessed the role of metaphor in utterance and exegesis, and by recognizing that language is the prime vehicle for ideas, he laid the groundwork for future genetic comparison of the myths of the same language family.

[8] Cf. Feldman and Richardson, *Rise*, p. 481.

[9] Cf. Richard M. Dorson, "The Eclipse of Solar Mythology," in Sebeok, *Myth*, pp. 25–63. Jan de Vries, *Perspectives*, pp. 87–88 neatly distils the essence of one of Müller's excesses: "To illustrate the type of explanation presented by Max Müller, I want to mention the Indian goddess *Saraṇyū*. With Kuhn, he attaches importance to the similar sound of the Greek *Erinys*. Still he does not consider her the personification of the thundercloud but, again, the dawn of day. Therefore, he compares her to Ushas, and particularly so because both are the mothers of twins (Saraṇyū is especially known as mother of the Aśvins, celebrated twin deities in the Vedic pantheon). However, Athena is also a mother of twins. Hence Athena is another goddess of morning twilight; proof is the myth of her birth from Zeus's head, as the morning twilight is born from the eastern sky. (After all, the east in India is called 'mūrdhā divaḥ' or forehead of heaven!) Now Athena's wisdom is explained, if only one thinks of the Sanskrit verb *'budh,'* which means both 'to awaken' and 'to know,' for the goddess who awakens men also leads them to knowledge."

As a way of repaying this debt to Müller, we should perhaps dwell a moment on the interrelationships among knowledge, metaphor, symbol, and myth. Knowledge is *intentional* existence. By becoming the thing known without ceasing to be itself, knowledge is both process and object. Knowledge expands by metaphoric translation of the unknown into what is already familiar. This interplay generates symbols that acquire new meanings by the process of recombination. Müller saw that myth in its early stages involved the contraction of raw elements of experience into a single concrete symbol charged with significance. He called this symbol a "diaphor," to underscore its creative novelty. Müller also realized that abstract symbols could follow the same line of semantic development, resulting in concepts that may be satisfying but bear no relation to experience. These concepts were mere names, not explanations of anything real—in Müller's words, *nomina*, not *numina*. But his criticism was misplaced by being thrust against the ancient mythographers. The true "disease of language" was to be found in the gaggle of free-standing reductive metaphors produced by many of his scholarly contemporaries. It is also a pity that Müller's critical eye failed to perceive the absurdity of giving his own solar metaphors a universal dimension.[10]

Looking back on the work of the early comparativists, Dumézil identified the key errors that made their strategy go awry. The linguists erred in not realizing that Indo-European dialects must have already reached an advanced stage of development well before the diaspora, so their work could not bear fruit until they ceased to linger over the unknown stages of evolution and began applying the comparative method to what was already known. The mythologists, for their part, made three basic methodological blunders: (1) in subject matter, they compared mythologies in isolation from the social and cultural contexts that had spawned them; (2) in method, they interpreted myth according to a priori systems; and (3) in assessing the relationship between language and myth, they relied too heavily on onomastic correspondences—

[10] Cf. Wheelwright, "Semantic," pp. 156 ff.

which do no more than confirm a common Indo-European origin—at the expense of functional correspondences which are a far more reliable index in comparative analysis.[11]

The importance of the sociological outlook to Dumézil is evident from these objections, which reveal his concern for cultural totalities, the workings of history, and a scientific method that is objectively verifiable. But it would be vain to think that the social metaphors of Vico or Durkheim were fully adequate to meet these concerns. Man has no more created society *ex nihilo* than he has created language, and the best minds of our species have had to admit that, in essence, they understand the one as dimly as the other. Nor are things so simple that they can be explained by saying that the social order serves as the model and touchstone for the collective creation of a supernatural order. There is reciprocity between the two, to be sure, but to ask which one came first would simply be to pose the problem of the chicken and the egg in other terms.[12] Dumézil came to realize the weakness of this conceit nearly a decade and a half after he had launched his own method of interpretation:

> I recognized toward 1950 that the "tripartite ideology" was not necessarily accompanied, in the life of a society, by a *real* tripartite division of that society according to the Indian mode; on the contrary, I recognized that, wherever one can establish its presence, the tripartite ideology is nothing (or is no longer, or perhaps never was) but an ideal and, at the same time, a method of analysis [*moyen d'analyser*], a method of interpreting the forces which assure the course of the world and the lives of men.[13]

---

[11] Cf. Georges Dumézil, *Mythe et épopée I: L'idéologie des trois fonctions dans les épopées des peuples indo-européens*, 2d ed. (Paris, 1974), pp. 9–11.

[12] See Alexander Goldenweiser, "Religion and Society: A Critique of Émile Durkheim's Theory of the Origin and Nature of Religion," repr. in Lessa and Vogt, *Reader*, pp. 65–72.

[13] Translation from C. Scott Littleton, " 'Je ne suis pas . . . structuraliste': Some Fundamental Differences between Dumézil and Lévi-Strauss," *Journal of Asian Studies* 34 (1974), 154, n. 12.

This "tripartite ideology" which Dumézil speaks of represents his unique solution to the problem of finding an object and a method proper to the science of comparative Indo-European mythology. It is the key to the thought patterns that characterized the Indo-European linguistic continuum, and a bare-bones sketch of it might look like this: on the abstract level, there is a set of three hierarchically ordered concepts; the first concerns the maintenance of cosmic and juridical order, the second involves the exercise of physical prowess, and the third governs health, wealth, fertility, and a host of related notions. In concrete terms, this pattern could be found endlessly replicated, from triads of diseases to three-fold conceptions of space;[14] but its important manifestations fall into three major modes: the social, the theological, and the literary. The prime example of the social level is the Indic class division into priests, warriors, and herdsmen–farmers (*brāhmaṇa, kṣatriya,* and *vaiśya*) which were paralleled in Rome by a similar division into *sacerdotes, milites,* and *Quirites,* respectively. The organization of the pantheon mirrors this configuration. Atop the Indic Olympus is Varuṇa, the cosmic sovereign, and Mitra, his juridical partner. They are followed by the war god Indra and, last, by the Aśvin, the twin equine tutelary divinities of the third estate. Their respective Roman counterparts are Jupiter and Dius Fidius, Mars, and Quirinus; each, with the exception of Dius Fidius who is little attested, is served by a high priest belonging to the order of *flamines maiores.* The literary level is too complex to allow a cursory summary to be adequate. It involves a transformation from either or both of the other two modes rather than a mirroring, and it encompasses a variety of genres ranging from epic to pseudo-history. The most important examples in this category are the *Mahābhārata,* wherein the five Pāṇḍava brothers serve as incarnations of the chief gods of the Vedic pantheon; the early history of

[14] Cf. Jaan Puhvel, "Mythological Reflections of Indo-European Medicine," in George Cardona, Henry M. Hoenigswald, and Alfred Senn, eds., *Indo-European and Indo-Europeans* (Philadelphia, 1970), pp. 369–382; also Dumézil, *Mythe et épopée I,* pp. 125–144 and M. Molé, "Le partage du monde dans la tradition iranienne," *Journal asiatique* 239 (1952), 283–298.

Rome, which contains the bulk of what evidence there is for the persistence of an Indo-European heritage there; and the folklore of the Ossets, which serves a similar preservative function for these descendants of the Scyths. It remains to be said that the articulation of this pattern loses complexity once one leaves the Indic sphere, so that the only other national traditions rich enough to offer an amplitude of comparative data are those of Iran, Rome, and Scandinavia.

There is a remarkable mixture of audacity and prudence in Dumézil's synthesis. Its appeal comes from its limitations. There can be no doubt that "tripartition" is also a metaphor, but what distinguishes it from the metaphors of other scholars is its empirical grounding in the textual data. The source of this cognitive model lies not in the mind of Dumézil but in the collective wisdom of the Indo-Europeans who produced it at some point during their period of unity as a "moyen d'analyser" or *Weltanschauung*. Thus, tripartition is not an a priori imposition but an a posteriori recognition. This, in itself, is no mean accomplishment, and Marcel Granet, who taught Dumézil how to conduct a proper *explication de texte*, must be given the lion's share of the credit for it. After all, Dumézil's initial insight, formed in the mid-1930s, that a typological nexus should exist between the pre-Capitoline triad of Jupiter, Mars, and Quirinus (based on the earlier Umbrian triad Juu—, Mart—, and Vofiono— found in the Iguvine tablets) and the class division of ancient India was not immediately apparent; it took discipline and digging to find the hypothesis confirmed in such details as the isomorphic links between the Vedic *rājan* and his brahman chaplain on the one hand, and the pair formed by the *rex* and the first of the *flamines maiores* on the other.[15]

---

[15] In his preface to *Mythe et épopée I*, esp. pp. 13–15, Dumézil recounts the history of his search for the right road. He published his first intimations in an article, "La préhistoire indo-iranienne des castes," *Journal asiatique* 216 (1930), 109–130. Émile Benveniste read Dumézil's original draft and suggested improvements. Two years later Benveniste adduced new arguments in support of the position in his "Les classes sociales dans la tradition avestique," *Journal asiatique* 221 (1932), 117–134.

The paradox of "less is more," so popular with the political ecologists of today, points to yet another strength inherent in Dumézil's limits. By eschewing the lure of false universality, Dumézil was left free to linger over the all-important details that make or break any comparison, and to achieve expertise in the various facets of Indo-European language and culture. It is no accident that the position created for him at Collège de France was called the Chair of Indo-European Civilization, and in that sense it is inexact to continue referring to Dumézil as simply a comparative mythologist. If Dumézil's integration of the best features of the sociological method with genetic comparativism at all altered the shape of his scholarly profile, then it made a historian of him, as much governed by Clio as were Thucydides and Toynbee. It is less easy to define his field of history, for its object is certainly not to reconstruct the values of proto-Indo-European society. Neither is its aim to analyze all cognitive aspects of the daughter cultures *in themselves.* Between these two poles rests the touchstone of Dumézil's solution, a construct that exists nowhere in time or space because it is a *typology*—a set of abstractions drawn from the evidence preserved in all the individual linguistic traditions and projected back as a scheme to measure the articulation of each piece of empirical source data. One must be clear that this typology is really a common denominator and is valid only for those fractions that have been fed into it. The contents this denominator encompasses are obvious reflections of the time of Indo-European unity, but one can hardly suppose that the sum of these reflections gives back the full picture. For this reason, it is somewhat misleading to follow the common practice and render Dumézil's terms "idéologie," "fonction," and "structure" into their English cognates, as these *faux amis* tend to give the impression of something far more monolithic than was conveyed by the original term. As an ideology in our sense, tripartition is somewhat like the tip of the iceberg, and thus hardly belongs in the same league with Scholasticism or Marxism. And while "function" may serve as a convenient shorthand to designate both the abstract principle (e.g., sovereignty) and its concrete unfoldings (e.g., priest, king), the term "structure," so readily transformed into a legitimate ideology by the suffix "-ism," has led to much misunderstanding and, indeed, bitterness. The structuralism that has its roots in the Prague school of linguistics, was first applied to narrative by Vladimir Propp,[16] and was carried to the utmost refinement by the ethnological analyses of Claude Lévi-Strauss, is indeed a monolith of universal dimensions, as it seeks to penetrate to their core the invariable workings of the human mind. However laudable this ambition, its operations exclude the kind of history that serves as a key distinguishing factor between Indo-European tripartition and universal binary opposition. And, as Dumézil has better sense than to mix metaphors, especially when they occur on different levels, he has strenuously resisted the *vade mecum* of the structuralist movement. That he should have been constrained to take public issue with its protagonists' indiscriminate criticism indicates the seriousness of the confusion.[17]

---

[16] *Morphology of the Folktale*, 2d ed. (Austin and London, 1968).

[17] The ahistorical bias of Lévi-Strauss is borne out in the last chapter of *Savage Mind*, pp. 245–269. A kindred spirit, A. J. Greimas, even went so far as to "improve" on Dumézil's analysis of certain Roman, Indic, and Celtic myths in "Comparative Mythology," from Pierre Maranda, ed., *Mythology* (Baltimore, 1972), pp. 162–170. In his introduction to *Mythe et épopée III* (Paris, 1973), p. 14, Dumézil makes his position clear: "In the course of the last several years the word 'structure' has become ambiguous. While retaining its former precise value when, for example, it is a question of the structure of a demonstration, of a novel, or of a state, it has taken on a much more ambitious technical usage in a philosophical system which today is very much in vogue, a system to which it has, indeed, given its name. The result has been confusion. Some have taken it upon themselves to rank my work—and, according to the several authors concerned, this has been either a matter of praise or a criticism—among the current manifestations or, given the dates involved, among the forerunners of structuralism. Indeed, it happens that some young structuralists are impatient about my slowness or my incapacity to follow the progress of the doctrine and the interpretative techniques which it inspires, and they would teach me by supportive examples of the use to which the more agile or orthodox spirits among them have already been able to put my data. I should like to put an end to these pointless favors: I am not, I have never been, nor will I ever be a structuralist." (Translation from Littleton, " 'Je ne suis pas,' " 151.)

Having defined Dumézil's field of inquiry as both the identification of what is unique about the Indo-European world-view and the analysis of the extent to which each of the individual national traditions has conserved the elements of its ancestral heritage, it becomes important to note two points: (1) tripartition is only the key cluster of a rich typology, and (2) the Indo-European pattern is cultural and hence organic, that is, subject to growth and development, both during the time of unity and certainly after the dispersion, when the migrators were exposed to shifting necessities and foreign influences. Thus, the comparativist must maintain a dynamic balance between the inflexible reality of the data and the contingent entelechy of its panoramic diaphor, the matter and form of his enterprise.

The fact that tripartition is the key but not the door, or what lies beyond, takes nothing away from its value; rather, it gives its role a certain precision. Most other Indo-European elements, when they are studied closely enough in their contexts, eventually manifest some relation to the tripartite order. Still, there are some divinities that appear to be outside the system. The Roman Janus and Vesta, the Indic Vāyu and Agni, and the Norse Heimdall, to name but a few, play relatively minor—though not unimportant—roles in the greater drama; others, like the Scandinavian Loki, act out larger portions of the central conflict.[18] Another main division of this nontripartite category encompasses highly developed rituals such as those involving the horse, which was so important to the ecology of the Indo-Europeans. Examples include the Indic *aśvamedha*, the Roman *October equus,* and similar Celtic practices involving royalty and fertility which have reflexes also in Scandi-

---

[18] Cf. Dumézil, "La tripartition indo-européenne," *Psyche* 2 (1947), 1348–1356, where he devised a category for the minor divinities typically concerned with beginnings and endings as the "épine du système." Although this term has not been much in evidence in Dumézil's subsequent writings, some form of comparison of the less prominent Indo-European deities, possibly leading to systematic classification, is highly desirable, if only to put tripartition into proper focus.

navia.[19] Finally, there exist narrative elaborations on the activities of members of one or another segment of the tripartite order. The most common of these cluster around the role of the Divine Twins, who are found engaging in the rescue of their sister, the sun-maiden, from the clutches of an abductor in examples that range throughout the Indo-European spectrum.[20] Two aspects of this category involve Camillus, as we shall see below: the parallelism between the Indic dawn goddess Uṣas and her Roman counterpart Mater Matuta, and the ritual articulation of Mater Matuta's role in Roman worship.

In speaking of process and change, one must be careful to distinguish between what occurred before the dispersion and what came after. For example, one is hard pressed to find within the touchstone tradition of India any elaborate attestations to the theme in which the two superior orders gang up on the third estate in a successful effort to integrate it into the system;[21] yet at Rome there is the account of the rape of the Sabine women—who literally represent fertility—by a Roman society consisting exclusively (and improbably!) of men acting as representatives of sovereignty and force. And this historicized myth is paralleled in Scandinavian mythology proper by the war between the gods of the Indo-European invaders, the Aesir, headed by Odin and Thor, and the so-called indigenous Vanir group of nourishment divinities, which included Frey, Njord, and the like. The independence of the Scandinavian account from the one given at Rome indicates that we

[19] Cf. Jaan Puhvel, "Aspects of Equine Functionality," in Puhvel, ed., *Myth and Law Among the Indo-Europeans: Studies in Indo-European Comparative Mythology* (Berkeley and Los Angeles, 1970), pp. 159–172.

[20] Cf. Donald Ward, *The Divine Twins: An Indo-European Myth in Germanic Tradition* (Berkeley and Los Angeles, 1968), which, despite its limiting subtitle, offers an adequate coverage of this theme throughout the Indo-European continuum.

[21] All Indic tradition tells us is that the canonical divinities of the third level, the Aśvins, were not incorporated into the society of gods until after a violent conflict with "two forces" (*ubhe vīrye*), which was followed by reconciliation and a pact. See Dumézil, *L'idéologie tripartie des indo-européens* (Brussels, 1958), p. 56.

have here a recounting of a quasi-origin myth from the time of Indo-European unity, whose earlier versions appear to have been lost. The fact that it concerns itself with the establishment of the tripartite order should be enough to attest to its antiquity, but one must proceed with extreme caution in assessing the degree to which such an account of the subjugation and incorporation of an indigenous population of husbandmen is based on historical fact.

An even more elemental version of the origin of the tripartite order is grounded in the paradigm of mankind's descent from a pair of primeval twins, attestations to which exist in Indic, Roman, and Scandinavian traditions. The algebraic model of this myth requires one of the twins, called "Man," to sacrifice his brother, who is functionally named "Twin," in order to shape the world and humanity from the remains of the victim. The implications are far-reaching. Man in his generative aspect (the third estate, it will be recalled, involves twins) sacrifices his alter ego—that is, himself—and thereby produces the two superior estates and all that can be schematized within the tripartite order. Jaan Puhvel has made a careful study of the Roman variant[22] in which, behind the veil of historicization, one can discern that Remus (I-E *Yemos) plays the role of the twin who is killed by his brother, the eponymous Romulus. The development of the world order from this beginning falls on the shoulders of the survivor, who accomplishes the task by rising from the third functional level to the first, following a quick stopover on the warrior rung, until he finally reaches apotheosis by

---

[22] "Remus et Frater," *History of Religions* 15 (1975), 146–157. It is important to note here that Puhvel makes a sharp distinction, in pristine Indo-European terms, between primeval twins and the Dioscuric variety. In his view, the combination of these two irreconcilable types, as it is found at Rome, is a systematizing invention of the Roman legend-mongers. He points out that India produced a different systematization, in that both the primeval pair Yama (plus Yamī) and Manu and the Aśvinic twins were fathered upon Vivasvant. My view of the situation is more speculative, but also more economical. It proceeds from the observation that Indo-European twinship is related to the source of life, and thus, at least on the conceptual level, Dioscuric re-creation through fertility appears as a most natural outgrowth of primeval creation.

being assimilated into Jupiter.[23] The weight of the evidence thus, again, points to a pre-diaspora Indo-European involvement with theological speculations on the coterminous origin of the world and the tripartite order, and on the internal dynamics inherent in both.

Examples of change and development after the various Indo-European tribes scattered in search of greener grass, or for whatever other motive, are obviously more difficult to pinpoint. The lack of profound or plentiful comparative evidence among speakers of Greek and Celtic dialects places most of the changes in their patrimony beyond the pale of recognition. Germanic tradition, however, does provide an interesting illustration. In the *Rigsthula*[24] one can observe a downward social shift wherein the three orders, as represented by the sons of the god Heimdall, are characterized as slave, peasant, and nobleman, thus leaving enough of the original pattern intact to enable identification of the divergences. It is interesting that this modification of the social ladder generated no corresponding changes in the conception of the supernatural order, thus attesting to the force of its persistence against a historical flux that favored the rise of the warrior role and the concomitant waning of the priest class. An even more dramatic example concerns the theme of the three sins of the warrior. According to Dumézil,[25] the Indo-European lone warrior–hero is ambivalent by nature and represents a danger as much to his own society as to the enemy. This is brought out in the accounts that describe the careers of three typical warriors, Śiśupāla of India, Herakles in Greece, and Starkad from Norse tradition, each of whom commits a threefold set of transgressions against the tripartite order. These are: impiety

---

[23] A similar promotion of the Norse hero Hadingus is described in Dumézil, *From Myth to Fiction: The Saga of Hadingus*, trans. Derek Coltman (Chicago and London, 1973); see also Littleton, *New Comparative Mythology*, pp. 108–109.

[24] See Dumézil, "The *Rigsþula* and the Indo-European Social Structure," trans. John Lindow, in Dumézil, *Gods of the Ancient Northmen*, ed. Einar Haugen (Berkeley and Los Angeles, 1973), pp. 118–125.

[25] *The Destiny of the Warrior,* trans. Alf Hiltebeitel (Chicago and London, 1970), pp. 53–64.

or insubordination, cowardice in battle, and sexual or venal excess. A triad of punishments, geared to each level and ending with the death of the hero, completes the thematic pattern.[26] The development that makes this theme significant as an index of change occurs in later Indic tradition, specifically the *Brāhmaṇas* and the epics, where the three transgressions become attributed to the god of war himself, to Indra, thus transposing a divine role into a heroic and mortal one.[27] The lack—so far—of any other divine tripartite sinner in parallel Indo-European traditions, coupled with the theme's obviously greater suitability to human heroes and the lateness of the accounts of Indra's sins, strongly supports the argument that the case of Indra the sinner was a local post-diaspora development and was not transmitted to any of the other migrating tribes.

The best and most plentiful sources that illustrate the varying developments of the Indo-European Weltanschauung, both before and after the migrations, can be found in the transposition of myth to epic. This phenomenon is of such pressing importance that Dumézil devoted a three-volume set to the study of its many manifestations, among which is included that of Camillus.[28] There is something about the process itself, however, which cries out for insights of a more theoretical nature. "Transposition" is a rather mechanical term for what has occurred. The transformation of myth to the literary mode involves, indeed requires, elaboration and invention. It is not merely a matter of stressing the flexibility of Indo-European mentifacts, for the conservatism of the supernatural order, even when the social structure was ready to accept change, demonstrates the selectiveness of that flexibility. When the propositions of myth, which are *sui generis*, are interpreted in terms of

---

[26] Yet another example of a sinning warrior was recently discovered in Celtic tradition by David J. Cohen, "Suibhne Geilt," *Celtica* 12 (1977), 113–124.

[27] That the motif of the sinning warrior belongs properly and essentially to the human level rather than to the divine was not brought out by Dumézil until *Mythe et épopée II* (Paris, 1971), pp. 17–132, where Śiśupāla is first mentioned.

[28] In addition to the three volumes of *Mythe et épopée*, the only other book completely devoted to this subject is *From Myth to Fiction*.

ritual and narrative, the theology undergoes a substantial readjustment. The dimension of inviolability wanes, while the dimension of human participation in the sacred increases. When a god from a myth becomes the man of an epic, nothing less than an *incarnation* takes place. As the two zones intersect, they produce a result that is either sublime or devastating. A god–man can transfigure a theology toward expansion into the heights and depths of mysticism, but a man–god could rob belief of its incommensurable "otherness" and bring about its degeneration into the bawdy stories of Olympus which Plato so condemned or the ridiculous apotheoses of Roman emperors.

It is for this reason that *euhemerism*, which is the operative principle in what Dumézil calls the transposition of myth to epic, has been so much misunderstood. When in circa 300 B.C. the Greek writer Euhemerus voiced the notion that later was to bear his name, he maintained that the gods represented deified historical heroes. The "euhemerism" found in Dumézil is quite the reverse of this, for he is able to show that certain key protagonists in the narratives he has investigated are, in fact, heroicized divinities or their hypostases or protégés. Euhemerus was later regarded as having quenched the divine spark of myth; Dumézil, by contrast, has been Prometheus and seen it kept alive, even nourished, in the world of creatures.[29]

The transformation of myth into the literary mode urges a change in the way it is perceived hermeneutically. Epicized myth is not merely another layer in the Indo-European cognitive model sandwiched between the supernatural and social sets, nor is it just a liminal mirror that reflects the systems above and below. Its function is more that of a vertical nexus, a metaphoric expression of the relationship between the sacred and profane orders, analogous to a hypothetical exchange where the bifurcated principles of sover-

[29] For a favorable view of Euhemerus, as opposed to what later thinkers made of him, see Kees W. Bolle, "In Defense of Euhemerus," *Myth and Law*, pp. 19–38.

eignty, the cosmic and juridical, find common ground. And emerging from this *coincidentia oppositorum* is a synthesis that brings something new.

Dumézil's series, *Mythe et épopée*, is replete with concrete instances of the novelty engendered by such transformations. But it is important to note that the main emphasis in Dumézil's presentation is motivated by his perennial concern to strengthen the corroborative links between the national traditions and the Indo-European heritage that served as their common source. Thus, the organization of the volumes follows an irregular growth pattern based on the occurrences of ad hoc analogies more or less loosely linked by a common factor, so that the division of each volume into three parts bears no significant relation to Indo-European functional tripartition.[30]

The first volume of *Mythe et épopée*, subtitled *L'idéologie des trois fonctions dans les épopées des peuples indo-européens*, focuses on a cluster of homogenous problems that go to the very heart of the national traditions they represent. The first of these major problems involves the *Mahābhārata*, the world's longest epic and India's greatest literary treasure. Dumézil recapitulates Stig Wikander's 1947 ground-breaking study[31] that had established the five Pāṇḍava brothers who appear in the epic as respective hypostases of the divinities in the tripartite hierarchy of the Indic pantheon. Then Dumézil goes beyond the parallelism to dwell on the import of this epiphany within the narrative context where an eschatological conflict between Good and Evil is depicted. The tripartite order incarnated in the Pāṇḍavas represents the liberating force of Good, which requires participation at the human level in order to prevail. Thus, while the values of the hierarchical concepts encompassed by tripartition are affirmed as an absolute positive, their involvement with the essentially theocentric theme of the

---

[30] Volume 1 actually consists of four parts, but the fourth part (pp. 577–628) is really a collection of odds and ends, or "epica minora," as Dumézil terms them.

[31] "Pāṇḍava-sagan och Mahābhāratas mytiska förutsättningar," *Religion och Bibel* 6 (1947), 27–39.

world's release from Evil has experienced a shift here toward a focus that is better described as anthropocentric.

The second problem in this volume concerns the origin and development of the particular form of consciousness that gave the Romans their identity. In finding the principal evidence for an Indo-European heritage at Rome preserved in the form of legends that had made their way into history and literature, as practiced by Livy, Ovid, Propertius, and Vergil, to mention but a few, Dumézil could conclude not only that Rome had a fully articulated native mythology but also that theological considerations were so wedded to the rise of the Roman *imperium* that the two became virtually indistinguishable, united in one flesh and one metaphor. The well-nigh total assimilation of Romulus into Jupiter stands as eloquent testimony to that feature of the Roman mind which, even at its earliest stages, saw itself as the center of the universe and could conceive of nothing more historical than the mythological heritage it had converted into signposts of a manifest destiny, and nothing more sacred than the history of its unfolding reign. Thus, Roman historicized myth goes far beyond any literary transformation, and its mediation between the supernatural and social orders is such that, here more than elsewhere, these two appear as obverse and reverse sides of the same coin. Given this point of view, any material (as opposed to formal) separation between Church and State in Rome is inconceivable.

The third problem focuses on the last descendants of the Scythians, the Ossets—who, like the Romans, have preserved the Indo-European "moyen d'analyser" in their folktales and epics. Again, these documents served as the ethnic self-identification of a people left to their own devices in maintaining their existence and integrity amidst hostile neighbors. The hardships of such a milieu provided a stimulus to the euhemerization process, which but mirrored the need for human ingenuity to achieve human survival. The end result was the embodiment of familiar theological and social abstractions in the concrete form of heroic narrative, which nonetheless remained faithful to the ancient spirit of the tripartite tradition.

The three hierarchically ordered concepts of that tradition were distributed among a set of three heroic families known as the Narts. Sovereignty is represented by the Alægatæ, who are collectively distinguished for their intelligence; heroism and strength are the hallmarks of the Æxsærtægkatæ from whom emerged the great hero Batraz;[32] the Boratæ with their riches personify wealth and fertility. Taken together, these families embody the essence of the Ossetic experience, one that is both Indo-European in its origin and uniquely its own creation. Their Scythian ancestors, already a distinct people, regarded the tripartite heritage as a gift from heaven. It was symbolized, as Herodotus 4.5–7 tells us, by three golden objects that fell burning from the sky: the cup of the sovereign, the warrior's axe, and a plow for the husbandman. Only the last of three brothers, Kolaxaïs, was able to gather them in without being burnt. A like sign of elevation later descends upon Batraz when he, too, receives three treasures that have the same functional significance. That a warrior figure like Batraz should become the focal point of the whole order highlights the stress that need placed on the role of force in the thinking of a people frequently exposed to strife. This is borne out by the Ossetic parallel to the Roman-Sabine war and the Aesir–Vanir conflict in that it differs from its siblings on two key points: (1) the combatants are confined to the two inferior strata, but as the Æxsærtægkatæ had become the leading family, they simply annexed the "intelligence" of the Alægatæ

---

[32] In the past few years a number of studies have suggested that the roots of the Arthurian tradition may be found here, in the corpus of tales surrounding such heroes as Batraz, and that they were transmitted by the Alans to France and the Sarmatians to Britain. See J. Grisward, "Le motif de l'epée jetée au lac: la mort d'Arthur et la mort de Batraz," *Romania* 9 (1969), 289–340; Helmut Nickel, "Wer waren König Artus' Ritter? Über die geschichtliche Grundlage der Artussagen," *Zeitschrift der historischen Waffen- und Kostümkunde* 1 (1975), 1–18; and especially C. Scott Littleton and Ann C. Thomas, "The Sarmatian Connection: New Light on the Origin of the Arthurian and Holy Grail Legends," *Journal of American Folklore* 91 (1978), 512–527 and its sequel by Littleton, "The Holy Grail, the Cauldron of Annwn, and the Nartyamonga: A Further Note on the Sarmatian Connection," *Journaal of American Folklore* 92 (1979), 326–333.

to serve in the struggle against the Boratæ, and (2) the war does not reach a constructive outcome, there is no reconciliation, and the Boratæ do not settle down in peace to become the third estate. The rise of the warrior class is not surprising here, as this conception is consonant with what occurred among the Germanic tribes, both in the development of their mythology and in the events that make up their history;[33] but the second divergence is rather interesting and illustrative. The ongoing struggle between these two Nart families depicts the persistence of the antinomy between the talented few and the overwhelming many. The Boratæ are by definition already part of the system, so the purpose of this euhemerized myth is not to reenact a primeval integration but instead to focus on the damages resulting from the lack of integration inherent in the social dynamics of competing estates. The accounts of a perpetual, inconclusive war represent a hardnosed look at an insoluble problem, but then even myth must be realistic if it is to survive.[34]

Dumézil concludes this volume devoted to great and sweeping themes with a section of sketches on a smaller canvas. There are vignettes such as the Judgment of Paris, the careers of the three sons of Ferīdūn and of William the Conqueror,[35] the Irish Macha, and the series of plagues in Iran and India. All of these manifest the Indo-European tripartite pattern, put to a special use in each instance. Dumézil then summarizes the varying ways in which the three concepts of tripartition may be represented in the literary mode: they may be distributed among various entities or united in

[33] Cf. Dumézil, *"Rígsþula."*

[34] In Livy, *Ab urbe condita* 1.8, Romulus solves the problem of populating a large city before it is forcibly occupied by greedy neighbors by inviting in all kinds of riff-raff; but the scheme backfires eventually when the descendents of these plebeians grow jealous of the patricians and discontented with their lot.

[35] Curiously enough, tripartition involving the career choices of three brothers is present in Dumézil's own family background. His grandfather sired three sons, one of whom became a vintner, another a government official (harbormaster at Noumea), while Dumézil's father achieved distinction as a general of artillery. Thus we have the third, first, and second estates represented, in that order.

21

a single personage, either simultaneously or successively. Finally, Dumézil addresses the crucial question of whether the tripartite conception is unique to the Indo-Europeans and concludes that, although sovereignty, force, and fecundity are notions critical to the survival of all peoples, there is simply no evidence for the existence of similar indigenous patterns among the non-Indo-European speaking peoples of the ancient world. This may be put another way: if there were any such systems or even competing conceptions of organizing the universe, they did not survive intact the ravages of time. The peculiar and specific Indo-European Weltanschauung is thus a gift of natural selection to posterity.

Volume two of *Mythe et épopée* broaches three problems of a different kind. Its subtitle, *Types épiques indo-européens: un héros, un sorcier, un roi*, promises a menagerie of figures tenuously linked by the fact that at least one person from each category can be found in a secondary episode of the *Mahābhārata*. That much is on the surface, as is Dumézil's stated intention to present a series of homologies too numerous and too consistent to allow each to be interpreted individually. But again, there is something deeper and more important about all this, something beyond the long-recognized similarities that hearken back to the creative efforts of common ancestors. The principal human actors are all personifications of a type cast in the role of mediator between certain gods and their counterpoles, whether these are other gods, demons, or mankind itself.

The first panel of this triptych showers new light on the problem of the sinning warrior. Dumézil's earlier study, *Destiny of the Warrior*, had defined the warrior's tripartite sins as an expression of social disintegration. The largest fly in that ointment was the exclusivity of Indra's role as a sinning god in a paradigm that otherwise contained only heroes. Dumézil's remedy here is to replace Indra with a human prototype, incarnated in the *Mahābhārata's* warrior Śiśupāla, and to redefine his sins as the by-product of an opposition between divinities of light and divinities of darkness, in the midst of which the hero is caught and buffeted to and fro. In the light of this interpretation, Dumézil takes a second look at the careers of his other two major sinning warriors, Herakles and Starkad, and concludes that they too are playthings of the gods, and in some sense are more sinned against than sinning. The case of Indra thus appears as a late extrapolation of this theme. This recasting shifts the problem from the sociopsychological level to the realm of theology, where it originated. The entry of a human agent through epicization allows the myth of divine conflict to develop the implications inherent in it, and therein lies the significance and novelty of this literary transformation.

The remaining two studies are both informed by the same operative principle. In the second panel, the role of the human figure is even more clearly liminal, for he is defined as a sorcerer who chooses to pass from the realm of Good to that of Evil, as embodied by the gods on the one hand and the demons on the other. Dumézil examines two representatives of this type of sorcerer, coming from the neighboring traditions of India and Iran and bearing the etymologically linked names Kāvya Uśanas and Kavi Usan, which attest to their common origin. While both are initially punished for having chosen the low road, the gods later relent and pardon each in a manifestation of divine supremacy.

The third panel examines the careers of three royal culprits: the Iranian Yima, the Indic Yayāti, and the Irish Eochaid Fedlech. In the nature of the Indo-European conception of order, the top level of the tripartite hierarchy controls the entire system. The king's sovereignty places him as a bridge between the gods and mankind, and thus, unlike the warrior, he need sin but once to suffer the triple loss that characterizes a total fall from grace. The case of Yima is the simplest, for when he sins, the sacred manifestation of his royalty—the $x^v arənah$—leaves him and splits into three parts to be distributed among representatives of the three canonical orders. The remaining two kings of fable are participants in more complicated plots. The action there involves the integration of a female element whose name contains the same sound as is found at the root of the word for *mead*, the Indo-European sacred drink. It is this female who controls all three functional aspects of the tripartite order. In Ireland she is called Medb. A series of successive marriages to male representatives from each of the three categories enabled her to incorporate the entire order within herself and thus to become the touchstone and source of all legitimate claims to royalty. In India this part is played by Mādhavī, the daughter of Yayāti and the mother of four sons who collectively embody the three functions. By sacrificing these tripartite qualities they are able to impart them to their grandfather so that he might reenter the heaven from which his sin had caused him to be expelled.

The implications of this epic expansion are themselves immense, and their exploration has scarcely begun. There is here the basis for a moral theology of guilt and innocence which deserves further attention. In addition, the role of women in Indo-European thought finds in the last essay of this volume a form of expression that cannot be overlooked. Clearly, there is the suggestion of a nexus between the transfunctionality of certain goddesses (e.g. Sarasvatī, Arədvī Sūrā Anāhitā, Athena) and woman's role as the giver of life. This connection stands, like the sacrifice of the primeval twin, at the bottom of the tripartite order. Yet at the same time, it is also central to the origin of the entire system. Thanks to the breakthroughs of Dumézil, the path has been cleared for a deeper understanding of the entire Indo-European ideology in all its splendid complexity.

Volume three of *Mythe et épopée* bears the shortest subtitle of all: *Histoires romaines*. That makes it, in a very real sense, a continuation of the second part of the opening volume. Here *Camillus* was originally published under the poetic title, "La saison de l'Aurore," sandwiched between the parallel opening essay, "La saison des rivières," and the concluding part, which consists of a Roman tripartite miscellany containing sections on Camillus, Publicola, Coriolanus, and so on. This part is followed by three appendices, of which the first two are included in this English edition.

In his introduction to the work Dumézil attempts vigorously to defend the subtitle. History here has two meanings, and both are apposite. The first refers to the events as narrated, the other to how they are interpreted. The stories under discussion are patently implausible; yet they were told as if they were true. Thus in a formal sense, they *are* history. And they are history in a hermeneutical sense as well: whatever is recorded serves a higher purpose in the pattern woven by the chronicler, whether it is based on incidents that actually took place or not. It is also history to observe how a people elects to look at its past. And if one historian can concern himself with balancing accounts that extol the virtues of the Gracchi against reports of their vices, then another can, with just as much validity, compare or contrast the apotheosis of Romulus with the political deification of Julius Caesar. It is vain to hope for a record of "wie es eigentlich geschehen," for even the most scrupulously objective historian will sooner or later fall prey to the necessity of adopting the Italian adage, "si non è vero, è ben trovato."

Dumézil demands his rightful place in the prytaneum of historians because he regards the same data with the same critical eye as they do, with this difference—that the history he practices is the history of ideas, specifically religious ideas. If the purpose of the historian is to distinguish the true account from the false, to obtain the facts as best he can by painstaking detective work, using the tools of textual analysis and borrowing from such neighboring fields as philology, archeology, and epigraphy, then that is precisely what Dumézil has been doing. And if the happy result of these probings among undisputed historians is, for example, a better understanding of what motivated Augustus' rebuilding program, then is not Dumézil's discovery of the religious value that masquerades as the overflow of the Alban Lake during the canicular days an accomplishment of commensurate importance?

The first of the two major essays in volume three of *Mythe et épopée* deals precisely with the problem posed by the account of the overflow of the Alban Lake. This essay shares with its sibling

Camillus a tightly knit complexity and a diminished reliance on tripartition as a major structural factor in its interpretation. Unlike *Camillus*, however, the key clue to its significance cannot be found elsewhere in Roman tradition but must proceed from a comparative analysis of two parallel accounts, one from Ireland and the other from Iran. The extreme closeness of the correspondences found in all three versions is truly remarkable, a clear indication that the original of the tale, its sequence of events, and its controlling metaphors, were all constructed at the time of Indo-European unity. The central elements of the tale are: (1) a sacred body of still water (lake, well) containing an element of fire, (2) protected by a figure whose name (Apąm Napāt, Nechtan, Neptunus) means "grandson of waters," (3) an approach is made to the water by someone who has no business doing so, (4) with the result that the standing water explodes into rivers, either to elude the unqualified claimant (Iran) or to punish the transgressor (Ireland). In the Roman account, the overflow of the Alban Lake occurs because some improperly created magistrates had offended the gods by performing rituals in its vicinity. The connection with Neptune lies in the date of the event, July 23, on which was celebrated the annual festival to the god known as the *Neptunalia*. The final outcome is positive. The waters of the lake, which represent Rome's sovereignty, are restrained from spilling this symbolic treasure into the sea when a communal effort succeeds in diverting them into canals that bring much needed irrigation to the drought-plagued farmers of the lowlands.

This particular study has been quite productive, leading to the publication of three articles that offer some interesting extensions of Dumézil's argument. The most important of these is Jaan Puhvel's "Aquam exstinguere,"[36] in which the author shows that Livy's use of "exstingues"—an odd metaphor to describe the act of controlling the lake's overflow—preserves the ancient concept of

[36] *Journal of Indo-European Studies* 1 (1973), 379–386.

"fire in water" present in the Irish and Iranian variants.[37] Patrick K. Ford's piece[38] concentrates on the potent essence contained in the watery substance and identifies it not with the validation of sovereignty—the $x^v arǝnah$ of the Iranian version—but with the old Irish notion of inspired poetry and its associated wisdom. The last of these spinoffs impelled by Dumézil's essay comes from the pen of C. Scott Littleton.[39] He focuses on the "grandson of waters" motif in the hope of including Poseidon under that rubric, and his conclusion, that Poseidon's role in the formation of the Lerna River is isomorphic with the functions of Neptune and his cognates, is easily the most daring and the most speculative of the lot.

The study following these introductory pages must be read against this backdrop of the Indo-European state of mind. The expansion of the core of myth through the artifice of epic and the peculiar historicization that marks its preservation in Rome resulted from processes that were as much psychological as they were ideological. Scholarship often tends to reduce such complexities to algebraic formulas, but Dumézil does not. Over thirty years of scrupulously detailed analysis in this area have allowed him to accumulate all the elements necessary for constructing a proper framework in which to understand the saga of Camillus, and without which this chronicle would deserve the condemnation of Theodor Mommsen as "die verlogenste aller römischen Legenden."

[37] The graphic image is that of a burning clear liquid whose fire must be "extinguished." One is tempted, briefly, to think of alcohol, the "firewater" that ruined so many red men in North America, remembering too that Irish "whisky" means "water of life" and that "vodka" is a diminutive of the word for "water." But if any natural phenomenon is at the root of this image, then it is more likely than not the natural seepage of naphtha from the soil of the oil-rich Caucasus.

[38] "The Well of Nechtan and 'La Gloire Lunineuse,' " in Gerald James Larson, C. Scott Littleton, and Jaan Puhvel, eds., *Myth in Indo-European Antiquity* (Berkeley and Los Angeles, 1974), pp. 67–74.

[39] "Poseidon as a Reflex of the Indo-European 'Source of Waters' God," *Journal of Indo-European Studies* 1 (1973), 523–440.

The fact that the chronicle of Camillus contains no epic analogs in other Indo-European traditions and that it can be explained adequately, *mutatis mutandis*, in terms that are basically Roman, highlights another aspect of Dumézil's methodology which requires mention here. For years, specialists in the various national traditions have criticized Dumézil for writing about their fields from the Indo-European point of view without taking into account all the features that make each tradition unique. They have argued that many of the elements that make up a particular national corpus are either not of Indo-European origin at all or have been so modified by syncretism, borrowing, independent development, and the like, that the total picture bears little resemblance to any set of values that might have animated their distant Indo-European ancestors.[40] Dumézil's response has been that, on the contrary, he has thoroughly familiarized himself with all facets of a specific tradition before venturing to isolate some segment of it and claim that it bears the imprint of the Indo-European ideology. This answer has failed to satisfy many specialists who, for whatever reason, fail to catch Dumézil's meaning or are reluctant to take him at his word, and by the mid-1960s Dumézil himself came to recognize the necessity of replacing these Indo-European segments in the national contexts where they were first found. The result of this foray into reciprocity was a work that encompassed both poles of approach. In 1966 Dumézil published *La religion romaine archaïque*, an "Indo-European" history of the religion of the Roman Republic, written from the Roman point of view.[41]

---

[40] A more detailed exposition of how this kind of criticism was leveled against Dumézil's writings on Germanic mythology can be found in my "Introduction, Part II," to Dumézil's *Gods of the Ancient Northmen*, pp. xiv–xliii. A partial response exists in my "History and Structure in Germanic Mythology: Some Thoughts on Einar Haugen's Critique of Dumézil," in Larson et al., eds., *Antiquity*, pp. 29–50.

[41] Dumézil, *La religion romaine archaïque* (Paris, 1966). The passage below, giving Dumézil's methodological blueprint for the work, is quoted from the author's preface to the English edition, *Archaic Roman Religion*, 2 vols., trans. Philip Krapp, (Chicago and London, 1970), pp. xvi–xvii: "It is not enough to extract from early Roman religion the pieces which can be explained by the religions of other Indo-

Introduction

The wealth of Dumézil's Roman writings and the complexity of the Indo-European heritage that Rome preserved as its own make it impossible to do justice to either, especially in a summary. However, it would be remiss not to identify the two consequences of his work which revolutionized Roman studies. The first we have already seen. In showing that the lion's share of the Indo-European heritage at Rome was concealed in the garb of history and legend, Dumézil opened up a whole new corpus of data for study, with all its implications about the Roman conception of culture. The second is even more important, for Dumézil was also able to show that by far the major and essential portion of Roman religion is Indo-European in origin and spirit. With these accomplishments Dumézil imposed order on a mass of data that otherwise would have remained a welter of confusion, united only by the language and geography of discord.

It is not difficult to imagine what the study of Roman mythology would be like had there been no Dumézil. One has only to look at the offerings of H. J. Rose, H. Wagenvoort, and Kurt Latte[42] to see Roman tradition as a babel of syncretism surrounding a core of primitive belief. According to these scholars, the roots of that belief are immersed in the magical concept of "numen," a latinized version of Polynesian "mana," which represents the mysterious

European peoples. It is not enough to recognize and to present the ideological and theological structures which are shown by the interrelations of these blocks of prehistoric tradition. One must put them back in place, or rather leave them *in situ*, in the total picture and observe how they behaved in the different period of Roman religion, how they survived, or perished, or became changed. In other words, one must establish and reestablish the continuity between the Indo-European 'heritage' and the Roman reality. At a very early stage I had understood that the only means of obtaining this solidarity, if it can be obtained, was to change one's viewpoint, to join those whom one had to convince. Without surrendering the advantages of the comparative method, or the results of Indo-European research, but by adding to this new apparatus, in no order of preference, the other traditional ways of knowing, one must consider Rome and its religion in themselves, for themselves, as a whole. Stated differently, the time had come to write a general history of the religion of the Roman Republic, after so many others, from the Roman point of view."

[42] The theories of these scholars are discussed, where appropriate, in Dumézil, *Archaic Roman Religion*, pp. 3–138 and passim.

powers inherent in nature. That there is some basis for "numenism" can readily be seen, especially in folk belief where the gods of hearth and home, the *lares* and *penates*, dominate the affairs of day-to-day life, and where each field, grove, and stream is believed animated by its tutelary *genius loci*. On the other side of the spectrum, there can be no denying that the Roman pantheon of the late period was perhaps overly sophisticated. According to the *interpretatio romana*, all nations had more or less the same group of gods, so it followed that a number of foreign deities, especially those of the Greeks, Celts, and Germans, were assimilated into known models already established in Rome. From there it was but a small step to allow for indiscriminate accretions to the pantheon, sometimes through the divinization of a local celebrity, other times by adopting the gods of a conquered tribe as a sop to their pride. But between the cultic detritus of an earlier civilization and the final phase of corruption there lies a body of myth that has every right to be called truly and uniquely Roman, and it is this body that occupies Dumézil's attention.

The writings that treat of this body are among the most important scholarly contributions of Dumézil's career, and they have made him the most important Romanist writing today. Dumézil has based his analysis of the Roman texts on the narrative structure and the functions of the dramatis personae. Ultimately, as we have seen, the key to interpreting these "histories"—or rituals, as the case may be (and often the two complement and corroborate each other)—lies in the evidence of other Indo-European traditions where structural and functional parallels of comparable value can be found.

Of course, the science of interpretation does not reach its fulness until it also comes to be practiced as an art. And it is the art of interpretation that can suddenly bathe even a seemingly "primitive" incident in a new light. Take for example the passage in Ovid's *Fasti*, 339–342, which recounts how an onion, human hair, and fish came to be prescribed as the specific apotropaic against thunderstroke. Numa Pompilius, Rome's second legendary king and successor to Romulus, desiring to protect his people from Jupiter's thunderbolts, captured the woodland spirits Picus and Faunus and compelled them, in exchange for their release, to draw Jupiter down from the heavens, so that Numa might parley with him. What followed was a masterpiece of contractual misconstruction. The god demanded a head, and Numa quickly agreed to a head of onion. "A man's," asserted Jupiter in an attempt to correct the king, but the latter was too quick and immediately added "hair." So, Jupiter tried a third time. "The life," he said. "Of a fish," came the response, as once again Numa beat the god to the punch. And at this the god laughed and agreed to be bound by Numa's artfully introduced substitutions.

At first, this incident might appear to have come from one of the cycles of Trickster Tales so prevalent in African and North American native lore, and to partake of the spirit manifested in the chaos–cosmos dichotomy, which Mircea Eliade[43] has identified as a universal archetype of early man's religious thought. Certainly we have a compromise here that allows the human order a degree of liberty within the larger sphere of divine jurisdiction. And later Roman life clearly mirrored this kind of arrangement by the separation of secular days from holy days according to the mystical concept of *fas* (as in *dies fasti* and *dies nefasti*), which validates and sustains every visible human relation and contract (*ius*).[44] However, this approach offers only a partial explication of the text. The full picture could emerge only after Dumézil was able to show that the first four legendary kings of Rome (Romulus, Numa, Tullus Hostilius, and Ancus Marcius) reflected, in descending order of hierarchy, the tripartite patterns of the Roman and Indic pantheons, even to the detail of the bifurcation of sovereignty into its magico-religious and juridical aspects. When Numa is thus seen as the embodiment of that aspect of the sovereign level that is concerned with regulating human affairs, then his role vis à vis Jupiter

---

[43] See *The Sacred and the Profane: The Nature of Religion*, trans. Willard R. Trask (New York, 1961).

[44] Dumézil, *Archaic Roman Religion*, pp. 131–132.

(for which name one could just as easily read Romulus) in Ovid's story becomes clear: he is not a trickster but a co-sovereign, dividing up spheres of influence with his colleague. Therefore, we are not dealing with an ancient and universal concept of magical expiation but with its replacement or metamorphosis into a more secular and legalistic symbology. This sophisticated Indo-European variant is fitted into a larger and more complex pattern of regulating the totality of things, each according to its nature.

There are many such items in Roman tradition which have gained their full meaning through the backward perspective of their Indo-European roots. Among the representations of the tripartite order are the three colors used to distinguish racing chariots: the *albati, russati,* and *virides,* linked to the deities Jupiter, Mars, and Venus respectively. Another example is the subsumption of all functional activities under the mantle of the queen of heaven in the formula IUNO S.M.R. (= *Seispes* [savior (or safety) in war], *Mater, Regina*) found on monuments to Jupiter's wife. A further instance of tripartition has been observed in the layout of the principal cultic administration in the *Regia* of the Forum where the main edifice of governance belongs to Janus and Juno, but especially to Jupiter, and surrounding it are two satellite *sacraria*: one to Mars, the other to Ops Consiva, patroness of abundance.[45] An old prayer to Mars recorded by Cato the Elder (*De agricultura* 141) echoes the farmer's tripartite concern, even when the specific object of his request is the protection of his property, his cattle, himself, and his family against all dangers, seen and unseen.[46] In addition, there exist a variety of literary references in Varro (*De lingua latina,* esp. "De hominibus"), in Propertius 4.1.9–32, and in Vergil,

[45] Ibid., pp. 171–172.

[46] Ibid., pp. 231–234. Dumézil makes an important distinction here between the god's direct action and its desired results, which spill over into the categories of sovereignty and fertility. This takes nothing away from Mars' extended role as a patron of agriculture, which is well attested. Mars is not unlike the Scandinavian Thor, whose control over the atmosphere was of such concern to the peasantry that it generated various forms of worship.

where, in addition to the mixture of oblique and transparent Indo-European remnants in the *Aeneid*,[47] book 2 of the *Georgics* offers the *Sabini, Remus et frater,* and *fortis Etruria* as the three quintessential components of "rerum pulcherrima Roma." All these examples, of course, are but a small portion of the vast and rich harvest that evidences the strength of the Indo-European heritage at Rome.

Of the more elaborate manifestations of this heritage, the Sabine War to acquire wives for Roman men (memorialized by Vergil, above) has already been mentioned. But there are several others. Perhaps the most prominent showcase of Dumézil's ingenuity lies in his interpretation of an incident from the Alban Wars, where the outcome is to be decided by the battle of two sets of triplets: the Roman Horatii and the Alban Curiatii. At first, the Albans appear to be winning, as they quickly despatch two of their opponents; but then the third Horatius seems to catch fire and is able to dispose of all three Curiatii without further ado. The pattern, as Dumézil saw it, was that of a *third* against a *triple* adversary. The parallel he adduced came from Indic myth where Indra, assisted by Trita Āptya (the name means "*third* of the Āptya"), kills a *three-headed* dragon, Triśiras. Because the dragon was also a Brahman and a relative of Trita Āptya, he and his accessory Indra must expiate the slaying. This amounts to undergoing ritual purification, a process traditionally entrusted to the Āptya clan, whose name is cognate with the word for "water." The taint of sin attached to this socially necessary murder is echoed in the Roman variant when the surviving Horatius slays his sister in anger at seeing her mourn the death of the Curiatius to whom she had been betrothed rather than shedding tears for the loss of her two brothers. As a result of this sororicide, Horatius, too, must undergo purification.[48] The more closely the correspondences between these two accounts are examined, the clearer it becomes that

[47] See Dumézil, *Mythe et épopée I*, pp. 337–422.
[48] See Dumézil, *Destiny of the Warrior*, pp. 12–28.

they are true variants of each other, sharing not only a common narrative structure but also the same ethical content. In each case, an act of rebellion—by Triṣiras against the gods, his cousins, and by Mettius Fuffetius against the lawful Roman overlords—justified, indeed required, the death penalty (Mettius is torn apart by horses for his treason), so that the subsequent need to purify the executors of the established order becomes more a means of solemnizing their vindication than of expiating their culpability.

The significance of Dumézil's method is that it provides both an analysis and a synthesis. Not only can Roman religion be recognized as inherently manifesting characteristic Indo-European traits —traits that are structurally complex and display a conscious socioreligious ideology far more sophisticated than the "numen" of earlier scholars—but also something of the unique Roman character comes through as well. It is the character of a people not satisfied merely with promulgating legal codes—that alone would not raise them above the rank of a Moses or a Hammurabi. They had to perfect the art of the legal loophole as well. In this way the burden of ritual which pervaded daily life was lightened by wit and sanity. Humans thus could foist ridiculous compromises upon gods, who then found themselves compelled to adhere to the letter of their own law rather than to its spirit; and by these means any soothsayer could turn aside the effects of an undesired omen by the simple recitation of the formula, "non consulto." (Variations on this theme have persisted throughout the centuries as the *Roman* spirit of Roman Catholicism!) This kind of mentality allowed a people to pull their gods into the framework of human time, where they assumed the position of civil servants.

Last, in addition to being both synthetic and analytic, Dumézil's method is also reciprocal, inasmuch as Roman comparative evidence brings to light previously undiscovered parallel motifs in other Indo-European traditions, and vice-versa. A noteworthy example of such reciprocity is provided by two seemingly unconnected events that occurred during the first war of the Republic.

Two heroes, acting independently for Rome, contributed vitally to the successful outcome of the struggle against the Etruscans. The first, Horatius Cocles, held off all alone the enemy at the Tiber bridge by casting terrifying looks at them. Given thus a chance to regroup, the Romans managed to avoid defeat. But the fortunes of war did not smile on them, and things began to look bleak once again, when a second hero, Mucius Scaevola, stepped in and single-handedly saved the situation. Perhaps "singlehandedly" is an inappropriate word, for he was fully limbed when he began his operation. After entering the enemy camp by stealth, he concealed himself in the tent of their king, Porsenna, and awaited an opportunity to stab him to death. Instead, fortuitously for Rome, he was captured. Interrogated by Porsenna, he claimed that he was but the first of three hundred "kamikazes" pledged to effect the king's assassination. In an effort to persuade the king of the truth of his statement, which was indeed false, he plunged his right arm into a brazier, burning it beyond remedy in a compelling charade of fanaticism. The shaken Porsenna sued for peace, and Rome was saved. The bynames borne by these heroes (Cocles = one-eyed; Scaevola = left-handed) as representative of their essence, led Dumézil to link them to the diptych formed by the Germanic joint sovereign divinities Odin and Tyr. Odin, it will be recalled, relinquishes an eye in exchange for more powerful insight into the secret of the runes, while Tyr sacrifices his right hand as surety for the false oath that allows the wolf Fenrir to be bound. Although the parallel between Odin and Cocles is admittedly far from exact, that between Tyr and Scaevola is remarkably close. The tantalizing incongruencies observed as the Roman and Germanic variants illuminated each other have led Dumézil to undertake further study of the problem and to investigate other possible parallels in Iranian and Irish traditions. While all the evidence is still being evaluated, one conclusion is certainly justified: the Roman and Scandinavian diptychs, as units, both involve sovereignty, albeit in different aspects. The Roman heroes who correspond to the Germanic sovereign gods act only as "citizens." In harmony with the fresh *repub-*

lican ideals of their state, they save Rome, without dominating her, from a hostile *royal* power whose chief aim is domination. This ongoing dichotomy in Roman political thought between the restrictive sovereignty of *regnum* and the extension of sovereignty through *libertas* is very much in evidence during the career of Camillus.[49]

When Dumézil first examined the saga of Camillus,[50] he recognized immediately that this was no historical chronicle and that its "truth" was more likely "poetic" in Aristotle's sense of the word. It was clear that the authors of this biography, or if not they then certainly their unknown sources, had in mind something more than to preserve a set of haphazard occurrences. The clues are numerous. Camillus begins his career as interrex after the previous government's failure to observe proper religious ceremonies had resulted in its fall. This incident foreshadows Camillus' later destiny as Rome's second founder, for it was charges of impiety in his use of a chariot drawn by four white horses—a symbol of the honors reserved exclusively for Jupiter—that, among other things, led to his convenient expulsion from Rome just as the city was threatened by advancing Gaulish forces. The remaining two charges against Camillus complete a tripartite pattern: the military complained of being denied their lawful booty or *praeda*, while the plebeian farmers were outraged when they failed to receive the rich agricultural fields of conquered Veii. None of the complaints was justified; in fact, it was the Romans who violated the tripartite order when they replaced Camillus with a multitude of inept commanders leading inexperienced soldiers drafted from the ranks of the Quirites, and when these citizens themselves neglected their religious sacrifices. This triple offense results in a triple calamity: the army is

---

[49] Dumézil's latest word on the evidence for this mutilated pair throughout the Indo-European spectrum can be found in his " 'Le Borgne' and 'Le Manchot': The State of the Problem," in Larson et al., eds., *Antiquity*, pp. 18–28. Strictly speaking, Cocles and Scaevola are not sovereign figures; see p. 19, n. 4.

[50] The two pertinent texts are Livy, *Ab urbe condita* 5 and Plutarch, *Lives* ("Camillus").

destroyed at the Allia; the Vestals and the Flamen Quirinalis are forced to flee Rome, which is generally abandoned except for the Capitol; and the remaining priests and senators are slaughtered by the enemy. The entire sequence of events has thus been cast unmistakably in the Indo-European ideological framework; and within this context it is Camillus' innocence that enables him to resume his post in just triumph after retaking the city.[51] That this tale bears all the earmarks of an *exemplum* in which doctrinal needs override factual probability is further manifested in the unusual character of Camillus' battle tactics. Not only his victory over the Gauls but also those in his other battles, notably against Veii, take place at daybreak, even when there is no strategic reason for them to do so.

Following a careful review of the evidence, Dumézil concluded that sometime between 445 and 365 B.C. there probably existed a Roman supreme commander who defeated Veii; but it was hardly credible that he also defeated the Gauls following a voluntary exile, or that *all* his attacks occurred at daybreak in startling replications of each other.

It was the stress placed by the story on the time of day and on the season of the year when the critical events were said to have occurred, that provided the key to unlock the riddle. The season was the summer solstice, when the days reach their maximum length and then begin to wane. The Roman feast associated with these developments is called the Matralia, and it consists of a ritual devoted to Mater Matuta, the dawn goddess. Its purpose is to commemorate the rebirth of the sun each morning and to ensure the continued repetition of this process. The counterpole to the Matralia is the Angeronalia, which occurs at the winter solstice on December 21, when the goddess Diva Angerona is invoked to reverse the trend of ever-shortening days which threatens to bring the final end of the sun and perpetual darkness.[52] Similar motives

---

[51] Cf. Plutarch 7 and 18.5–7; Livy 5.25, 5.38, and 5.54. For full discussion, see Dumézil, *Mythe et épopée III*, pp. 216–238.

[52] Cf. Dumézil, *Archaic Roman Religion*, pp. 335–339.

appear to attend the June 11 celebration of the Matralia. The sequence of events is as follows: Roman matrons proceed to the temple of Mater Matuta before the first light, bringing with them a slave woman whom they then expel from the enclosure with slaps and blows. Following this, they take into their arms the infant sons born to their sisters, honor the babes, and commend them to the goddess. The actual mothers of these children represent the night that gives birth to the sun. The slave woman portrays an evil aspect of night, one that desires to linger on and thus delay—if not prevented—the sunrise. The matron aunts reenact the dual role of the dawn goddess, who is the sister of night, by driving away the persistent shadows and by delivering the newborn sun to his mission.[53]

Lest this interpretation appear to be in unreconstructed imitation of Max Müller, let it be noted that these equations had a basis in the texts before they were ever touched by the tools of exegesis; and further, that Dumézil has adduced a conclusive parallel in the dawn mythology involving the Vedic goddess Uṣas. The hymns of the *Rig Veda* portray the coming of day as a violent struggle between the dawn goddess Uṣas and the inimical shadows that strive to prevent the birth of the sun, the child of her twin sister the goddess of night, Rātrī. The one major difference is that what India preserved as mythical narrative Rome, typically, maintained as ritual.[54]

The saga of Camillus, then, represents a third stage in the metamorphosis of this myth, for in it ritual has returned to narrative, this time costumed as history. The original title of Dumézil's study of this saga, "La saison de l'Aurore," highlights the weight

[53] Jaan Puhvel points out (in a personal communication) that there seems to have been some *glissement* in Dumézil's interpretation of the expulsion of the slave woman. In Dumézil's *Déesses latines et mythes védiques* (Collection Latomus 24) (Brussels, 1956) she symbolized the "tarrying dawn," thus a basically good but occasionally dilatory figure, while in *Mythe et épopée III*, p. 321, she seems to personify "evil darkness" in a more general way. Puhvel prefers the earlier explanation, which allowed a neat interpretation of the "demonized dawn" in Iranian tradition as Būšyąstā.

[54] Cf. Dumézil, *Archaic Roman Religion*, pp. 50–55.

Dumézil places on the links that mark Camillus as protégé of the dawn goddess, although Jupiter and Juno are also to be counted among his patrons. The symbolism of Camillus' dawn victories is decisive in making him a solar figure. Camillus can be distinguished favorably from the types adduced by Müller by the concreteness and clarity of the evidence, whose unbroken roots reach far back into Indo-European tradition, and by something else as well: his ambiguity. In spite of Dumézil's interpretation—or perhaps because it is scrupulously non-reductive—Camillus continues to retain his uniqueness and some of his mystery. One is left with the impression that he is more than merely solar. He is primarily (in terms of the human narrative) a wartime leader, yet he does not possess any of the less palatable characteristics of a warlord, and his talents for administration appear far from shabby. He touches on each of the three Indo-European "functions," yet he is not unequivocally contained by any of them.[55] Perhaps the answer lies in the fact that the saga of Camillus has no parallels as such in the traditions of any of the other Indo-European peoples. Its protagonist appears to be a uniquely Roman phenomenon, the embodiment of speculative theological extrapolation that drew on its Indo-European base to develop something that occurred nowhere else. Dumézil's study does not illuminate all facets of this character with equal force, but it has masterfully dissected the central problem and brought a wealth of evidence to bear on the questions that relate to it.

Now that *Camillus* has been situated within its proper context, it is time to let the work speak for itself.

---

[55] It is interesting to note that Dumézil chose not to include the section dealing with Camillus' putative "three sins of the warrior" (*Mythe et epopee III*, pp. 216–238) as part of his original essay on Camillus which appeared earlier in the same volume, and that he requested this section not be translated for the English edition. The author's reluctance in this matter may be indicative of a desire to avoid any misleading emphasis on tripartition and its relation to the central character.

The Dawn Season

1

Camillus and Aurora

The figure of Camillus dominates the last century of "Roman history before history." He was considered the city's second founder until a third nudged *libertas* into a slow shift toward the principate. The title founder, or rather restorer, is justified, but Camillus is first and foremost the savior of Rome, and more integrally so than Publicola had been at the time of the violent transition from *regnum* to *libertas*. At that time Rome had been neither conquered nor destroyed. Its noble adversary, the Etruscan Porsenna, in contrast to the Gallic Brennus, had declined to press his advantage. On lifting the siege, he had even generously provisioned the exhausted Romans.[1]

There is not one episode from Camillus' biography, among the few versions which have come down to us, which is not an *exemplum*, even for Romans of the most diverse types: there are *exempla* in the military arts, with their calculations, boldness, ruses, and precautions ranging from the difficult capture of Veii, which destiny was reserving for the *fatalis dux*, to the rout of the second Gallic band that wanted to renew Brennus' exploit. But there are also *exempla* in military ethics, for this eminent general is not bloodthirsty: honesty toward the Faliscan enemies, generosity

---

[1] See my *Mythe et épopée III* (Paris, 1973), pp. 265–266 and 290.

toward the strayed Tusculans; in both instances moderate conduct proves more efficacious than victory. Then, *exempla* of personal morality: with absolute power so often at his disposal, he has no other ambition than to serve Rome, even when she is ungrateful. At the time of his triumph he is reproached for being a bit too vain— this must still be examined more closely—but later, calumnied, unjustly banished, he refrains from invoking by his prayers the wrath of the gods on the city and asks them only to cause the Romans to regret his absence. Then when a catastrophe that surpasses his expectations does occur, he resumes serving without arrogance, even securing, under acrobatic conditions, his investiture from what remains of the State surviving on the Capitol. Perhaps he gives way to a personal antipathy toward Manlius; but if he pursues him to the Tarpeian Rock, it is first and foremost to rescue *libertas* once again. Finally, *exempla* of political wisdom: he sets in motion the "new society," where the plebeians will no longer only be defended by their revolutionary magistrates, the tribunes, or reduced to subordinate magistracies, but will participate at all levels of command. It is Camillus who opens the consulate to them, and his public life is completed symbolically by his vow of a temple to the goddess Concord.

CAMILLUS AND HISTORY

To what extent does this harmonious collection, this constant demonstration in perfect acts of the virtues necessary for Roman grandeur, belong to history? As always, this has been debated; but in view of the magnitude of Camillus' success, even the historians most inclined to recognize the facts underlying the splendid traditional accounts have expressed doubt. One of the greatest and most open-minded of them, Theodor Mommsen, wrote that the chronicle of Camillus had become the falsest of all the Roman legends, "die verlogenste aller römischen Legenden,"[2] and quite recently, as level-headed a critic as Robert Flacelière, the most recent editor of Plutarch's *Lives*, began his introduction to the *Life* of Camillus with this warning:[3]

> Does the personage of M. Furius Camillus have much more historical consistency than Publicola's? Doubt is justified. Nevertheless, his epoch is more than a century later, since, according to tradition, he lived from 445 to 365 B.C. But the majority of the accounts which concern him have such a marked legendary character that one might wonder if he ever really existed. It is nonetheless possible that a Roman of this name seized Veii around 396 B.C.; but that he subsequently conquered the Gauls who had seized and set fire to Rome is hardly believable.

Where does credibility begin or end? The first sentences of the sixth book of Livy can never be cited too frequently. After recounting the capture of Veii, the destruction of Rome, and after recomposing the poignant speech by which Camillus prevents the Romans from emigrating to Veii, the historian stops to declare that all he has written up to this point is uncertain. And he gives his reasons:[4]

> In the five preceding books I have related everything which occurred from the founding of Rome until its capture by the Gauls. These events are obscure, not only because of their antiquity, which makes them escape attention because of the great distance from which they are viewed, but also because of the meager use of writing, which is still the only means of saving the past from oblivion. But beyond that, a great part of

[2] Friedrich Münzer used this phrase of his great predecessor as the conclusion of his article on the 44th Furius: August von Pauly and Georg Wissowa, *Real-Encyklopädie der classischen Altertumswissenschaft* (Stuttgart, 1912), vol. 7, col. 348.

[3] Plutarch, *Vies*, ed. Robert Flacelière (Paris, 1961), vol. 2, p. 141.

[4] See my *Archaic Roman Religion*, trans. Philip Krapp (Chicago and London, 1970), vol. 1, p. 4.

what was preserved in pontifical books, in the state archives, or in individual memoirs perished in the fire which consumed the city.

In fact, the uncertainty of events in Roman history is not limited to the account of Rome's resurrection, itself manifestly laden with as many edifying features as was that of her ruin. The year 390[5] does not suddenly transform the quality of the evidence; the Camillus following this date does not become overnight a more consistent figure, and his actions do not become better substantiated.

THE VOW TO MATER MATUTA

Escaping as it does the customary grasp of history, on what does this exemplary novel rest? If there were only the personage of Camillus, the description of his virtues and merits could pass for a construction *ex nihilo* intended to educate, an edifying image of the "Roman as he should be." But there are events—uncertain events—which support him, or which he initiates. There is, in the manner in which he endures, gets through, or dominates these events, an abundance of precise detail, at times strange and without moral value. What is the source of this rich material, which forms an array as coherent as that of the virtues and serves as a background for him?[6]

For many long years I tried in vain to learn if one could use

---

[5] Or whichever year one prefers, at about that time.

[6] The bibliography of Camillus is extensive. What is essential, from Theodor Mommsen and Friedrich Münzer to Jean Hubaux, can be found in the first note of Arnaldo Momigliano, "Camillus and Concord," *Secondo contributo allo storia degli studi classici* (1960), 89–108 (repr. from *The Classical Quarterly* 36 [1942], 111–120). Add K. Günther, *Plutarchs Vita Camilli in ihren Beziehungen zu Livius und Aurelius Victor*, Progr. (Bernburg, 1899); Alfred Klotz, "Quellen der plutarchischen Lebensbeschreilbung des Camillus," *Rheinisches Museum für Philologie* 99 (1941), 282; Jean Bayet's edition (Guillaume Budé collection) of the fifth book of Livy, appendix 4 ("M. Furius Camillus"), pp. 140–155; and two articles in the *Revue des études*

either the teachings of the new comparative mythology or the recent progress in the direct study of Roman religion for a total or partial interpretation. The example of the *Lives* of Romulus, Numa, and Publicola, abundant with transformed myths, encouraged the exploration of the first path, the attempt to discover for Camillus an approach of the same type. Twenty years of effort brought no results. The second path, the examination of the religious behavior of Camillus, did not seem any more promising; his

---

latines 48 (1970): Joseph Hellegouarc'h, "Le principat de Camille," 112–132, and Christian Peyre, "Tite-Live et la 'férocité' gauloise," 277–296. In spite of all these works, the problems of Camillus remain as indeterminate and as elusive as they were in Mommsen's day. Even the points on which there is considerable agreement today are somewhat arbitrary. In particular, we do not have the right, despite current opinion, to decide that the version by Polybius (where the capture and evacuation of Rome are recalled in only a few words, without mention of Camillus or any other Roman chief, in the lengthy but schematic catalog of Gallic expeditions toward the South) or the version of the "mysterious source of Diodorus of Sicily" represent the "first" stages of tradition, the rest being formed by successive alluvions. As for Polybius, it is more likely that, considering the event from the Celts' point of view and placing it in the full context of their movements, he felt no need to give any details whatsoever (because he does not give any others) on the "Roman side" of the affair. And as for Diodorus, one has rather the impression that he summarizes poorly, carelessly, mixing or shifting the elements of a biography of Camillus similar enough to the one we know (see below, n. 22). Have we not known for a long time that in his account of 14.116 (where Camillus is not mentioned even though he fills the following chapter), the escalade of the Capitol by the young Pontius Cominius, devoid of reference to Camillus, remains, one might say, up in the air; or that, as Momigliano wittily said (p. 91), "Pontius Cominius climbs the beleaguered Capitol not to obtain the approval of the Senate for Camillus' dictatorship but simply to give an indirect occasion for the miracle of the geese and the feat of Manlius (Ch. 116)"—which is scarcely satisfying? By contrast, it is probable that the writers of the time of the Scipios, the Gracchi, Sulla, and Augustus slanted certain episodes of the chronicle, certain character traits of the hero, to give the impression that they themselves were thinking of their great contemporaries and of the current political scene; but the search for traces of these intentions, to which an extraordinary fecundity has been attributed, has at times been carried to the point of childishness—for example, the *humanitas* of Camillus expressed for all that in the original episodes of Falerii and Tusculum was given *in toto* to Scipio the African! At the risk of being censured for ignorance, I shall not discuss any of these hypotheses. Many of them will weaken of their own accord if the information brought together here warrants consideration.

respect for the Capitoline gods, affirmed so many times, could not characterize him, except perhaps by opposition to Manlius who nearly considered them his debtors. The two great divinities whom Camillus solicits and who help him take Veii are foreign: Apollo of Delphi and Juno of the city, probably an *interpretatio romana* of some Etruscan Uni. At least for Apollo, the general simply continues the politics of the Senate which, according to legend, had already linked the Delphic god to the Veian enterprise at the time of the marvel at Lake Alban. Among the beneficiaries of the vows of Camillus was indeed a properly Roman divinity, Mater Matuta, to whom he promises, on leaving Rome for the camp before Veii, to dedicate her temple if he returns with a victory. But Mater Matuta is a minor goddess, for whom Camillus may well be thought to have had, privately, an individual or occasional devotion. More than one Roman general, in the midst of history, permitted himself the originality of addressing his vow to a modest, unexpected protector.

It was, however, Mater Matuta who, at the beginning of 1971, provided the key that step by step quickly opened a large number of doors in Camillus' career. The details of the progress of the research have little importance. Here are the stages and the results.

To recall the facts: "And now the senate, in the tenth year of the war, taking away all other commands, created Camillus dictator, who chose Cornelius Scipio for his general of horse. And in the first place he made vows unto the gods that, if they would grant a happy conclusion of the war, he would celebrate in their honor the great games and dedicate a temple to the goddess whom the Romans call Matuta, the Mother."[7] Here is one of the opportunities Plutarch took, in his copious polygraphic work, to include annotations he had written about this goddess which, with a few verses of Ovid, remain our principal source of information about her.[8]

Livy says the same after a more solemn opening (5.19.1–6):

---

[7] πρῶτον μὲν εὐχὰς ἐποιήσατο τοῖς θεοῖς ἐπὶ τῷ πολέμῳ τέλος εὐτυχὲς λαβόντι τὰς μεγάλας θέας ἄξειν καὶ νεὼν θεᾶς ἣν Μητέρα Ματοῦταν Ῥωμαῖοι καλοῦσι, καθιερώσειν.

[8] See below, appendix 1: "The Two Rites of the Matralia: Texts."

Camillus and Aurora

The games and Latin festivals had been renewed, the water from Lake Alban had been drained across the countryside, and the fates lay in wait for Veii. Consequently, the general whom they had chosen for the ruin of this grand city and for the salvation of the country, M. Furius Camillus, was named dictator and he in turn designated P. Cornelius Scipio as Master of Horse. The change from general to chief altered in one fell swoop the entire situation. The hopes, the men's morale, the very fate of the city took a new course.

First of all, he punished according to martial law the soldiers who, during the past panic, had fled from the camp before Veii, with the result that it was no longer the enemy that the soldier feared the most.

Then, having established the day of enlistment, he hurries meanwhile to Veii to strengthen the courage of the troops. Back in Rome, he proceeds to raise a new army; there is no attempt to escape serving. Even better, the young foreigners, Latins and Hernici, volunteer to take part in the war. The dictator thanks them before the whole Senate. All the military preparations having been completed, he vows, by *senatus consultum*,[9] to celebrate the Games after the capture of Veii

[9] The customary formula *ex senatus consulto* causes no problem when it is a question of an ordinary magistrate: the Senate decides and the magistrate ensures the execution of this decision (the formula is not only Roman; at Praeneste we find *de zenatuo sententiad*, the magistrate being a *preto(r)*, Vetter, no. 320; in Oscan, with or without the preposition, *(dat) senateís tanginud*, σενατης ταυγινοδ, the magistrate being for example, a ϗραιστορ, who "commands," *faamat*, the execution: Michel Lejeune, "Il santuario Lucano de Macchia de Rossano de Vaglio," *Atti della Accademia Nazionale dei Lincei, Memorie, Classe di Scienze morali, storiche e filologiche*, Serie VIII, 16 no. 2 [1971], 68–69). But what is its significance here concerning a dictator? Probably Camillus, who has all the initiative in this chapter, insists on associating the Senate with his vow, either to heighten its solemnity or because the *ludi magni* imply a large expenditure of which the State is to assume charge and thus take responsibility (cf. Livy, 36.36.2). Even though all-powerful, αὐτοκράτωρ, a dictator may desire and, if need be, obtain by pressure such senatorial decisions (cf. *peruicit ut . . .* of the dictator Fabius after Trasimene, 22.9.9). The only text of Livy that is exactly parallel to this one, concerning a dictator (30.39.8), includes a similar pledge of expense: "Cerialia ludos dictator et magister equitum ex senatus consulto fecerunt." I heartily thank André Magdelain for having given me learned advice on these words. After utilizing David W. Packard's *Concordance to*

and to dedicate the temple of Mater Matuta which the king Servius Tullius had formerly dedicated, and which had been restored.[10] He leaves Rome with his army. . . .

After the victory, the vow was naturally fulfilled. Livy notes the fact in three words (5.23.7). Plutarch does not speak of it, probably because it goes without saying.

There is nothing mysterious about Mater Matuta.[11] In spite of the strange repugnance of several contemporary authors, she was what the second part of her name implies—from which the adjective *matutinus* derives—and what the poet Lucretius, for example, states explicitly: the goddess of dawn. She received no daily worship, or at least nothing of it has been handed down. On the other hand, once a year the passage of the seasons gave her importance. Her festival was set, in fact, on June 11—that is, when the calendar was well corrected, shortly before the summer solstice.[12] This is the moment when the day's duration, which for six months has continued to lengthen to the detriment of that of the night, seems to stabilize and soon will begin the reverse movement. This reverse movement will result six months later in the "narrow days" at the height of the winter solstice administered by another goddess,

---

Livy (Cambridge, Mass., 1968), vol. 4, pp. 588–589, he concludes: "After all, for Livy, isn't it a question of a certain kind of preference to underline that a vow is proper thanks to the Senate's authorization of it?"

[10] "Ludos magnos ex senatus consulto uouit Veiis captis se facturum aedemque Matutae Matris refectam dedicaturum iam ante ab rege Seruio Tullio dedicatem." I do not think one can understand this to mean "he promised . . . to restore and to consecrate the temple of Mater Matuta . . . " (Gaston Baillet, trans., *Tite-Live Histoire Romaine* [Paris, 1940]). The fulfillment of the vow, which occurs immediately after the return to Rome and the triumph (23.7), precludes Camillus' having had time to do the restoration work. If, however, this translation is adopted, nothing of the following argument is changed.

[11] See below, appendix 1. The first public exposé of the interpretation of Mater Matuta was given at a conference at the University of Liège in April 1956.

[12] See below, appendix 1: "Significance of the Matralia," for information about the probably narrow interval (except for periods of exceptional negligence), within which were included, before the reform of Julius Caesar, the discrepancies between the calendar and natural phenomena, particularly the solstices, corresponding to certain annual festivals (or groups of festivals).

Angerona. It is therefore probable that at least the naturalistic intention of the festival, placed as it is, was to encourage the dawn, the daily dawns, against the offensive—the imminent increase of nocturnal time—or to strengthen them against their own lassitude. The two rites we know of for this festival are the following: a female slave allowed into the temple of the goddess was violently expelled from it by the Roman ladies; then they took in their arms and commended to the goddess not their own children, but those of their sisters. If, as is normal for acts of sympathetic magic, these two mimicries claimed to reproduce the actions of Aurora herself, they could only represent on the one hand the expulsion of the invader, the villainous darkness, by the coming dawns, and on the other hand the welcome that the dawns extend each day, the care they give, to the young sun whom the benevolent night, and not the ephemeral dawns themselves, carried in her womb and to whom she has just given birth.

This is the goddess to whom the *fatalis dux*, or rather because of his uncertain person, the authors of his chronicle, chose to entrust his fate.[13] Is this predilection a detail without significance or has it indeed resonances or consequences in the rest of the *Life*?

SOLISQUE, 1

The first component of a response was proposed in 1956 by Jean Hubaux.[14] After hearing my analysis on Mater Matuta in

[13] R. M. Ogilvie, *A Commentary on Livy, Books I–V* (Oxford, 1965), p. 681, explains in a surprisingly modern way, as if it were a diplomatic operation, the attention that Rome gives to Mater Matuta at that time. Caught between two enemies, the Etruscan to the north, the Volscian to the south, the Romans would have tried to neutralize the second enemy or even to join with it against the first: "The foundation of the temple of Mater Matuta is to be seen . . . as a matter of policy, as a step to promote friendly relations with the inhabitants of the key city of Satricum." But the calendar proves that Mater Matuta was also an old Roman goddess who did not need to be introduced to Rome.

[14] See above, n. 11. Whence a note in my *Déesses latines et mythes védiques*

April at the University of Liège, he was struck by a detail of the account with which Livy concludes the Veian episode, namely the triumph[15] that the victorious general celebrates just before fulfilling his vows to the Juno of Veii and to the Latin Aurora (5.23.4–7):

> At the return of the dictator, all the orders of the State went to meet him, forming a crowd such as had never been assembled for any other general. As for his triumph, it surpassed considerably the extent of honor usually marking this ceremony. What attracted attention above all was Camillus himself entering the city in a chariot drawn by white horses, an equipage which seemed indecent not only for a citizen of a republic but likewise for a simple mortal. It was even considered sacrilegious that a dictator had usurped the horses of Jupiter and the Sun—and this is the main reason which caused his triumph to have more renown than he had approbation. He then chose the location of the temple of Juno Regina on the Aventine and dedicated the one of Mater Matuta. Once these divine and human ceremonies were accomplished, he abdicated from the dictatorship.

This Sun, which was rather quickly interpreted as Apollo, is surprising. If a sacrilege[16] was necessary, was it not enough of a major sacrilege to offend the father of the gods, the god who had been the greatest in Rome before as well as after the establishment of the Capitoline cult? In fact, all the other sources name only Jupiter. Thus Plutarch (*Camillus*, 7.1–2):

> Camillus, however, whether puffed up with the greatness of his achievement in conquering the city that was the rival of Rome, and had held out a ten year siege, or exalted with the felicitations of those that were about him, assumed to himself

---

(Collection Latomus 24) (Brussels, 1956), p. 26 n. 5, and another in Jean Hubaux, *Rome et Véies* (Paris, 1958), p. 114 n. 1.

[15] Diodorus of Sicily, 14.117.5, points out variants.

[16] See *Mythe et épopée III*, pp. 232 and 293 regarding the problem caused by this interpretation of sacrilege for conduct that, on the contrary, was ritually imposed.

more than became a civil and legal magistrate; among other things, in the pride and haughtiness of his triumph, driving through Rome in a chariot drawn with four white horses, which no general either before or since ever did; for the Romans consider such a mode of conveyance to be sacred, and specially set apart to the king and father of the gods.

In short, the impression given is that Livy alone was desirous of evoking here, without apparent advantage for the Roman interest, a solar quadriga that can only belong to the Greek Helios, familiar to cultivated Romans of his time; by this contrivance he could show "Sol" among the divinities to whom Camillus is reputed to have pridefully wanted to compare himself at the time of his Veian triumph. Livy must have had a reason, especially since this mention of the sun god is the only one found anywhere in his legendary history, in the first six books of *Ab urbe condita*.[17] For what reason?

THE VICTORIES OF THE DICTATOR CAMILLUS AT DAWN

Jean Hubaux's observation and these simple reflections should have impelled us, in 1956, to open an investigation on a particular point: would not the goddess Aurora have continued her protection after the affair of Veii, where she had served Camillus under her name and according to the usual procedore of the *uotum* —would she not, at one time or another, have helped in his career through that which constitutes her material domain and her own means of action: the daily sunrise, daybreak? The truth is, this necessary and easy research waited fifteen years.

Judging by the annotations that Plutarch, recording Camillus'

---

[17] It was a question of Sol only in the enumeration of the "gods of Titus Tatius" (Varro, *De lingua latina*, 5.74; Dionysius of Halicarnassus, 2.50.3): see my *Archaic Roman Religion*, p. 169 and n. 34. On the Sol as a Roman cult object, see below, chapter 3: "The Day Begins during the Night," n. 4.

vow, attached as an explanatory parenthesis to the name of Mater Matuta, he does not seem to have been aware that this goddess was Aurora. For him she is only the Latin form and name for the Greek Leucothea, and it is by the fable of this unfortunate and devoted aunt of Bacchus that he explains the curious rites of the festival of the Matralia. And yet, an uninterrupted reading of his *Life* of Camillus reveals a trait, which until now has gone unperceived and which can only be explained by one purpose: that of manifesting a fundamental rapport between the hero and the phenomenon of dawn.

After holding the dictatorship that permitted him to take Veii, Camillus received this exceptional office four more times, during which all power and all responsibility were concentrated in his hands.[18] Only one of these dictatorships, the penultimate, was necessitated by wholly domestic concerns, when Rome was occupied with the difficult problems of adjusting the relationships between the patricians and the plebeians; no foreign wars were waged during this period. But each of the three other dictatorships —the second, the third, and the fifth of the complete picture—is the result of a state of war that causes great peril to Rome; and each time Camillus wins an unqualified victory in the first battle. *Now each of these three battles is begun under conditions that assure victory, exactly at dawn.* Here, in succession and without commentary, are the narratives.

The first is placed at the end of the Gallic catastrophe. During Camillus' exile the Romans were defeated on the Allia by the hordes of Brennus; and Rome, with the exception of the Capitol, was captured and destroyed. From outside Camillus succeeded in forming an army with the remnants of the legions which had escaped the disaster of the Allia. The senators, having sought refuge on the Capitol, declared or had him declared dictator for the second time. Then Camillus marched toward Rome. Meanwhile,

[18] Concerning the sovereign power of the dictator (of whom the orders are *pro numine*, Livy, 8.34.2), see pp. 273–274 of André Magdelain's "Praetor maximus et Comitiatus maximus," *Iura* 20 (1969), 257–285; cf. above, n. 9.

the Capitol had to negotiate, to buy the departure of the Gauls at a heavy price of gold, duly weighed. All Western children will remember from their history books the barbarian chief adding his sword and his buckler to the weights that load the scales, and his cry has come down through the centuries: "Vae uictis," or, as Plutarch says, τοῖς νενικημένοις ὀδύνη. But now the army of Camillus arrives (chapter 29):

Whilst this difference remained still unsettled, both amongst themselves and with the Gauls, Camillus was at the gates with his army; and having learned what was going on, commanded the main body of his forces to follow slowly after him in good order, and himself with the choicest of his men hastening on, went at once to the Romans where all giving way to him, and receiving him as their sole magistrate, with profound silence and order, he took the gold out of the scales, and delivered it to his officers, and commanded the Gauls to take their weights and scales and depart; saying that it was customary with the Romans to deliver their country with iron, not with gold. And when Brennus began to rage, and say that he was unjustly dealt with in such a breach of contract, Camillus answered that it was never legally made and the agreement of no force of obligation; for that himself being declared dictator, and there being no other magistrate by law, the engagement had been made with men who had no power to enter into it; but now they might say anything they had to urge, for he was come with full power by law to grant pardon to such as should ask it, or inflict punishment on the guilty, if they did not repent. At this, Brennus broke into violent anger, and an immediate quarrel ensued; both sides drew their swords and attacked, but in confusion, as could not be otherwise amongst houses, and in narrow lanes and places where it was impossible to form in any other form. But Brennus, presently collecting himself, called off his men, and, with the loss of a few only, brought them to their camp; and rising in the night [νυκτός] with all his forces, left the city, and, advancing about eight miles, encamped upon the way to Gabii. As soon as day appeared [ἅμα δ̣ ἡμέρᾳ] Camillus was upon him, splendidly armed himself and his soldiers full of courage and confidence; and then engaging with him in a sharp conflict, which lasted a long while, overthrew his army with great slaughter, and took their camp. Of those that fled, some were presently cut off by the pursuers; others, and these were the greatest number, dispersed hither and thither, and were dispatched by the people that came sallying out from the neighboring towns and villages.

And Camillus receives the honors of a second triumph.

In his third dictatorship, Camillus confronts a coalition of Volscians, Latins, and Etruscans. The situation is very serious. The Roman army, commanded by the consular tribunes, let itself be hemmed in and besieged in its camp. It must be freed (34.1–5).[19]

Camillus, being the third time chosen dictator, and learning that the army under the tribunes was besieged by the Latins and the Volscians, was constrained to arm, not only those under, but also those over, the age of service; and taking a large circuit round the mountain Maecius, undiscovered by the enemy, lodged his army on their rear, and then by many fires gave notice of his arrival. The besieged, encouraged by this, prepared to sally forth and join the battle; but the Latins and the Volscians, fearing their exposure to an enemy on both sides, drew themselves within their works, and fortified their camp with a strong palisade of trees on every side, resolving to wait for more supplies from home, and expecting, also, the assistance of the Tuscans, their confederates. Camillus, detecting their object, and fearing to be reduced to the same position to which he had brought them, namely, to be besieged himself, resolved to lose no time; and finding their rampart was all of timber, and observing that a strong wind constantly at sunrising [ἅμα φάει] blew off from the mountains, after having prepared a quantity of combustibles, about break of day [περὶ

[19] According to Plutarch, *Camillus*, 33.2, this account was concurrent, at this point in Camillus' life (third dictatorship), with the etiological legend of the Caprotine Nones: περὶ τούτου τοῦ πολέμου διττοὶ λόγοι λέγονται.

τὸν ὄρθρον] he drew forth his forces, commanding a part with
their missiles to assault the enemy with noise and shouting on
the other quarter, whilst he, with those that were to fling in the
fire, went to that side of the enemy's camp to which the wind
usually blew, and there waited his opportunity. When the
skirmish was begun, and the sun risen, and a strong wind set
in from the mountains [ἐπεὶ δὲ συνεστώσης τῆς μάχης 'ο θ' ἥλιος
ἀνῄει καὶ τὸ πνεῦμα λαμπρὸν ἐξέπιπτε], he gave the signal of
onset, and heaving an infinite quantity of fiery matter, filled
all their rampart with it, so that the flame being fed by the
close timber and wooden palisades, went on and spread into
all quarters.

The Latins, having nothing ready to keep it off or extin-
guish it, when the camp was now almost full of fire, were
driven back within a very small compass, and at last forced by
necessity to come into their enemy's hands, who stood before
the works ready armed and prepared to receive them; of these
very few escaped, while those that stayed in the camp were all
a prey to the fire, until the Romans, to gain the pillage, extinguished it.

The coalition breaks up, Camillus accepts the surrender of the
Volscians, energetically pushes his success, and wins his third
triumph.

In his fifth and final dictatorship, Camillus, an old man now,
again finds the Celts as adversaries. Coming from the Adriatic, a
huge band of Gauls advanced as far as the immediate boundaries of
Rome. The Senate and the people unanimously make him dictator
(41.1-6, 42.1):

When the Gauls drew near, about the River Anio, dragging a
heavy camp after them, and loaded with infinite spoil, Camillus drew forth his forces, and planted himself upon a hill of
easy ascent, and which had many dips in it, with the object
that the greatest of his army might lie concealed, and those
who appeared might be thought to have betaken themselves,
through fear, to those upper grounds. And the more to increase this opinion in them, he suffered them, without any

disturbance, to spoil and pillage even to his very trenches, keeping himself quiet within his works, which were well fortified; till, at last, perceiving that part of the enemy were scattered about the country foraging, and that those that were in the camp did nothing day and night but drink and revel in the night-time [τότε δὲ νυκτὸς ἔτι] he drew up his lightest-armed men, and sent them out before to impede the enemy while forming into order, and to harass them when they should first issue out of their camp; and early in the morning [ὄρθου] brought down his main body, and set them in battle array in the lower grounds, a numerous and courageous army, not, as the barbarians had supposed, an inconsiderable and fearful division. The first thing that shook the courage of the Gauls was, that their enemies had, contrary to their expectation, the honor of being aggressors. In the next place, the light-armed men, falling upon them before they could get into their usual order or range themselves in their proper squadrons, so disturbed and pressed upon them, that they were obliged to fight at random, without any order at all. But at last, when Camillus brought on his heavy-armed legions, the barbarians, with their swords drawn,[20] went vigorously to engage them; the Romans, however, opposing their javelins [that is, those which Camillus had ordered made for precisely this circumstance] and receiving the force of their blows on those parts of their defences which were well guarded with steel, turned the edge of their weapons, being made of soft and ill-tempered metal, so that their swords bent and doubled up in their hands; and their shields were pierced through and through, and grew heavy with the javelins that struck upon them. And thus forced to quit their own weapons, they endeavoured to take advantage of those of their enemies, laid hold of the javelins with their hands, and tried to pluck them away. But the Romans, perceiving them now naked and defenceless, betook themselves to their swords, which they so well used, that in a little time great slaughter was made in the foremost ranks,

---

[20] Regarding this motif of the Celts' swords, of which Polybius also is aware (2.33.3), apropos of a much later event, see Flacelière's edition of Plutarch, p. 147.

while the rest fled over all parts of the level country; the hills and upper ground Camillus had secured beforehand, and their camp they knew it would not be difficult for the enemy to take, as, through confidence of victory, they had left it unguarded. . . .

This was the last military action that ever Camillus performed; for the voluntary surrender of the city of the Velitrani was but a mere accessory to it. But the greatest of all civil contests, and the hardest to be managed, was still to be fought out against the people.

Thus, these three decisive acts of war, the only ones in which Camillus commands as dictator, are undertaken at dawn and practically won from the outset, without *the outcome ever in doubt.*

This detail is particularly striking in the first instance. If it had not been essential to the story, Roman pride would have reveled in having the entire revenge—the annihilation of the Gauls—occur during the afternoon or the previous evening, and in Rome itself. What a beautiful spectacle: the insolent barbarian chief beaten right away and punished on his famous scales, this time weighting the trays with his cadaver; the Gauls massacred on the spot where they had dared to strike the priests of Rome and the consuls. In place of this "ready-made scene" Plutarch offers the reader a juridical debate between Camillus and Brennus, followed by a skirmish which the narrowness of the streets prevented from developing into a battle. Very quickly, without even being harassed, without many losses, Brennus extricates himself and retreats to his camp somewhere in the city. Then, during the night, he leaves the city as a tactical retreat. And it is there, a few hours later, that Camillus, who let him leave the city, overtakes and surprises him. The Greek expression stresses the suddenness of attack, the disarray of the Gauls: "As soon as day appeared, Camillus was there, upon him" (ἅμα ἡμέρᾳ παρῆν ὁ Κάμιλλος ἐπ' αὐτόν). And what a Camillus! ὡπλισμένος λαμπρῶς, "clothed in brilliant armor." Why this detail? It is never mentioned again and even here, it is surprising, since Camillus, drawn out of exile, must have had greater worries than obtaining rich armor. Why, if not to add an almost supernatural note to the military genius of the character? His surging apparition before Brennus is a luminous epiphany, at dawn.

That the second victory is won at dawn is no less an important detail. If Camillus attacks at daybreak it is not to effect a surprise but because the maneuver that he has conceived needs the natural phenomenon which, at this location, occurs habitually and only at this moment of the day. For we must, of course, understand that the violent wind of dawn does not blow only that day, but regularly, and that Camillus was informed of this event on his arrival during the night, since he has the idea and the time to have the combustible materials which can only be useful to him at dawn brought and amassed, and since once these preparations are finished, he in fact waits for dawn and the atmospheric breeze that will facilitate the conflagration.

For the third victory, the dawn participates to a lesser degree. She allows only the surprise attack. But even that is not insignificant; it is striking that Camillus chose this battle plan and no other.

Are we to accept as fortuitous, without meaning, a repetition so regular, so complete, since these three victories are all won by Camillus during an unshared command, so varied also, since here dawn's motive is different each time—and a repetition in which a detail, that daybreak as such does not logically imply and does not necessarily call for, comes to reinforce in the first two cases: the armor of the general shimmering in the nascent light; the violent wind that blows neither night nor day but just when the sky lightens?[21] It is more logical to think that Camillus, who had successfully placed the task of his first dictatorship under the tutelage of the goddess Aurora and which the goddess Aurora had then favored, continues through his life, when he is supreme chief, to vanquish by means of the same hope and the same favor, at the precise hour of the day when the goddess is active. In other words, perhaps

---

[21] Different from the "themes and clichés" studied by Henry Bardon, *Revue des études latines* 24 (1946), 82–115.

the authors of his *gesta* intended to make of him, not only at the seizure of Veii, but throughout his military life, a typical protégé of Mater Matuta, emphasizing rather than putting aside the solar traits that this honorable definition implied.

SOLISQUE, 2

Let us return to Livy to ascertain that in his accounts of the same events nothing remains of this sort of leitmotif. On the first two occasions, the historian is concise to the extreme: he does not specify the time, the hour of the exploit, and eliminates the auroral detail. As for the third occasion, he curiously displaced it in such a way as to dismantle the theme.

Against Brennus (5.49.6):

> In a second more regular battle engaged in at the eighth milestone on the road to Gabii, the Gauls who had regrouped there after their flight were vanquished under the leadership and auspices of the same Camillus. The carnage was total. The camp was taken and no one remained to spread the news of the disaster.

Against the Volscians (6.2.9–13):

> The Volscians had entered into battle by mistake, believing that the Gauls had nearly annihilated the Roman youth. But the news that Camillus commanded as chief threw them into such terror that they closed themselves into an entrenchment, itself fortified by a pile of trees which was supposed to prevent the Romans from entering. Seeing this, Camillus gave the order to set fire to this obstruction of branches. By chance, a wind of great violence blew in the direction of the enemy [*forte erat uis magna uenti uersa in hostem*]. Not only did the fire open a passage but as the flames reached the camp, the vapor, the smoke, the very crackling of this mass of green material discouraged the enemy to the point that the Romans had less

trouble forcing open the entrenchment than they had had crossing the brazier. The enemy was routed and cut to pieces.

Thus dawn and the weapons which she causes to dazzle on Camillus have disappeared from the first victory. Dawn has also disappeared from the second and the wind is no longer hers but blows "by chance," *forte*, God knows when.[22]

Against the second Gallic invasion (6.42[23]):

> This was the year that the dictator, M. Furius Camillus, opened battle against the Gauls on Alban territory. Although the memory of their former defeat had left the Romans in extreme terror, their victory was neither doubtful nor difficult. The barbarians were massacred by the thousands during the battle, by the thousands also at the capture of their camp. Most of the survivors, in disorder, reached the Apulia, escaping the enemy as much by the remoteness of this refuge as by the dispersion caused by the panic and the hazards of the flight.

This time again dawn has disappeared from the scene.

With the second listing, it is difficult not to assume that the omission constitutes a new example of the well-known repugnance that Livy manifests toward any tradition that, exceeding the general protection of the gods to which the history of Rome and the biography of its great men brilliantly bear witness, proclaims the particular intervention of a divinity in the life of an individual, the closeness between a human being and a supernatural being. In his work from the very beginning he did not hesitate to accuse the

---

[22] Diodorus of Sicily (14.117.2) by contrast neglects the wind and fire but does specify that the victory over the Volscians was prepared by Camillus at night (νυκτὸς ἐξῆλθον) and won at dawn (καὶ καταλαβόντες ἅμ' ἡμέρᾳ τοὺς Οὐολούσκους τῇ παρεμβολῇ προσμαχομένους). Diodorus does not specify the time of the victory by which Camillus takes back the Roman gold from the Gauls and "nearly all their booty," a victory evidently moved from the day after their departure from Rome to the day after Camillus' deliverance of Satricum (117.4). Neither is a time given for a victory by Camillus as dictator over the Eques and the Equicoles (117.3).

[23] Livy writes these words after a discussion of sources; concerning this discussion see Flacelière's edition of Plutarch, p. 147.

Vestal who had claimed intimacy with Mars (1.4.3) of being an impostor. Then he let it be understood that he did not believe in the amicable relationship between Numa and the nymph Egeria (1.19.5) either. Much later, when it is necessary for him to speak of the rumors circulating about Scipio, son of Jupiter, his uneasiness is as apparent as his discretion (26.19.1–8).

This impression is confirmed by the way Livy used what constitutes the mainspring of the third auroral victory. Slighted, as has just been seen in 6.42, at the apogee of Camillus' military life, the dawn was placed much sooner, in the fifth book, at the beginning of his "post-Veian" career. Indeed, Camillus has just celebrated the triumph where he left himself open to criticism for imitating "Jupiter and the Sun." He has also just fulfilled his vows to Juno and Mater Matuta; but he has difficulty with the people and the reader cannot, in this victory where dawn intercedes only in a purely human hourly calculation, perceive any resonance, suspect any supernatural connivance—and all the less since this isolated mention of dawn does not follow the other two more picturesque and less human instances which the historian purely and simply refused to utilize. Here is the narrative where the enemies are no longer the Gauls but the Faliscans (5.26.4–8):

> Even though the enemy, for greater security, had at first shut themselves behind their walls, Camillus, by ravaging the countryside and setting fire to the farms, obliged them to leave the city. But fear prevented their going very far. They therefore built a camp, a few thousand feet from the site, relying above all for protection on the difficult access, surrounded as it was by rocks and ravines which allowed only very narrow or very steep passages. But Camillus, leaving from the plain, had a prisoner guide him. He pulled up camp in the middle of the night [*multo nocte*] and at the first glimmer of day [*prima luce*] appears in rather high positions dominating the enemy. Three detachments were raising fortifications when the enemies undertook to hinder the work. Camillus fights them and puts them to flight. From then on the fright of the Faliscans

was such that, in their desperate flight, they did not stop at their camp, which was closer, and reached the city. Many were killed or wounded in the panic prior to reaching the gates. The camp was taken.[24]

That is what Livy retained of the tradition of which Plutarch gives a complete picture in his three episodes: Livy displaced, and in so doing, devalued the only one of the three that he did not eliminate. Must we not then assume that the mention *Solisque,* in the account of the triumph, is intended subtly to replace all the rest by demythifying it, by reducing to a man's momentary pretension what had been, in a less skeptical version, the triple sign, perceptible to all, of · the special benevolence of the goddess Aurora and of her understanding with the hero?[25] The probability that Plutarch literally and faithfully retains here an authentic Roman tradition is so much the greater since, let us repeat, he seems unaware of what Livy could not ignore, namely that the protectress of Camillus, Leucothea, alias Mater Matuta, is the goddess of dawn, adoptive mother and protectress of the Sun.

FIRST BATTLE AT DAWN

Camillus encountered dawn much earlier, at the very beginning of his public life. Prior to him, says Plutarch (2.1-3) the house of the Furii was not illustrious:[26]

[24] The analogies with the account of the third "victory at dawn" in Plutarch are apparent: occupation of high ravines by the Romans during the night, unbeknownst to the enemies; descent by the Romans at daybreak; refusal of the fugitives to use their camp.

[25] Ogilvie, *Commentary on Livy,* p. 680 (to Livy, 5.23.6) note: "*Solisque*: the mention of the Sun as well as Jupiter as an object of comparison must post-date the introduction of the Hellenic mythology about the Sun, i.e., after the beginning of the third century B.C." (see Stefan Weinstock, "Two Archaic Inscriptions from Latium," *Journal of Roman Studies* 50 [1960], 117). "I think, for reasons developed in the text, that none other than Livy himself is responsible for this isolated mention."

[26] Plutarch, i.e., the tradition that he represents, is categorical on this point in

He by his own acts, first raised himself to honor, serving under Postumius Tubertus, dictator, in the great battle against the Æquians and the Volscians. For riding out from the rest of the army, and in the charge receiving a wound in his thigh, he for all that did not quit the fight, but, letting the dart drag in the wound, and engaging with the bravest of the enemy, put them to flight; for which action, among other rewards bestowed on him, he was created censor, an office in those days of great repute and authority.

This "great battle," which suddenly pulls Camillus from obscurity and opens up the finest of careers for him, beginning with the unlikely post of censor,[27] is familiar; it is the battle fought in 431 B.C. on Mount Algidus well before the war against Veii. And this battle, in the very detailed, moving epic account of Livy (4.27–29), is a victory "at dawn."[28]

It is, in fact, on Mount Algidus, a row of hills which extends from Preneste to the Alban Mountains, that the dictator A. Postumius Tubertus destroyed the army of the allied Æquians and Volscians—the same enemies that Camillus and his contemporary generals are reputed to have vanquished so often half a century later. Roughly speaking, the dictator spent the night preparing a complex offensive for dawn (4.28.1)—with the express prohibition to move *ante lucem* "because this corps is difficult to direct in the disorder of night combat." Thus the plan is to put into action at daybreak:

By this time the day was breaking [*et iam lucescebat*] and everything could be seen. Fabius had delivered a charge with his cavalry; the consul had made a sally from the camp against the enemy, who were already wavering; while the dictator, in

such a way that he nearly reconciles his declaration with the glories attributed to several Furii before Camillus and assembled by Hellegouarc'h, "Principat," 16; cf. below, chapter 2: *"camillus?"*

[27] Flacelière's edition of Plutarch; pp. 231–232: "According to other sources, Camillus did not become censor (with M. Postumius Albinus) until 403 B.C., i.e., 28 years after his deed (on Mt. Algidus)."

[28] Hereafter I use this expression in the sense of "victory where dawn plays a decisive role."

another part of the field, attacking the supports and the second line, had fallen upon the foe from every side, as they wheeled about to meet the wild shouts and sudden onsets, with his victorious foot and horse.

Total victory would have been immediate had the heroism of one Volscian not succeeded in prolonging the combat. But the die had been cast and the allied army was finally destroyed. The dictator (4.29.4), "entrusting the command to the consul, returned to Rome in the triumphal chariot [*triumphans inuectus urbem*], then abdicated the dictatorship."

In four verses of the *Fasti* (6.721–724) we learn more about this triumph and about the season, the day of victory:

> During the following night [i.e., between June 17 and 18], the constellation of the Dolphin will appear. In times past this constellation had seen the flight of the Æquians and the Volscians in your countryside, Algidian territory, an exploit which made you famous, Tubertus, by a victory gained over these close neighbors. Victor, you advanced, Postumus [sic], in a chariot which snow white horses pulled.

It is the very quadriga of Camillus.

The date of the victory is instructive. Dawn on June 18 occurs in the midst of the period of preparation for the summer solstice, which is opened by the festival of the goddess Aurora on June 11. This period harbors, still closer to the solstice on June 20, the *dies natalis* of the temple of another divinity, Summanus, whom we will soon meet again and whose period of activity is limited to the second part of the night. These details about the season of the victory and the manner of triumph must have had significance in the exploit of Tubertus, since they were retained by Ovid. In this victory, as in the subsequent triumphal entry, they make of this old dictator a rough draft of Aurora's great protégé, Camillus. Indeed, it is under his orders that the future protégé of Aurora, participating as a cavalryman, comes into glory at a very young

age. The leitmotif of Camillus' biography is thus sketched in from
the beginning.

DAWN BATTLES IN THE FIRST TEN BOOKS OF LIVY

This demonstration would not be complete without verifying
that, in all the legendary and semilegendary history of Rome—that
is, until approximately the beginning of the third century—the
theme of the victory won (or at least assured) at dawn, far from
being commonplace, is scarcely utilized.

At that, the only example I know is but a poor copy of the
battle of Mount Algidus. It occupies, in Plutarch, the penultimate
chapter (22) of the *Life* of Publicola and, in the *Roman Antiquities*
of Dionysius of Halicarnassus, three chapters (5.41–43). As on
Mount Algidus, the Roman attack is carried out here by three
separate corps which must operate jointly and suddenly, at dawn,
this time against the Sabine invaders.

> Publicola, however, soon advertised of these designs by de-
> serters, disposed his forces to their respective charges. Postu-
> mius Balbus, his son-in-law, going out with three thousand
> men in the evening, was ordered to take the hills, under which
> the ambush lay, there to observe their motions; his colleague,
> Lucretius, attended by a body of the lightest and boldest men,
> was appointed to meet the Sabine horse; whilst he, with the
> rest of the army, encompassed the enemy. And a thick mist
> rising accidentally [κατὰ τύχην], Postumius, early in the morn-
> ing [περὶ ὄρθρον] with shouts from the hills, assailed the am-
> buscade, Lucretius (at the same time (ἅμα)] charged the light-
> horse, and Publicola besieged the camp; so that on all sides
> defeat and ruin came upon the Sabines.

Not only the hour and the planned maneuver of the three corps
correspond to the battle of Mount Algidus, but the name of one of

the commanders, in spite of a variant (Βαλβός), is the same. The *legatus* Postumius Balbus, commander of one of the three corps in the army that another Postumius, the dictator Tubertus, leads corresponds at Mount Algidus to Postumius Albus, son-in-law of Publicola and commander of one of the three corps. This is therefore another utilization of a scheme, several of which are found in the "history" of the first centuries. But the first ten books of Livy contain no other battle voluntarily begun in *prima luce* by the Romans and ending in victory.

In 2.25.2 it is the Sabines who attack *prima luce* the *fossae* and the *uallum* of the Roman camp; but the Roman general waits (*parumper moratus*) to test his soldiers and does not begin (*tandem!*) combat until after being convinced of their ardor, as in 2.59.6 it is the Volscians who surprise *prima luce* a Roman marching column and put it to flight. In 2.51.7 the consul Servilius imprudently attacks the Janiculum *orta luce* and is unsuccessful. In the battle of 2.64-65, the dawn sees only the conclusion of the operations, which continued all night and tired the enemy. Likewise in 3.38.8 the second battle that begins *luce prima* is in fact but the complement of the long nocturnal battle, as the Prussian engagement prolonged the English battle during the evening of Waterloo. Similarly, in 5.28.9-13, the combat having been started at night, *ante lucem*, the *prima lux* only convinces the general that his troops can pursue the vanquished without fear of ambush—or again as in 7.12.1-2, a sudden nocturnal alarm hurries the Romans to the ramparts of their city until the *prima lux* shows the small number of Tibertines who attack it and whom they liquidate immediately. In 9.24 Sora is captured at night and the consuls arrive *prima luce*, when all is finished. In 9.35-37, the Roman attack is made not at dawn but in the predawn, *paullo ante lucem*, because on summer nights it is the time of deepest sleep, *quod aestiuis noctibus sopitae maxime quietis tempus est.* In 10.20 the general, informed by spies a little before daylight, *aliquanto ante lucem*, that the enemy is pulling up camp, *nocturna trepidatione*, does not wait for the day and attacks close to but short of dawn *iam lux appitebat.* In 10.43 the consul prepares *prima luce* to storm the position of the Samnites enclosed in Cominium, but twenty enemy infantry corps sighted in the vicinity make him suspend the order to attack.

That is the lineup. By contrast, the accumulation of four "victories at dawn" to the credit of Camillus—the one that brings him to the fore and the three that he wins during his dictatorships—no less than the picturesque and unpredictable role dawn plays in two of these last victories, must be significant. The authors of the chronicle truly wished Camillus to appear lastingly as the protégé of Mater Matuta.

THE LIFE OF CAMILLUS

It would be irresponsible to try to draw from this first investigation inferences, most likely important ones, for the formulation, if not the solution, of fundamental problems: when, by whom, by what means was the history of the first centuries of royal as well as republican Rome fabricated? I shall limit myself to four remarks that concern only the chronicle of Camillus and the theology of Mater Matuta.

First, we must recognize that this theology was still clear and familiar to the Romans when the chronicle was composed—that is, as clear as was all ancient history—at some point between 350 and 270,[29] probably more likely at the beginning of this period, shortly after the traditional date of Camillus' death.

Second, the relationship between Camillus and Aurora implies that, already at that time, the Romans were prepared to accept a type of hero singled out in the following centuries for great renown: Scipio, still a modest offshoot of Jupiter; above all the successive

---

[29] This, of course, does not preclude subsequent retouching, even the fabrication of new variants.

and increasingly showy protégés of Venus, up to the most illustrious, her beloved *nepos*, Julius Caesar; Augustus who owed victory and sovereignty, but above all his birth, to Apollo. Camillus, to be sure, is neither the son nor the nephew of Mater Matuta, but, by his copying the solar chariot at the time of his first victory (Livy) or by his dazzling epiphany at the time of his "victory at dawn" over the Gauls of Brennus (Plutarch), he appears as the epic equivalent of the star that Aurora introduces and protects each morning and for which the nephews, caressed and commended by the Roman ladies during the second rite of the Matralia, provide the ritual equivalent.[30]

Third, Livy is neither the sole nor the principal source for Plutarch.[31]

Fourth, Plutarch's principal source—probably Livy's also— must have presented completely and continuously the double picture of the relationship Camillus maintains with Aurora: first with the very individualized Mater Matuta of the annual Matralia, then with the goddess who opens each new day, one more discreet and veiled by her phenomenon. Plutarch retained the two aspects; but, not understanding the true significance of the goddess of the Matralia,[32] as is demonstrated by his annotations, he did not maintain or express the connection between these aspects. He linked the first to the inconsequential mention of the vow of Camillus; then, on three occasions, each time Camillus is victorious as dictator, he retained for the victory an auroral character that, in the first two instances, is more than an indication of time—without realizing, of course, that dawn is the domain of Matuta. Livy more carefully kept the first aspect, the first part, while removing moreover all originality: the *uotum* made to Mater Matuta and the *dedicatio* of

[30] Camillus thus prefigures the solar pretensions, nourished by the religions and speculations of the Mideast, which Henry Seyrig discovered in the coinage of Anthony. Pierre Grimal has just demonstrated the importance of these pretensions in the personage created by Nero at the beginning of his reign (*Comptes rendus de l'Académie des Inscriptions et Belles-Lettres* [1972], 225–230).

[31] See Flacelière's edition of Plutarch, pp. 144–147.

[32] This precludes the hypothesis, scarcely admissible of itself, that Plutarch systematically added the note "aurora" to the three victories of Camillus as dictator.

the promised temple form only a specific, banal case of an ordinary procedure; but since he still knew, as did Lucretius, the true naturalistic value of Matuta and since his philosophy of history was loath to admit a special link between a man and a divinity, he purely and simply omitted the dramatic scenes—barely evoking them through the enigmatic *Solisque*—which expressed in terms of everyday life the too constant favor, extended well beyond the *dedicatio*, which Aurora shows to her hero.

2

Aurora and Camillus

At this point in the study we are faced with two complementary tasks. On the one hand, it is a priori probable that the chronicle of Camillus, comprising, as we understand it, the action of the goddess and the behavior of the hero, has something to teach about the rather brief theology of Mater Matuta. On the other, it may be that other singular episodes of the chronicle are explained by the aspects of this theology known elsewhere and by the acts of worship dependent thereon.

THE GODDESSES OF JUNE 11

The goddess Aurora, then, by means of and under the guise of her daily phenomenon, favors Camillus each time he, as dictator, engages in a decisive battle. We must further understand that she was a good patroness, granting not only victory but also personal protection. Jean Hubaux has remarked that, except for the wound Camillus had received as a young horseman in the affair of Mount Algidus (where, moreover, each of the Roman chiefs was reputed to have received a famous wound), he is never touched by an enemy weapon:[1]

---

[1] *Rome et Véies* (Paris, 1958), p. 111.

Furius Camillus is invulnerable. No matter how eagerly he rushes forward to meet all possible enemies—Eques, Volscians, Veians, Faliscans, Gauls, Etruscans, Latins, other Gauls—he comes out unscathed from all these battles. When he finally dies, after an incredibly long military career, it is from the plague. Barring error, of all the great Romans of ancient times, he is the only one to succumb to a death apparently so incongruous with his many exploits.

Reflecting on these lines of the Belgian scholar, a reader who is not yet familiar with the chronicle of Camillus would unhesitatingly give a name to the divinity capable of providing such happiness: Fortuna. In fact, at first glance, Matuta acts as a type of Fortuna. And this is an important, moreover well-known, element of her theology. Here it will suffice to recall the principal facts:

First, the temples of the two goddesses on the Forum Boarium are close to each other. In 211 they burned in the same fire and were rebuilt together the following year by the same magistrate.

Second, the *dies natalis* of the two temples, that is, their dedication day, is the same: the eleventh, two days before the Ides of June.

Third, theologically the two goddesses are perceived as relatives. In 196, a general, L. Stertinius, coming back from Outer Spain with a fine booty, put 5,000 liras of silver in the public treasury, and with the profit from the sale of the rest, *de manubiis*, had two entrance porticos built on the Forum Boarium, "before the temple of Fortuna and Mater Matuta," and a third in the large Circus, and put gold statues on these porticos. The close proximity of the two Forum Boarium temples is not sufficient to explain their simultaneous foundation since a third one was built far away, in the Circus.

Fourth, the legendary founder of the two temples is the same. The king Servius Tullius, famous for his devotion to Fortuna, erected a sanctuary not only to his favorite divinity, but also to Mater Matuta, as Livy tells us when he speaks of Camillus' vow.[2]

---

[2] The authentic history that may be hidden under this tradition matters little

Of these two purveyors of luck, Fortuna is by far the more popular at this period of history, and perhaps she was strengthened very early by the Greek concept of Τύχη. It is, however, the other goddess who gave her name to the festival of their common day, Matralia, thus bearing witness that formerly she was of no less interest than Fortuna in the eyes of society or of individual Romans. Consequently, it is through her that the poet of *Fasti* begins his long bipartite exposé of the rites and legends of June 11. The plan of this exposé is most informative.

FASTI 6.473–624

Ovid, as he often does, first summons a character from mythology to cloak him in a two-verse periphrasis signifying simply that a new day is beginning. The character this time is chosen for the occasion: Tithonus, husband of the Greek Aurora (6.473–476):

> Now, Phrygian Tithonus, thou dost complain that thou art abandoned by thy spouse and the watchful Morning Star comes forth from the eastern waters. Go, good mothers (the Matralia is your festival), and offer to the Theban goddess the yellow cakes that are her due.

The Theban goddess is Leucothea, otherwise called Ino, the maternal aunt of Dionysus–Bacchus, who was deified after her death. That is, in fact, the learned and necessarily inadequate interpretation of Mater Matuta. Until verse 568 everything concerns her, including the rapid description and longer explanation of the two rites. Then the second goddess follows her, vigorously called forth:

> The same day, Fortune, is thine and the same founder, and the same place.

And until the end, up to verse 636, Fortuna alone is treated.

In the first part, after recording in a few words the name, the

---

here; see Arnaldo Momigliano, *Terzo contributo alla storia degli studi classici* (Rome, 1966), 597 n. 105 and 666.

place (Forum Boarium), the founder (Servius Tullius), and the first rite (the expulsion of the slave woman) of the Matralia, Ovid amply develops the Dionysian legend of Ino-Leucothea. He then moves on to the second rite (the attention of the celebrants toward the children "other than their own") and finishes by recalling the two relatively late historic events that occurred June 11.

In the second part, after the concise but dense transition quoted above (common date, place, founder of the two cults), the poet points out the only particular, unusual trait of Fortuna's cult; her temple contains a strangely garbed statue (570–572):[3]

> But who is yonder figure that is hidden in robes thrown one upon the other? It is Servius: so much is certain, but different causes are assigned for his concealment and my mind, too, is haunted by a doubt.

An honest investigator, Ovid passes in review three incompatible explanations, which go on to verse 624. Then, in eleven verses, he recalls the fire that, at this period of history, destroyed the temple, sparing only the statue. This gives him the opportunity to recount briefly the marvelous birth of Servius: Volcanus, god of devouring fire, was his father.

The union of the two goddesses must be an ancient trait justified by ideology. In the *Rig Veda*, where the mythology of Aurora —Uṣas—is so close to that of Mater Matuta, a similar link is many times established between Uṣas and Bhaga, "Attribution" personified, the god who is giver of goods and luck. A proverb, recorded in the *Brāhmaṇas*, says that Bhaga is blind for the same obvious reason that later made Westerners put out or blindfold the eyes of Τύχη—Fortuna.[4] But in the hymns, Bhaga is merely a beneficent

---

[3] The symbolism of this statue and the personage represented are subjects for discussion; see Plutarch, *Roman Questions*, 36 on the "bedroom" of Fortuna (Τύχης θάλαμος), which is beside the Fenestella.

[4] See my *Mitra-Varuṇa: Essai sur deux représentations indo-européennes de la souveraineté*, 2d ed. (Paris, 1948), pp. 194–199; idem, *Les dieux des Indo-Européens* (Paris, 1952), chapter 2 (ameliorated in the Spanish edition *Los dioses de los Indo-Europeos* [Barcelona, 1970], particularly pp. 48–50); idem, *Mythe et épopée I* (Paris, 1968), p. 150.

god. His connection with daybreak and with the goddess who presides over it is so close that in the only hymn consecrated to him he constitutes, according to Louis Renou,[5] "a kind of masculine double of Uṣas." Moreover, nothing is more natural than this solidarity. Aurora is not limited to producing the young Sun for humanity in a particularly brilliant instant. She also opens a long day with a personal and social, religious, political, economic, even military content, a content unforeseeable and uncertain. Reversing the Turkish proverb, we might say: "Until nightfall who might know with what the day was pregnant?" Here is Fortuna, or rather the multiple Fortunae: one of the peculiarities of this figure is that she fragments herself into small specific entities according to time and place: *Fortuna huius diei, Fortuna huius loci, Fortuna muliebris, Fortuna equestris,* and so on.

MATER MATUTA AND FORTUNA

But we are in Rome, the home of born jurists, experts in definitions and distinctions, for whom ambiguities are repugnant. In spite of a generally admitted postulate, there are no theologic doublets in Rome. For example, all their common or alternate traits and honors notwithstanding, Tellus is not a doublet but a complement of Ceres. Ovid (*Fasti* 1.671–674) says clearly that they are distinct as the *locus* and the *causa* of growth.[6] Likewise Bellona, who dominates war even in its diplomatic aspects and who can thus anticipate it, is not a feminine equivalent of Mars, who is totally engaged in the melée.[7] In sum, the closer two or three divine figures

---

[5] *Études védiques et pāṇinéennes* (Paris, 1957), vol. 3, p. 9 n. 2. Yāska, *Nirukta,* 12.13, says that Bhaga presides in the late morning. In *Rig Veda*, 1.123.5, Uṣas is called sister of Bhaga.

[6] See my *Archaic Roman Religion*, trans. Philip Krapp (Chicago and London, 1970), pp. 370 ff.

[7] Ibid., pp. 390 ff.

are, the more the Romans in their taste for order and clarity endeavored to distribute among them the aspects of one task, of one domain, which from a distance appear uniform. This is also the case of Fortuna and Mater Matuta. They divided between themselves two ways, opposed in their principles and in their consequences, of administering divine favor, and constitute an articulated couple whose formula stands out sufficiently in the exposé of Ovid. Briefly, Matuta, the goddess of the Matralia, is a mother, or rather an aunt who behaves like a mother. When she has chosen to protect a man, one can expect to see her act with feelings suitable to a mother, and first with indefectible fidelity. In contrast, Fortuna is a mistress who treats her favorites as women who are simultaneously amorous and imperious treat the men who interest them—a treatment often pleasant, sometimes uncomfortable, occasionally dangerous. Let us look more closely at the two panels of the picture of the *Fasti*.

The first, that of Matuta, is impregnated from beginning to end with a maternal spirit which, though expressed in Greek, Dionysian scenes, is nonetheless significant. The tone is given by the first verses (*Fasti*, 6.485–488):

> Through the compliance of Jupiter with her request Semele was consumed by fire: Ino received thee, young Bacchus, and zealously nursed thee with the utmost care. Juno swelled with rage that Ino should rear the son who had been snatched from his leman mother; but that son was of the blood of Ino's sister.

This theme of maternity, and a maternity that is not carnal but adoptive and moral, runs through the entire story with many variations—devotion, heroism, troubles, and pains—until the last verses, related to the second rites of the festival (559–562):

> Nevertheless, [that is, in spite of all that Leucothea did for Palemon, her own son, which has just been recounted], let not the affectionate mother [*pia mater*] pray to her on behalf of her own offspring: she herself proved to be no lucky parent. You will do better to commend to her care the progeny of

78

another [*alterius prolem*]; she was more serviceable to Bacchus than to her own children.

Let us compare with this the opening of the section devoted to Fortuna; we recall the beginning: (569–572):

> The same day, Fortune, is thine, and the same founder, and the same place. But who is yonder figure that is hidden in robes thrown one upon the other? It is Servius: so much is certain, but different causes are assigned for his concealment, and my mind, too, is haunted by a doubt.

And the poet, without further reflection, moves on to the first of the three justifications proposed for this strangeness (573–581):

> While the goddess timidly confessed her furtive love, and blushed to think that as a celestial being she should mate with a mere man (for she burned with a deep, an overmastering passion for the king [Servius Tullius], and he was the only man for whom she was not blind), she was wont to enter his house by a small window (*fenestra*); hence, the gate bears the name of *Fenestella* ("the little window"). To this day she is ashamed and hides the loved features beneath a veil, and the king's face is covered with many a robe.

The opposition of the two goddesses is clear, and one now sees why Servius Tullius is reputed to have dedicated their temples on the same day, at the same site. His career, begun in the domain of Mater Matuta, developed and tragically ended in the domain of Fortuna.

Mater Matuta shaped, in fact, his birth and his early childhood. He was no more reared by his mother than was the nephew of Ino. Son of a captive who served in the palace of the first Tarquin and his wife Tanaquil,[8] he was brought up by the queen, and

---

[8] About this feminine figure out of whom some scholars have attempted at times to make a goddess, see the discussion of Arnaldo Momigliano, "Tre figure mitiche: Tanaquil, Gaia Cecilia, Acca Larenzia" (1938), repr. in *Quarto contributo alla storia degli studi classici e del mondo antico* (1969), 455–479 (particularly pp. 461–463): "Tanaquil è insomma semplicemente una figura di donna su cui la tradizione leggendaria ha lavorato."

the queen only, *alterius prolem*, as Ovid says concerning the second rite of the Matralia. Thus, in the beginning, through the care of his second mother, he bears the mark of a divine protectress who is not Fortuna. Florus expressed well the moral values, which are constant through all the variants of this famous narrative (1.6):

> It is Servius Tullius who then took over the government of the city. Though born of a slave mother, his obscurity presented no obstacle to him [*nec obscuritas inhibuit*]. In fact, owing to his exceptional nature, the wife of Tarquin, Tanaquil, had given him the education of a free child, and a flame which appeared around his head had promised that he would be famous [*clarum fore*]. This is why, thanks to the queen's artifice, he succeeded Tarquin after his death, as if he had been designated for this role in advance. But so deftly did he exercise this royalty acquired by ruse, that he seemed to have received it by right.

This is Mater Matuta's part in his life—the queen playing for the foreign child, the adopted, moreover marvelous, son, the role that the "Theban goddess" plays for Bacchus.

The remainder of Servius Tullius' career, however, depends on Fortuna his mistress, as Ovid says. He accumulates extraordinary successes; and when he is old, probably too old to be loved even by a goddess, his luck turns and he suffers one of the cruelest deaths of Roman legend. Incited by his daughter, his son-in-law rebels, Servius is killed, and his daughter forces the reluctant coachman to drive the wheels of her chariot over the cadaver.

Reading further in the *Fasti*, one finds for June 24 a reference to another cult of Fortuna, also founded by Servius Tullius (*Fasti*, 6.771–784):

> Time slips away, and we grow old with silent lapse of years; there is no bridle that can curb the flying days. How quickly has come around the festival of Fors Fortuna! Yet seven days and June will be over. Come, Quirites, celebrate with joy the goddess Fors! On Tiber's bank she has her royal foundations.

. . . The common folk worship this goddess because the
founder of her temple [Servius Tullius] is said to have been of
their number and to have risen to the crown from humble
rank. Her worship is also appropriate for slaves, because
Tullius, who instituted the neighboring temples of the fickle
goddess, was born of a slave woman.

Dubia dea: this is Fortuna's part in the life of this king, of all great
men. Did not a friendly voice advise the triumphant general,
advancing in a chariot, to turn around "in order to exorcise Fortuna, the executioner of glory," "ut sit exorata a tergo Fortuna
gloriae carnifex"?[9]

We can return to Camillus. The difference that separates him
from Servius Tullius is simple, and evident to whoever follows his
life in Plutarch. Until his death, Camillus enjoys the protection of
Mater Matuta alone and is ignorant of Fortuna. Let us reread chapter 36, where Camillus is rendered more directly responsible for the
downfall of Manlius Capitolinus than he is in Livy and in other
sources. The story commences (36.1–2) with one of Camillus'
triumphs, the third. This distinction was accorded him after his
second "victory at dawn" (chapter 34), quickly exploited (chapter 35).

> For all which actions he received a triumph, which brought
> him no less honour and reputation than the two former ones;
> for those citizens who before most regarded him with an evil
> eye, and ascribed his success to a certain kind of luck [εὐτυχίᾳ
> τινί] rather than real merit [μᾶλλον ἢ δι' ἀρετήν], were com-
> pelled by these last acts of his to allow the whole honour to his
> great abilities and energy [τῇ δεινότητι καὶ τῷ δραστηρίῳ τοῦ
> ἀνδρὸς ἀποδιδόναι τὴν δόξαν]. Of all the adversaries and enviers
> of his glory, Marcus Manlius was the most distinguished, he
> who first drove back the Gauls when they made their night
> attack upon the Capitol and who for that reason had been
> named Capitolinus.

[9] Pliny, *Natural History*, 28.39.

After the execution of the ambitious Capitoline, condemned for *affectatio regni*, the story concludes with a few words, which deliver him over definitely to this Fortuna who had had no hold on his rival (36.8):

> He was convicted, carried to the Capitol, and flung headlong from the rock; so that one and the same spot was thus the witness of his greatest glory, and monument to his most unfortunate end [τὸν αὐτὸν τόπον ἔσχε καὶ τῶν εὐτυχεστάτων ἔργων καὶ τῶν μεγίστων ἀτυχημάτων].

In other words, the career of Manlius is marked by the two opposing aspects of the Τύχη, of Fortuna—the Capitol and the Tarpian Rock—while Camillus owes nothing to "good fortune," to luck, εὐτυχία. The protection of Mater Matuta would not have permitted a demise like that of Servius Tullius, his predecessor, or of his adversary, Manlius. Plutarch, we have seen, recognizes in the form of his hero's death the worthy crowning of a happy career (43.1–2):

> In the year following, a pestilential sickness infected Rome, which, besides an infinite number of the common people, swept away most of the magistrates, among whom was Camillus; whose death cannot be called immature, if we consider his great age, or greater actions, yet was he more lamented than all the rest put together that then died of that distemper.

To die in the general affection, to die "at the right time," "in the nick of time" (ὡραῖος, *maturus*), what better sign of an indefectible divine protection?

THE ETHICS OF MATER MATUTA

The assortment of qualities displayed by Camillus during his lifetime is remarkable. These qualities dispense with resorting to luck to explain his successes. In fact, Plutarch carefully avoids using the derivatives, good or bad, or τύχη when the hero is referred to,[10] while he uses them frequently, in the course of his *Life*, with regard to other personages or even to Rome. Pontius Cominius, the messenger sent by the Roman troops at Veii to the magistrates of the Capitol, succeeds in his perilous mission ἀγαθῇ τύχῃ (23.2); Camillus himself explains to the young people of Ardea that the catastrophe at the Allia is a stroke of τύχη (23.3); the *omen* of the centurion who prevents the Romans from deserting the ruins of their city occurs κατὰ τύχην (32.2). The word εὐτυχία is applied to Camillus only once, placed by Plutarch in Camillus' own mouth; but the circumstances are extraordinary. In recently conquered Veii, the triumphant general, overwhelmed by felicitations, humbles himself in the Roman manner before Jupiter, *minor* before a *maiestas*. He prays to the great god that, if a mystical ransom is necessary in return for the present success (τῆς παρούσης νέμεσις εὐπραξίας), it strike neither Rome nor the Roman army, but rather himself, and at the least cost. Scarcely has he pronounced these words than he loses his footing while turning around, and falls. He rises immediately and says the god has already granted his prayer, satisfied with a small tumble to balance his very great good fortune ('επ' εὐτυχίᾳ μεγίστῃ). Thus, in his profound piety and in his religious modesty, Camillus himself is ready to attribute to luck a success for which he knows, as do his biographers and we ourselves, that he carefully and rationally assembled the conditions.

Likewise, what Plutarch emphasizes throughout the entire *Life* are his personal strengths rather than external luck: first, his intelligence and his character and also his experience (9.1; 38.1); then his justice (10.6), his caution, and his καλοκαγαθία (24.4), his prudence in battle (37.3), his moderation (38.2-3), and his humanity

---

[10] It is significant that Plutarch, in his treatise *Of the Fate of the Romans* where the multiple chances of Rome and the great Romans are amply exploited, mentions Camillus only to say that, after the liberation of Rome, he erected a temple to Aius Locutius in acknowledgement of the nocturnal counsel given to M. Caedicius (see my *Mythe et épopée III* [Paris, 1973], pp. 228-231); now the counsel was not concerned with Camillus and Aius Locutius is not Fortuna. Servius, on the contrary, establishes many cults of Fortuna which Plutarch enumerates (*Of the Fate of the Romans*, 322C-323D; *Roman Questions*, 36, 74, and 106).

(38.4–6), without counting his meritorious conversion, in politics, to liberalism (42). These are the factors of his enduring success.[11]

Textual analysis of Livy seems to express another balance. He agrees with Plutarch as far as the personal strengths of Camillus. Throughout his entire life, *consilium* and *consilia*, as opposed to *temeritas* (6.24.6), dominates his action and this intellectual superiority rests on more ethical qualities: *iustitia* (5.27.11; 28.1), *fides* (5.28.1), *moderatio* (6.25.5–6; 27.1), *patientia* (6.27.1), and *uirtus* (6.27.1)—to which must be added a piety toward the gods that never weakens. But in contrast to Plutarch, Livy (who, one recalls, eliminated as much as possible the marks of a continuous favor from Mater Matuta) seems to reintroduce Fortuna into this extraordinary destiny.[12] He uses her name no fewer than seven times in direct relation to Camillus. But a distinction must be made in that *Fortuna* in Latin has a very wide usage, much wider than τύχη in Greek.

While Camillus, heading an army composed of Ardeans, crushes a horde of Gauls, the remnants of the Allia army, regrouped at Veii under the command of a centurion, obtain a victory over the Etruscans. Of this victory it is said (5.45.8): "tantum par Camillo defuit auctor, cetera eodemque fortunae euentu gesta." *Fortuna* is most likely not the goddess here but simply designates the uncertainty of any battle, which may have a good or a bad *euentus*. Similarly, several times *fortuna* is only an appellative, designating the course of events, good or bad, with its resulting good or bad situation. For example, after the capture of Veii, when Camillus begs the gods—if they take offense at such a success—to transfer their jealousy and that of the men to him and not to Rome and when he says (5.21.15) "si cui deorum hominumque nimia sua

---

[11] The detailed multiplicity of qualities advises against reducing the debate for Camillus to a simple commonplace "ἀρετή or τύχη; uirtus or fortuna?" (Plutarch, *Of the Fate of the Romans*, 316C–326C; etc.).

[12] Besides the general reason that Fortuna always remained a familiar figure to the Romans, a sort of *lectio mythica facilior* in relation to Mater Matuta, other points of consensus probably played a role, which Hellegouarc'h (see following note) keenly analyzed.

fortuna populique Romani uideretur," the adjective "excessive" indeed proves that *fortuna* is not the goddess. Here *fortuna* is but a tally sheet, appreciable if not measurable and given to fluctuation. Again, in his exile at Ardea, at the news of the disaster at the Allia and of the occupation of Rome by the Gauls Camillus is "maestior fortuna publica quam sua" (5.43.7). This signifies nothing other than that he is "sadder about the national misfortune than about his own." A little further on (5.44.1) when he addresses the Ardeans saying "my old friends and my new fellow citizens" and justifies this title by saying "quando et uestrum beneficium ita tulit et fortuna hoc egit mea," "since your kindness has permitted it and my misfortune has reduced me to it," *fortuna mea* is not a goddess, but an objective fact, parallel to *uestrum beneficium*, an aspect of what he calls in the next sentence his *condicio*. Likewise when Livy, wishing to oppose the success of the army Camillus commands against the Volscians and the unfavorable situation of the allies on the Etruscan borders, writes (6.3.1) "cum in ea parte in qua caput rei Romanae Camillus erat, ea fortuna esset, aliam in partem terror ingens ingruerat," the word *fortuna* has no meaning other than that of an "advantageous or disadvantageous situation." It does not evoke the intervention of the goddess. In the same way, in Camillus' funeral eulogy (7.1.8) "uir unicus in omni fortuna" signifies only "in all circumstances, good and bad, of his life": *omnis* demythifies *fortuna*.

These texts aside, and also, of course, those (5.19.3, 37.1, 40.1, 43.7, 49.1, 51.2 and 3, 6.3.1, and 34.8 and 9) dealing with the fortune of the Romans, the city, or armies, and not of the general, there nevertheless remain two texts where Fortuna is an active force, a responsible will, a goddess favorable to Camillus. In 5.26.10, the war against Falerii would surely have been perpetuated like the one against Veii "ni Fortuna imperatori Romano simul et incognitae rebus bellicis uirtutis specimen et maturam uictoriam dedisset." And in 6.23.9, objecting to the temerity of his colleague L. Furius, Camillus tries to persuade his soldiers that they must not open battle under unfavorable conditions and reminds them that, until this day, the Romans have had no cause to complain about his plans or his Fortune: "aut consilii sui aut Fortunae paenituisse." Do these two texts suffice to make Livy's Camillus a protégé of the goddess Fortuna, as has again been recently affirmed?[13] I think not. The first is obviously a rhetorical expression whose words must not be exaggerated. The second seems to equate *consilium* with *Fortuna* as conditions of the success. It should be clarified by what the historian says at the beginning of the chronicle of Camillus before the capture of Veii, regarding the first victory that the *fatalis dux* obtains for his troops, in a sort of trial operation in *agro Nepesino* (5.19.8): "omnia ibi summa ratione consilioque acta Fortuna etiam, ut fit, secuta est," "all was carried out with the highest perfection of reasoning and judgment so that, as usually happens, Fortuna followed." The hierarchy is clear; it is not Fortuna that leads or acts, but *ratio* and *consilia*.

The overview of Camillus' qualities enables us to perceive another difference between the protection given by Mater Matuta and by Fortuna. Not only is one maternal and faithful, the other passionate and capricious, but Mater Matuta seems to act less from without by means of discreet help and circumstances than from within, in the head and the heart, through the thought and the character of the man she favors, immunizing him against any form of *superbia*. Fortuna, on the other hand, acts only from without, or rather, when she acts from within she leaves her favorite exposed to or even predisposes him to the intoxication of power, the delirium of pride. Among Camillus' "victories at dawn," even in the second, there is no miracle *per se*. If he allows himself, once in the first victory, the pleasure of appearing before the enemy at the time and in the attire of the rising sun, or if, according to Livy, he triumphs in a chariot that too closely resembles that of the sun, we can

---

[13] Jean Bayet, edition of Livy (Guillaume Budé collection, 1954), vol. 5, pp. 145–146. Joseph Hellegouarc'h, "Le principat de Camille," *Revue des études latines* 48 (1970), 112–132 (on this point particularly 117–119), considered only the Camillus of Livy. It is clear that the four uses of the adverb *forte* in the chapters of Livy concerning Camillus do not involve Fortuna.

assume, based on his general deportment, that he does not claim to equal the star but simply that he recognizes, expresses, and accepts the benefaction of the goddess Aurora. Under all circumstances he gives the appearance of a man entirely in command of himself, because in the assortment of qualities that result from the "rule of Mater Matuta" one of the most valuable for a chief (and the opposite of the perilous stupors of Fortuna) is prudence, reflection before action—even, on occasion, the refusal to act. Aside from the *Life* of Camillus, this truth is expressed, directly linked with the goddess, in the six verses that conclude the development of the *Fasti* devoted to Mater Matuta, which are at first surprising. The unreserved eulogy of Mater Matuta, the moving explanation of the beneficial intentions of her festival, conclude with the mention of two military disasters that took place the same day and which one would more likely expect to see attributed to Fortuna (6.563–568). However, a close look is sufficient to show that they are in their right place:

> They relate that she [Mater Matuta] said to thee, Rutilius, "Whither dost thou hasten? On my day in thy consulship thou shalt fall by the hand of a Marsian foe." Her words were fulfilled, and the stream of the Tolenus flowed purple, its water mingled with blood. When the next year was come, Didius, slain on the same day, doubled the forces of the foe.

These two regrettable accidents occurred at the beginning of the century just before our era, during the Social War. The second mention is, moreover, erroneous, Didius' name having replaced that of the consul L. Porcius Cato who, in fact, perished in 89 B.C., a year after the consul P. Rutilius Lupus. But this has little bearing on our subject. If Ovid gives no indication of the cause of the second setback, he throws light on the first and mixes therein the goddess of the day in an instructive manner: Rutilius makes the mistake of remaining deaf to the very clear warning the goddess had been careful to give him. Fortuna might have let him become involved and perish by surprise. Matuta did what she could to save him, to restrain "his haste" (*quo properas?*).

This intervention of Matuta thus confirms that the idea Ovid has of her and of her modus operandi is indeed the one we have extracted. It further confirms that the foremost quality of the men whom she protects is the very one that explains all the successes of Camillus, *ratio consiliumque*, the accurate appreciation of the risks and the advantages of a given situation.

Two scenes from the *Life* of Camillus illustrate the two sides of the *consilium* by which he governs himself. Both bring into play, not the goddess directly, but Satricum,[14] the city which is one of the chosen seats of her cult. It is as if Mater Matuta favored Camillus not only through her daily *time* but through the *territory* that belongs to her, and caused him to amass not only the "victories at dawn" but the "victories at Satricum."

In one of the scenes (Livy, 6.23–25; Plutarch, 37), Satricum, a Roman colony, has just been captured by the Volscians. Camillus, who is not dictator but one of the *tribuni militum consulari potestate* who at the time hold the position of the consuls, receives the mission to oppose them. Having arrived before the enemy, he refuses to start a combat that he judges too uncertain and toward which his impetuous colleague L. Furius, the young officers, and even the soldiers want "to hurry." The fate of the battle which presents itself, *praesentis dimicationis fortuna*, says this entire group, is delayed only by the judgment and command of a single man, *unius uiri consilium atque imperium*. Camillus does not give in, but leaves the initiative to L. Furius, who starts the battle. It is nearly a disaster; only the adeptness of Camillus succeeds in turning it into a victory, following which, moreover, he gives a good example of *moderatio animi* (self-control) in regard to his guilty colleague. Livy, before the event, summarizes its lesson well (22.6):

> The Volscian war was entrusted, out of the regular course, to Marcus Furius. Of the other tribunes, Lucius Furius was assigned him by lot for his assistant, not so much (it would

[14] Satricum occupied the site of the present Borgo Montello, on the River Astura. Antium, a Latin city, had passed under the domination of the Volscians after the end of the Roman royal era.

seem) for the good of the commonwealth as that he might be the source of all honour to his colleague; who gained it in his public capacity because he made good what the other's rashness had lost, and as a man because he used the error of Lucius to earn his gratitude rather than glory for himself.

But, for the help of Matuta to be efficacious, the beneficiary must collaborate, must listen to the call of *ratio*, to the objective appreciation of the facts which, depending on circumstances, will compel him to caution or audacity. Rutilius did not listen and hurried when he should have waited—preferring to provide Ovid with an excellent transition between the description of Matuta, which he has just completed, and that of Fortuna, which he undertakes immediately thereafter.

In the other scene, where the *consilium* of Camillus commands audacity, the mention of the location is certainly significant. Through their two cities, Mater Matuta of Satricum and Fortuna of Antium manifest opposite feelings toward the Roman general. Livy is the lone witness here (6.8–9). A coalition of Latins, Hernicians, and Volscians has taken up arms and has concentrated its troops in front of Satricum. Camillus is sent against them not as dictator but again this time as one of the military tribunes. The Roman army does not fail through temerity—quite the contrary. Frightened by the enemy's number, the army hesitates. Then Camillus seizes a standard and darts forward. The soldiers follow him, terror invades the other camp, and the victory would be complete had sudden and violent rain not interrupted the combat. During the night the Latins and the Hernicians withdraw, abandoning the Volscians, who leave their camp and sequester themselves in Satricum. But Camillus rouses his soldiers: isn't the victory within their reach? In a great burst of enthusiasm, they attack the walls with ladders from all sides. They take the fortress where the refuged Volscians abandon the fight. Camillus immediately conceives a greater plan. He wants to turn his efforts to Antium, one of the large Volscian cities and the origin of the war. But he needs the approbation of the Senate because Antium is so well fortified that immense stores for siege must be set up. Leaving the army to his colleague, Camillus thus goes to Rome "to exhort the Senate to destroy Antium." But while he is in Rome news arrives that in the north the Etruscans have attacked allied Roman cities, which now call for help. It is to defend them, *omisso Antio*, that the Senate appoints its best general. Livy concludes: "eo uim Camilli ab Antio Fortuna auertit," "it is by this means that Fortuna averted from Antium the force of Camillus." Thus, the city of Mater Matuta yields to the assault of the soldiers of Camillus without their striking a blow, delivering to him the Volscians who occupied the city. By contrast, the city of Fortuna is seen protected from Camillus through the only means left to the gods: preventing the attack, dispatching the invincible Roman to another front. It is interesting to see that Livy, despite the inverse symmetry of the two scenes, clearly shows Fortuna acting against Camillus before the walls of Antium. Yet he does not even suggest that Mater Matuta facilitated for him the scaling of the walls of Satricum—probably another effect of the bias that makes him blur the special bonds of his hero and the goddess.[15]

There seems to be an exception to this constant protection of Mater Matuta. Between the capture of Veii by the Romans and the capture of Rome by the Gauls, human wickedness and unjust accusations drive Camillus into exile. But is this really an exception? If we consider that this disgrace prepares the most brilliant reparation and is pregnant with the incomparable glory, we will sense rather a

[15] During Camillus' life, but in a situation in which he is not involved, Livy saw no problem in showing Mater Matuta of Satricum intervening against the enemies of Rome in a more personal way even than did Fortuna of Antium against Camillus. In 6.33.4–5 while the Latins, in revolt against Rome, burned Satricum without respect for the sacred edifices, only the temple of Mater Matuta was saved, "neither by their own scruples, nor by their reverence for the gods, but by an awe-inspiring voice that issued from the temple and threatened dire retribution if they did not remove those impious fires to a distance from the sacred walls." Later, in 7.27, the consul M. Valerius Corvus, occupying Satricum which had been reconquered, rebuilt, and colonized by the Volscians of Antium, demolished and burned the city that had thus become enemy territory; but, naturally, "only the temple of Mater Matuta was saved from the flames."

useful detour from the divine benevolence. We will come back to this point in the next chapter.[16]

Another trait of Camillus draws him closer to the maternal goddess who protects him: a great and communicative ability for compassion and even tenderness. We will soon find manifestations of this in more ample contexts. Listing them is sufficient at this point.

When the children of Falerii are delivered to Camillus by their schoolmaster, he sends them back to their parents, calling them "eam aetatem cui etiam captis urbibus parcitur" (Livy, 5.27.7). If he does not cry as do his soldiers at the sight of the pitiful band of Sutrians chased from their city with women and children, he is ἐπικλασθείς, "seized with pity" (Plutarch, *Camillus*, 35.3), and hastens to reconquer their homes for them. When, on his way to punish the unfaithful Tusculans, he sees them all, men, women, children, express a repentance a little too theatrical, he has pity on them, οἰκτίρας, even though he is not duped, and becomes their intercessor with the Senators (ibid., 38.5). These, in turn, are moved and welcome the envoys of these traitors as brothers (Livy, 6.26.3). These three instances of behavior—in all three there are children to save, alone or among other unfortunate persons—are consistent with a fundamental quality of "Mater" Matuta. It is this quality that supports the second rite of the "Matralia" and probably provoked or favored the assimilation of the goddess to Ino-Leucothea. In fact, the Greek legend that supposedly founded the rite, the safety and education of the child Bacchus, is one of pity, tenderness, fidelity, and protection.

CAMILLUS?

If it is true that the external, direct interventions of Matuta in the life of her hero are not obvious, there is yet another external

---

[16] See below, chapter 3: "Victories at Night."

trait that we expect in the interventions because of its recurrence in the mythology of dawn and the rising sun among the various Indo–European peoples.[17] In the Vedic expressions, at least in one of them, the Sun is not the son of Aurora but rather her nephew, whom she takes in. In the epic transposition that the *Mahābhārata* makes of the oldest mythology, the hero offspring of the Sun who expresses anew the essential traits of his father, has two mothers of whom only the second, the adoptive one, counts. In the Ossetic and Caucasian legends, the hero Soslan (Sosryko), who presents so many solar elements, is formed in a rock from which the wise Satana extracts him, rears him, and treats him as a mother would, constantly calling him "my son whom I did not beget." In Rome the theologem subjacent to the second Matralia rite and the legend of the childhood of Servius Tullius, first and partial devotee and protégé of Mater Matuta, also presents us with this motif. Did Camillus depart from this convention?

We will never know anything about this because his chronicle, as we read it, says nothing about his origin and his beginnings. Plutarch limits himself to introducing the biography by the very vague words: "At that time" κατὰ τοῦτο δὴ καιροῦ (1.4); then he broaches his subject, not just when Camillus is already adult (or adolescent), but when he is at the point of accomplishing his first feat (2.1): "The house of the Furii was not, at that time, of any considerable distinction;[18] he, by his own acts, first raised himself to honor."

This brief and negative indication moves along at least in the expected direction. Only for the gift of life are the "heroes of dawn" indebted to their real parents, especially their real mothers, whom they don't know or subsequently neglect. A second indication is perhaps provided by the very surname of M. Furius. The *camillus* is in fact a free child (*ingenuus*), even patrician (*nobilis*), and prepu-

---

[17] The converse is obviously not true; many heroes reared by an adoptive mother or parents have nothing solar about them. See my *Mythe et épopée III*, pp. 327–328.

[18] See above, chapter 1, n. 26.

bescent (*impuber, inuestis*) whose father and mother are still living (*patrimus, matrimus*) but who is attached to the religious service of a priest, namely the head priest, the *flamen Dialis: flamini Diali ad sacrificia praeministrabat.*[19] This implies that, for his demanding liturgical activity, the priest take a child from another family and put him under his orders, even if he has children of his own. Is this the kind of situation—of which *Camilla*'s in the *Aeneid* seems to be a transposition[20]—that earned Camillus his surname? This would be a specifically Roman adaptation of the "bifamilial" status of solar heroes.

THE FALISCAN PEDAGOGUE

These are the probable or possible extensions allowed by the chronicle of Camillus for the theology of Mater Matuta, as herself and in contradistinction to Fortuna.

Inversely, we ought to investigate what has been preserved for us of the rites of Mater Matuta's festival—not of her most ancient theology—to see if they were used by the first people responsible for "Roman history" to constitute the chronicle of a hero whom they considered the devotee, the protégé, and, in his character, the imitator of the goddess. A happy surprise awaits us. One of the most famous episodes of this chronicle was produced by a simple and intelligent alteration of the two consecutive rites of the Matralia.

To recall them once again: several days before the solstice that begins to lengthen the nights at the expense of the days, thus to

[19] See the fine article "camillus" by Samter in Pauly-Wissowa, *Real-Encyklopädie der classischen Altertumswissenschaft* (Stuttgart, 1899), vol. 3, col. 1431.

[20] The Queen Camilla is the very type of child taken from her mother at a very young age and brought up by others—her father, to be sure, but above all by Diana to whom he gives her as "her own." (*Aeneid*, 2.557–560: *accipe testor, / diua, tuam*).

hinder, to retard the dawns, the Roman ladies intervene. Through their mimicry, they encourage the goddess in her increasingly difficult office, and through sympathetic action probably give her energy. Just as the dawn, or by multiplication the chorus of successive dawns jointly threatened, must first chase from the sky the evil, demonic obscurity that occupied it, so the Roman ladies brutally expel from the temple of the goddess a slave woman whom they have introduced in violation of the rule forbidding access to the servant class. That done, the Vedic Auroras, like Aurora, take in and each day care for the young Sun whom their sister, the good, useful Night, has just produced. They take their sisters' children in their arms, give them affection and respect and entrust them to the goddess. Conservative as always in religious matters, the Romans of more cultured centuries scrupulously maintained the cult that was given to her, but everything takes place as if the meaning had ceased to interest them. Despite the date of the festival they neglected its seasonal value and, in compensation, emphasized the various social relationships of the participants in the accomplishment of the rites. The opposition between the ladies and the intruded slave and the attention they give to the children who are not theirs were no longer perceived as symbols of the double mechanism of the beginning of the day, but as scenes of a strange human theatre. The darkness, the dawns, the young suns of each day vanished before the ladies and the children who were representing them: the guilty *serua*, the severe and tender matrons, the *alterius proles* as such. In brief, sentiment covered over the magic and very little would have sufficed to compose a little novel from these two mythodramatic scenes. It would only have been necessary to add a unitary human plot since once the naturalistic mythology, which unified the two scenes, had disappeared (the expulsion of the gestating Darkness, allowing the reception of the young daily Suns), the succession remained without a causal link, without any link.[21]

[21] Similar comments could be made on the formation of the legend of the Horatii and the Curiatii, in particular the murder of the sister. See my most recent

This is what the authors who composed the chronicle of the goddess Aurora's protégé accomplished. They created a new psychological relationship between the two scenes. In addition, in composing a heroic narrative, they changed all the feminine characters who came into it into the masculine.

Two years have passed since the conquest of Veii. Camillus is no longer dictator but *tribunus militum consulari potestate* along with five other colleagues. His *prouincia* is the war against Falerii whose inhabitants, after rousing and supporting the Veians, are now Rome's most dangerous enemies. Following a battle—won by Camillus at dawn, according to Livy—the Faliscans barricaded themselves in the city besieged by the Roman army. Lines of surrounding ramparts were established at some distance from the walls and the two sides observe each other, limiting themselves to brief skirmishes. The story of the evil schoolmaster is placed here (Livy 5.27):

> It was customary amongst the Faliscans to employ the same person as teacher and attendant of their children, and they used to intrust a number of lads at the same time to the care of one man, a practice which still obtains in Greece. The children of the chief men, as is commonly the case, were under the tuition of one who was regarded as their foremost scholar. This man had in time of peace got into the way of leading the boys out in front of the city for play and exercise, and during the war made no change in his routine, but would draw them sometimes a shorter, sometimes a longer distance from the gate, with this and that game and story, until being farther away one day than usual, he seized the opportunity to bring them amongst the enemy's outposts, and then into the Roman camp, to the headquarters of Camillus. He then followed up his villainous act with an even more villainous speech, saying that he had given Falerii into the hands of the Romans, having delivered up to them the children of those whose fathers were in power there. On hearing this Camillus answered: "Neither

comment in *From Myth to Fiction: The Saga of Hadingus,* trans. Derek Coltman (Chicago and London, 1973), pp. 122–123.

the people nor the captain to whom you are come, you scoundrel, with your scoundrel's gift, is like yourself. Between us and the Faliscans is no fellowship founded on men's covenants; but the fellowship which nature has implanted in both sides is there and will abide. There are rights of war as well as of peace, and we have learnt to use them justly no less than bravely. We bear no weapons against those tender years which find mercy even in the storming of a city, but against those who are armed themselves, who, without wrong or provocation at our hands, attacked the Roman camp at Veii. Those people you have done your best to conquer by an unheard-of crime. I shall conquer them, as I conquered Veii, in the Roman way, by dint of courage, toil and arms."

Camillus had the traitor stripped and his hands tied behind his back; then, telling the boys to escort him home, gave each of them a stick with which to beat him back into the town. A crowd gathered to see the sight, and later, when the magistrates had called a meeting of the council to discuss this odd turn of events, the feelings of the whole population were completely changed: where once fierce hatred and savage rage had made even the destruction of Veii seem a better fate than the tame capitulation of Capena, there was now a unanimous demand for peace. In street and council chamber people talked of nothing but of Roman honor and the justice of Camillus; by universal consent representatives were sent to him, and were allowed to proceed to Rome to lay the submission of Falerii before the Senate.

All ends well. The Faliscans are simply requested to pay the cost of the Roman troops engaged in the year's campaign. As for Camillus, enemies and fellow citizens, vying with each other, express their gratitude to him.

Plutarch's account, where the traitor is defined as διδάσκαλος, schoolmaster or pedagogue (*Camillus*, 10) is much the same with a few unimportant differences. For example, at the time of the children's return (10.6): "By this time the Faliscans had discovered the treachery of the schoolmaster, and the city, as was likely, was full of lamentations and cries for their calamity, men and women of worth running in distraction about the walls and gates; when, behold, the boys came whipping their master on naked and bound, calling Camillus their preserver and god and father."

This noble legend, a classic illustration of both the advantages resulting from humane and loyal conduct and the risks that treason carries, is not an ordinary theme in folklore or history. It is specific to the life of Camillus[22] and the material is highly improbable. Yet evoking the two rites of the Matralia is enough to understand its formation. The innovations are the following:

First, all the feminine roles of the rites are taken by men. Camillus has the role the Roman ladies had in the two rites, expulsion–punishment, care of the "children of another." The despicable schoolmaster who penetrates the Roman camp occupies the place of the slave woman who was supposed to have entered the temple voluntarily and criminally. The sons of the leading citizens of Falerii are substituted for the children of the sisters.

Second, Camillus, being a general and the hero of the chronicle, is put in the spotlight, acts alone, while the Roman ladies act collectively, with no one to lead them. But we must not forget that in the Indian myth the goddess Aurora appears at times in the singular, at times in the plural form, denoting the indefinite number of Auroras. Also in the Matralias themselves, the goddess is one, while the celebrants who imitate her are multiple, *bonae matres*.

---

[22] The presence of a pedagogue, a schoolmaster, at Falerii in an anecdote originating in the fourth century—two centuries before Rome was familiar with this type of graeculus—has been explained by the precocious and close relations of this city with the Greeks. Others think that the particular character of the pedagogue was introduced into the anecdote after the fact. In any case, there is no Greek prototype for the anecdote itself which has not been explained when it is placed in the vast group of accounts that folklorists label "the hunter hunted." We naturally think of Fabricius, sending back to Pyrrhus a deserter who offered to poison the king—a trait that, moreover, belongs to an exchange of propriety and courtesy between the Romans and the Greeks. But what is peculiar in Camillus' chronicle and sets up our proposition is the fact that the deserter is a schoolmaster and the stake is made up of "the children of others."

Third, the opposition between two social groups which supports the first rite—that of the noble Roman ladies and, through the single and unfortunate figure, that of the impure slave—is replaced by the ethnic and political opposition between two historic peoples at war, the Romans and the Faliscans.

But above all, the two scenes that in the rites are successive and independent, with only the identity of the "good" celebrants in common, are mingled in the narrative: (a) the schoolmaster does not simply violate a prohibition, is not only an intruder in Camillus' camp, as the slave woman is supposed to be in the temple of Mater Matuta. He is a traitor and it is through him that the children find themselves in Camillus' hands, which gives Camillus the opportunity to make known the tender respect he has for their "age group"; and (b) it is the children whom Camillus charges to beat the schoolmaster and to lead him to disgrace out of the camp. In the first rite it is the Roman ladies who wield the rods and expel the slave without the intervention of the children; in the second rite these ladies take the children in their arms without the slave's intervention.

These are the four principal innovations, in part interdependent, which permitted a Roman and ethical plot to be made starting with the reinterpreted liturgical mimicries. The correlation would be almost perfect if the two rites already meshed, if "the children of others" were introduced into the temple by the intruded slave and if the ladies violently expelled the slave only after expressing affection and respect for the children. But that was impossible, given the first, naturalistic significance of the rites. The villainous Darkness could not entrust to the Auroras the infant produced daily by their sister, the benevolent Night. Nor could each Aurora wait until she had called her own Sun before driving out the villainous Darkness.

Inversely, two important traits of the rites were retained in the Roman reinterpretation: the opposition between a single "villain" (the traitorous schoolmaster) and the plurality of the "children of eminent families," and the opposition—only implicit in the Roman ritual but stated in the Indian myth—between the good Night allied to Aurora and mother of the Sun (or the Nights, mothers of the daily Suns) on the one hand and the villainous or demonical Darkness who menaces or restrains the nascent Suns on the other hand. The episode from Camillus' life transposes the first one(s) into the Faliscan notables. They are temporarily enemies of Rome but can be won back by Rome—as they finally are. Camillus himself emphasizes their relationship with Rome as members of the great human family.[23] The second is transposed into the despicable schoolmaster, worthy of an infamous and violent expulsion.

The grouping of these remarks is easily arranged in the table at the end of this chapter. In the first column the two naturalistic myths of dawn, subordinate to the two rites of the Matralia, are recalled according to the formulas of the *Rig Veda* applicable to Rome. In the second, these two Roman rites are briefly described. In the third, the plot of the legend resulting from a literary reinterpretation of the two rites is analyzed. This completely literal reinterpretation cuts the two rites from their ancient mythical support and combines them according to a new causality.

The evidence of this derivation, this systematic transformation, uncovers new material and a new process in what must be called the making of the chronicle of Camillus.

We first know Camillus as a hero of the goddess Aurora. He honors her, she protects him. Either in time or space, her daily moment and the main seat of her cult favor the victories of this protégé: at the moment of dawn each time that he acts as dictator, and at Satricum several times, when he acts as one of the consular tribunes. We have also seen that this protection carries the very mark of Mater Matuta, the opposite of Fortuna, and that the type of goddess determines the character of the hero: like her, he is reasonable, faithful, and sensitive. But here we find ourselves—in the extension of this last virtue—confronted with something quite different. In the sequence of the schoolmaster and the Faliscan children, Mater Matuta is simultaneously present and absent. She is

[23] R. M. Ogilvie, *A Commentary on Livy, Books I–V* (Oxford, 1965), p. 688.

present since the episode was fashioned on the rites of her festival. She is absent because the gestures, the behavior taken from these rites delineate no more than the exterior of the episode and because the entire plot, which gives it beauty and logic, is a new creation. Also, she is present since Camillus behaves morally, as do the Roman ladies in the two rites where they themselves mime the actions of the goddess, and absent since all the feminine roles, including her own, are given to masculine characters.

It therefore appears that the authors of the chronicle, in addition to presenting the scenes intended to manifest the nature and auroral links that they lent to Camillus, embellished this material, which they had found insufficient, through other episodes. One such episode, where Aurora no longer plays a role, was freely and ingeniously taken from the form of her festival's rites. Simply stated, on a point where form was inseparable from sense, something—the essential aspect—of the goddess' character subsists in Camillus: the regard for the "children," the protection he gives them, and more generally the profound humanity which, during the siege and after the capitulation of Falerii, enables him to be moderate, to be good.

This freedom of the transposers explains the cleavage between this episode where Camillus, as an exception, plays a role copied from that of Aurora herself, and in all the others where he is only the protégé of the goddess—that is to say, ultimately plays the role of the rising Sun.

*Myth	Rites	Literature
Light and darkness oppose each other constantly.	I.1. The Roman ladies and the slave women form two opposing classes.	I.1. The Romans and Faliscans are at war.
	I.2. Shortly before the summer solstice, the Roman ladies assembled in the temple of Mother Aurora,	I.2. Camillus and his army are before Falerii in their camp,
	I.3. the entrance to which is normally forbidden to any slave.	I.3. where normally no Faliscan can enter.
	II.1. A slave woman brought into the temple by the ladies is supposed to be guilty of this intrusion.	II.1. A Faliscan schoolmaster, despicable traitor, enters the Roman camp, presents himself to Camillus,
		III.0. and turns over to him the Faliscan children entrusted to his care.
Aurora, the Auroras, expel from the sky the villainous Darkness who occupied it improperly.	II.2. She is ignominiously chased from the temple by the ladies with cuffs and blows.	II.2. Camillus expresses his anger and his disgust, delivers the traitor over to the children and gives rods to them,
		III.4. so they can lead him back to Falerii while insulting him and thrashing him.
Aurora, the Auroras, care for the young Suns, the offspring of their sister, the benevolent Night.	III.1. The Roman ladies show respect and affection for the children, pray to the goddess for the children, who are not theirs,	III.1. Camillus, expressing his respect for the Faliscan children and for all children,

*Myth	Rites	Literature
	III.2. but are those of their sisters;	III.2. and emphasizing that the Romans and the Faliscans —parents of the children—are united despite the war by the natural ties of human kinship,
	III.3. [naturally, once the rites are over, the children are returned to their parents.	III.3. sends the children back to their parents.
	IV. The rites are probably intended to favor all those— except Darkness, the woman slave —who enter into or behind the symbolic scenes:	IV. The adventure ends well for all the characters but the schoolmaster:
	mythically: the goddess Aurora herself is duly honored and the Suns strengthened; socially: the family ties are drawn closer (aunts and nephews) and the children put under the protection of the goddess.]	Romans and Faliscans become friends, Camillus is universally praised and the children, saved by Camillus, give him the names of father and god.

3

Night and Day

At this point the sphere narrows, the means of proof end. In the preceding chapters, it was only a question of exploring the points of contact between the biography of Camillus and the theology, mythology, and rituals of a goddess who, we are expressly informed, was his preferred divinity[1] at the decisive moment of his career. We were only developing, therefore, a theme whose origin was firmly documented. But to stop the research at this point is impossible. Two problems already confront us, regardless of whether they are susceptible of solution or not.

PROBLEMS

We formulated the first problem in passing.[2] The people's hostility, calumny, and exile stand between the actual fulfillment of

---

[1] Whatever warning I make, there will be no lack of critics to recall that Napoleon "also," and with a greater array of arguments, was qualified to be promoted to the level of solar hero, and his career—from Corsica to Saint Helena, with twelve field marshals, and so on—interpreted as a solar myth. But the cultic rapport of Camillus with Aurora (vow, dedication) is contained *in the texts* as well as is the accusation of *imitating the Sun* at the time of his triumph (Livy) and his victories (Plutarch, Diodorus), even his epiphany (Plutarch) *at sunrise*. The exploration of this theme is therefore necessary.

[2] See above, chapter 2: "The Ethics of Mater Matuta."

the vow he had made to the goddess Aurora—the dedication of a temple—and the first and dazzling manifestation of the affinity he has and will always have with her—the epiphany on the road to Gabii and the attack on the Gauls of Brennus at the first glimmer of day. Do not such vicissitudes carry more the mark of Fortuna, in whom he does not confide, than of Aurora, to whom he is already devoted? Granted, tradition places the episode of the Faliscan schoolmaster at the beginning of the unfavorable period; but in this situation, by which the authors of the chronicle only intended to show, in transposing the Matralia rites, that the hero had indeed assimilated the "spirit" of the goddess, she does not intervene, does not have to aid a career that is not put in *discrimen* by the siege of Falerii. Then why this somber digression in the life of her protégé?

The second problem arises in the wake of the first. After annihilating Brennus and the Gauls in his first "victory at dawn," Camillus never knows failure. But dawn, and through it the goddess who presides at this brief instant, intervenes only twice as an explicit and decisive factor: each time Camillus, as dictator, has sole command; both times at Satricum where, being one of the consular tribunes, he obtains his victory. Yet this long period contains many other military episodes, certain of which are no less singular than, for example, that of the Faliscan schoolmaster. From where do they come? Are they or are they not related to the central "matutinal" interpretation of Camillus' career?

For the benefit of well-intentioned critics, we repeat that henceforth we are no longer aiming for a demonstration. Like the analyst, the comparativist should carefully delimit the point where the arguments cease, having served their purpose, and the attempts at more or less plausible extension begin. If an argument is found erroneous, the demonstration is shaken, if not ruined; if an extension is found illusory, it and it alone must be either eliminated or corrected while the demonstration that preceded and suggested it can remain intact. We are at this point. With full knowledge, we go beyond this point, under the constraints of the two problems just formulated.

One possible a priori response would eliminate both problems at once. Could the authors of the chronicle, having exhausted their supply of "matutinal" information, not have padded the biography of Camillus with entirely different subject matter? Have we not moved a little quickly in speaking of a "hero of Aurora"? If one concedes (and it is not unreasonable) that the authors' design was only to construct the character and the life of an exemplary man and not—like the poets of the *Mahābhārata*—to transpose as completely as possible a mythological grouping into a single epic,[3] is it not natural to think that they drew from diverse sources and simply used the relatively brief material provided by Aurora concurrently with other elements unrelated to her?

Two facts work against this concept. First is the unity and stability of the character of Camillus, as noble, faithful, and moderate in misfortune as in glory, a character that we have seen marked constantly by the spirit of Mater Matuta, in contrast to the at times excessive imprudence of the "heroes of Fortuna." Second is the distribution of the "auroral" scenes from one end of his life to the other, from the first battle to the last: the "victory at dawn" on Mount Algidus reveals his valor; he requests the victory over Veii from the goddess Aurora, who grants it; after the exile, each of his three military dictatorships gives rise to a "victory at dawn." Thus, this theme does not sustain a limited period of his career, but encompasses it and marks it completely in a manner as coherent and uniform as is his very character. We are thus justified in attempting to determine if the authors of the chronicle did or did not conceive and execute a whole, unitary project.

PLAN OF THE LIFE OF CAMILLUS

Let us place our problems with greater precision in the overall scheme of the narration. The life of Camillus falls naturally into four parts.

[3] See the first part of *Mythe et épopée I* (Paris, 1968).

Since Camillus has no "childhoods" and the battle of Mount Algidus is mentioned only as a point of departure already passed when the narration begins, the first part contains the Veian war, with the intervention of Mater Matuta clearly defined.

In the second part, from the dedication of the temple of Mater Matuta to the exile, the goddess is not named: but this part is dominated by the episode of the Faliscan schoolmaster, for which the Matralia rites provided the raw material.

The third part—the exile—is the difficult one, as nothing evokes the favor of Mater Matuta or the advantages of dawn. It is subdivided into two sections.

First: for a certain period of time, Camillus lives secluded at Ardea, leading a completely private existence. It is during this same time that the Romans experience the misfortune at the Allia: generals who are incapable and negligent in their religious duties lead the one army of the Republic to disaster.

Second: once Rome is occupied by the Gauls of Brennus, Camillus without resentment prepares his country's deliverance. Symmetrically, the remnant of the army that was defeated at the Allia, having taken refuge at Veii, prepares to collaborate with him. These preparations occur in three stages: (1) When the Gauls who occupy Rome send out a detachment of foragers into Ardean territory, Camillus emerges from his life of seclusion and leads the young Ardeans to victory. Meanwhile the Romans from Veii battle the Etruscans, who had hoped to profit from the misfortunes of Rome in order to recover their city. (2) Sought by the Romans from Veii to take their command, Camillus accepts only on condition that he be officially invested by what remains of the State, which is now under siege on the Capitol. The rash and fortunate temerity of a messenger allows the establishment of a liaison and the transmittal of the proper nomination: Camillus becomes dictator. (3) He takes command, prepares his army for combat, and finally marches to Rome's rescue.

The fourth part of the scheme includes all the rest of Camillus' life. We already know the three "victories at dawn" that punctuate

it, decisive victories that he obtains during his three military dictatorships. But this very long period contains, along with important
civil acts, the other military episodes of which we have spoken,
where he commands as one of the *tribuni militum consulari
potestate*. In these he also obtains success, the two principal ones—
aside from the "victories at Satricum"—being unusual types.

Our twofold task concerns the third and fourth parts.

THE DAY BEGINS DURING THE NIGHT

Let us not mince words: in the protégé of Aurora we find ourselves, as much as is possible in Rome, confronting a solar personage. Rome probably never had many solar myths or even rites
properly called autonomous:[4] There is nothing reminiscent of the
conflict between the sun and the storm, of the Vedic Sūrya and
Indra, or of the Vedic myth of the wheel detached from the Sun's
chariot, whose importance is confirmed by its transformation in
the epic. The sun interested above all the Roman, the Roman
society, the Roman state by the multiple framework that its annual
uniform birth and its daily births, variable according to the seasons, proposed or imposed on their activity. In other words, rather
than an astral religion, what we observe is a juridico–religious concept, expressed in beliefs and practices, of the star as a regulator of
time periods during which man envisages his action. Would not
one of these beliefs give the key to our first problem?

[4] See my *Archaic Roman Religion*, trans. Philip Krapp (Chicago and London,
1970), pp. 389 n. 29 and 563. Perhaps one should acknowledge the existence of an
ancient solar symbolism of the Circus and races, which subsequent speculations did
no more than develop. For the colors of the factions see my third essay ("Albati,
russati, uirides") in *Rituels indo-européens à Rome* (Paris, 1954). The book by Carl
Koch, *Gerstirnverehrung im alten Italien* (Frankfurter Studien zur Religion und
Kultus der Antike 3) (Frankfurt, 1933), contains abundant material but the method
is objectionable. See again G. K. Galinsky, "Sol et le *Carmen saeculare*," *Latomus*
26 (1967), 619–633 (Sol et les Latins, Sol Indiges, etc.).

The Roman day begins at midnight, thereby containing at the outset half the night. This mode of division, which we inherited and which was easily imposed throughout the world created by Rome, seems natural to us. Natural it is not, and the Romans, who saw other astral systems functioning around them, noted its originality. Sunset, sunrise, and noontime had furnished a very convenient beginning of day to other peoples—"Athenians, Babylonians, Umbrians." Rome herself had adopted the middle of the night and from this concept flowed religious or civil rules that the erudite Romans, first among them Varro, collected. We read in Macrobius (*Saturnalia*, 1.3.6–8):

> As for the custom of the Roman people, noted by Varro, of counting the days from midnight to midnight, there are many illustrative examples. . . . The rites and practices of auspication conform to this way of calculating. In fact, one rule requires that the magistrates take the omens and perform the act for which they took them within one day. So, taking the omens after midnight and performing the act after sunrise, they are reputed to have taken the omens and acted the same day. By the same token, the plebeian tribunes are not permitted to be away from Rome an entire day. So, when they leave after midnight and return after the lighting of the first torch, but before midnight, it is not considered a full day's absence.

In the eighty-fourth *Roman Question*, Plutarch wonders why the Romans began the day at midnight and his response is interesting, though insufficient. According to him, the Roman State was first of all essentially military. After all, in battle most of the plans are made "in advance" during the night, daybreak being the time of execution, night that of preparation. But this specific and quite practical consideration would probably not have sufficed to cut the night ritually and juridically into two parts, and to attach the second part to the following day. The reason is rather a religious one and results directly from the mythology of Aurora subjacent to the Matralia rites as we understand them. Let us recall that these rites imply: (1) that there is a "bad," but also a "good" Darkness, one the enemy of the day, expelled from the sky by Aurora, the other pregnant with the sun, transmitting to Aurora the luminous infant being born; and (2) that Aurora is not the mother of the Sun, but his adoptive mother. Alone she is incapable of producing him; she gathers him up after he has been prepared and brought into the world by "the other"—*alterius proles*—by the good Darkness who is incapable of accompanying him in the life she has just given him. In other words, in the couple, each of the two—those whom the Vedic hymns willingly call "the two sisters"—is indispensable for the accomplishment of the common act. For Aurora to be able to take charge of the Sun, the Night must first perform her office of pregnant and parturient female. For the Night's maternity to be fruitful, Aurora must be ready to take her place. The Roman concept of day does no more than translate this theologem: the second part of the nocturnal darkness, carrying within it the sun to be born, is inseparable from the day that follows; it is in fact the first part of the day.

SUMMANUS

This remark, by the way, allows clarification of an often poorly understood section of Roman theology, that of the god Summanus whom all sources define as the one who hurls nocturnal lightning, *nocturna fulgura*.[5] But the Roman theory of the bipartition of night—before and after midnight, yesterday and today—has the following consequence. The only nocturnal lightning that can be retained as signs concerning the future is the lightning

---

[5] On pages 785–795 of a recent essay, "Etimologie di teonimi" (see *Mythe et épopée III* [Paris, 1973], p. 81 n. 1), M. A. L. Prosdocimi attempted an interpretation of *Summanus* using *summus* as a point of departure and challenges the interpretation *sub* + *mane*. In a corrective note (p. 785 n. 20), with fine loyalty, he criticized himself.

observed after midnight, during that part of the night, its length dictated by the seasons, which already belongs to this future. A Greco–Latin glossary is therefore correct in specifying *fulgur submanum* as κεραυνοβόλιον ἀπὸ πρωὶ ἢ νυκτήρινον "lightning before dawn, or nocturnal,"—a formula that confirms the etymology of the god's name which I advanced some thirty years ago,[6] "at the approach (*sub*) of morning (*mane*)." The expression is analogous to that which provided the general name of night in Armenian, *c-ayg* "until (*c*) dawn (*ayg*)" parallel to the name of day *c-erek* "until evening (*erek*)." Summanus, more modest and more precise, is active in that portion of the night belonging to the day for which his lightning, his signs are valid. This interpretation takes into account the two known traits of the god's cult:

First, the *dies natalis* of his temple[7] is June 20, nine days after the festival of Mother Aurora and a few days before the summer solstice. This date on the calendar can scarcely be fortuitous, and the bringing together of the protectress of the newborn light and a god active during the declining night is significant, especially when it occurs during the days that precede and prepare for the day on which diurnal time will begin to decrease to the gain of nocturnal time. The purpose of the Matralia rites on June 11 is to fortify the light (dawn, sun) menaced by an impending withdrawal. The date chosen for the dedication of Summanus' temple, June 20, results from an opposite, or rather complementary, need: to con-

---

[6] The etymology of *Summanus* through *sub* and *mane* is already in W. Warde Fowler, *The Roman Festivals of the Period of the Republic* (London, 1899), p. 181. Regarding the dark aspect of the Vedic Aurora, see Ananda K. Coomaraswamy, "The Darker Side of Dawn," *Smithsonian Miscellaneous Collection* 94 no. 1 (1935), 4–6.

[7] The temple situated in the Circus Maximus was dedicated in 278, after the statue of Summanus on the Capitoline Temple of Jupiter had been struck by lightning and thunder and the head cast into the Tiber. Only the day chosen for the dedication is important here. Ovid, *Fasti*, 6.729–732, introduces it with words suitable for the occasion:

Jam, tua, Laomedon, oritur nurus [= Aurora]
ortaque noctem pellitt . . .

ciliate at an opportune time the good graces of the "ascending divinity," the personage whose domain will not cease, for six months, to encroach on the day.

Second, Festus (p. 475L[1] = p. 438L[2]) gives the gloss: *summanalia, liba farinacea in modum rotae ficta* "the *sumanalia* are cakes of flour made in the shape of a wheel." The symbolism is clear: the portion of the night that concerns Summanus is the one that prepares for the appearance of the solar "disc." One will note that the festivals that mark or announce the two points of retrogression of the day's curve call for special cakes.

Ovid appears to give to a third rite, included in the Matralias, the same importance as that of the two rites already mentioned. At the beginning of his description of the festival, we read (*Fasti*, 6.475–476):

> Go ahead, noble mothers—the Matralias are your festival— and offer the yellow cakes to the Theban goddess.

Ovid is careful to justify this usage by referring to the etiological legend: when the Greek Ino–Leucothea and her son Palemon arrived at the future site of Rome, where they would become, through the will of the intellectuals, Mater Matuta and Portunus, they were cordially received by Carmentis, mother of the Arcadian Evander (6.529–534):

> It is said that as a guest thou didst enter the home of loyal Carmentis and there didst stay thy long hunger. The Tegean priestess is reported to have made cakes in haste with her own hand and to have quickly baked them on the hearth. Even to this day she [= Ino–Matuta] loves cakes at the festival of the Matralia. Rustic civility was dearer to her than the refinements of art.

We know a little more about these yellow cakes. Varro (*De lingua latina*, 5.106), dealing with names of various kinds of cakes, says that these of Mater Matuta were called *testuatium* because they were prepared in *testu caldo*, probably a covered receptacle of (preheated?) terra-cotta. The importance thus given to the container should allude to one of the poles in the auroral theology. The yellow cake offered to the goddess Aurora is cooked in a mold, as the sun is prepared in a hidden manner in the womb of the night before being released, received by Aurora. In sum, by a kind of chiasma of values Aurora's cake, defined by its being cooked in a mold, refers to what precedes the birth of the sun, while the cake of the god of declining night, characterized simply by its "wheel" shape, refers to the sun, born or incipient.

The other cakes are prepared shortly after the second solstice, at the Calends of January; these take their names from Janus, *ianual* (Paulus Diaconus, p. 93L[1] = p. 227L[2]; cf. Lydus, *Months* 4.2). At the beginning of *Fasti* (1.127–128) Ovid, or rather Janus himself, gives the recipe, unfortunately very vague and without specifics so that the symbolic value, which is still very probable, cannot be deduced:

> When the priest consecrates cereal cake and barley seasoned with salt, you will laugh at the names he gives me because, in the ritual language of his offering, he calls me sometimes Patulcius, the one of the Beginning, sometimes Clusius, the one of the Closing.

One can imagine, if one wants to go beyond the data, that this double aspect—mentioned on the occasion of the offering—of the god who in January closes and opens the annual time, found, in some way or other, symbolic expression in the cakes themselves, probably in their shape.

VICTORIES AT NIGHT

After this digression, wherein direct analysis and analogies allowed us to define Summanus and to perceive the articulation that he constitutes—as a god who acts with the goddess of day-break when the night is declining, at the approach of the summer solstice—it seems possible to justify the design of Camillus' career by the same concepts. Here is the proposal, expressed in the affirmative for simplification.

The authors who intended Camillus to be the protégé of Aurora in the fourth part of his chronicle and the human counterpart of the rising sun in the epiphany of his first "victory at dawn," were led by the Roman concept of day to have this destiny begin in a sombre, obscure period, under cover of which he prepares for his luminous career. If he did not emerge from some sort of night, Mater Matuta could do nothing for him, no more than she could take the infant sun in her arms in the mythology subordinate to the second rite of her festival—if he had not first been fashioned and brought to maturity by her tenebrous sister. Here again, it may be permissible to identify the correspondents of the evil shadows and the useful night.

The Gallic barbarians overrun Rome; the Ardean hosts shelter Camillus. Camillus, reduced to the condition of private individual, first does nothing, has no activity either as a Roman citizen or as an Ardean wanderer; during the same time Rome is almost annihilated. The negative side of the epic manifestation of night is completion, or rather destruction, of the preceding glorious period. After the disaster, Camillus and those of the Roman forces subsisting in Veii, actively, progressively, and happily prepare the resurrection: this is the positive side of the night, the gestation of the time about to be born, a time destined to be no less glorious than that which preceded it. Objectively, there is reason to think that the symbolic interpretations are not illusory.

We have often said that one of the dominant themes in the fourth part of the chronicle is the "victories at dawn" that Camillus obtains each time he has sovereign power. Yet in the third part, contrariwise, *all the operations through which Rome's deliverance ripens, at Ardea as well as at Veii and on the Capitol, are carried out during the night, in the middle of the night, before dawn.*

Let us consider first the initial moves of the exiled Camillus at Ardea, according to Plutarch (*Camillus*, 23):

And now, the siege of the Capitol having lasted a good while, the Gauls began to be in want of provision; and dividing their forces, part of them stayed with their king at the siege, the rest went to forage the country, ravaging the towns and villages where they came, but not all together in a body, but in different squadrons and parties; and to such a confidence had success raised them, that they carelessly rambled about without the least fear or apprehension of danger. But the greatest and best ordered body of their forces went to the City of Ardea, where Camillus then sojourned, having, ever since his leaving Rome, sequestered himself from all business, and taken to a private life; but now he began to rouse up himself, and consider not how to avoid or escape the enemy, but to find out an opportunity to be revenged upon them. And perceiving that the Ardeans wanted not men, but rather enterprise, through the inexperience and timidity of their offices, he began to speak with the young men, first to the effect that they ought not to ascribe the misfortune of the Romans to the courage of their enemy, nor attribute the losses they sustained by rash counsel to the conduct of men who had no title to victory; the event had been only an evidence of the power of fortune; that it was a brave thing even in danger to repel a foreign and barbarous invader whose end in conquering was, like fire, to lay waste and destroy, but if they would be courageous and resolute he was ready to put an opportunity into their hands to gain a victory, without hazard at all. When he found the young men embraced the thing, he went to the magistrates and council of the city, and, having persuaded them also, he mustered all that could bear arms, and drew them up within the walls, that they might not be perceived by the enemy, who was near; who, having scoured the country, and returned heavy-laden with booty, lay encamped in the plains in a careless and negligent posture so that, with the night ensuing upon debauch and drunkenness, silence prevailed through all the camp. When Camillus learned this from his scouts, he drew out the Ardeans, and in the dead of night [περὶ μέσας νύκτας], passing in silence over the ground that lay between, came up to their works, and, commanding his trumpets to sound and

114

his men to shout and halloo, he struck terror into them from all quarters; while drunkenness impeded and sleep retarded their movements. A few, whom fear had sobered, getting into some order, for a while resisted; and so died with their weapons in their hands. But the greatest part of them, buried in wine and sleep, were surprised without their arms, and despatched; and as many of them as by the advantage of the night [νυκτός] got out of the camp were the next day [μεθ' 'ημέραν) found scattered abroad and wandering in the fields, and were picked up by the horse that pursued them.

Livy (5.43.4–45.4) gives the same account, with more rhetoric. He also specifies that Camillus delivers the Gauls to the Ardeans *uinctos somno, uelut pecudes*; that the preparations are made early in the night, *prima uigilia*; that the troops leave the city *primae silentio noctis* and that everything is completed quickly, *nusquam praelium, omnibus locis caedes.*

But Livy gives one, even two Roman versions of this nocturnal battle of the Ardeans, conceived and won by the greatest Roman. What remain of the legions destroyed on the Allia are at Veii and watch angrily as the Etruscans in cowardice take advantage of the situation—"without pity" the historian dares say—to make incursions into Roman territory, even to prepare, while laden down with spoils, to attack Veii, *spem ultimam Romani nominis*, and, for that purpose, to set up camp very close to the city. Indignant, the Romans would like to attack immediately, *extemplo*, but

> restrained by the centurion Quintus Caedicius, whom they had chosen to be their commander, they postponed the affair till dark (*rem in noctem sustinuere*). The only thing wanting was a leader like Camillus; in all else the order followed was the same, and the same success was achieved.

That is not all:

> Indeed, under the guidance of captives who had survived the nocturnal massacre, *qui caedi nocturnae superfuerant*, they set

115

out on the following night, *nocte insequenti*, and came to another band of Etruscans, at the saltworks, whom they surprised and defeated with even greater carnage; and so, rejoicing in their double victory, returned to Veii.

Thus, here we have Rome in possession of an army that warrants the name, and the only military leader at her disposal has resumed service. General and soldiers could not but reunite, as head and members of the same body. But whether the soldiers did not want to approach the general (Livy) or he refused to respond to their call (Plutarch) until receiving the authorization or investiture from those Romans still in Rome, a means had to be found to consult these august phantoms on the Capitol where they were holding their own against the Gallic blockade, and to know their answer. Then one of the young Romans of Veii, Pontius Cominus (or Cominius) volunteered to cross the Tiber, climb to the top of the Capitol and, his mission accomplished, return by the same route.

He succeeds. But the trip, of course, could only be made at night. If Livy, in short, does not consider it useful to give this detail, Dionysius of Halicarnassus, in the fragment preserved from the twelfth book (7.9) which relates this famous episode, indicates neither the time, nor the means of the trip to Rome, but indeed says "at night" 'υπὸ νύκτα 'απηλλάγη for the return. Plutarch, by contrast, is explicit (25.2–3) about the trip to the Capitol. Having memorized Camillus' message to the Senate and carrying with him pieces of cork, Pontius sets out:

> He boldly traveled the greatest part of the way by day ['ημέρας], and came to the city when it was dark [ἤδη σκοταῖος]; the bridge he could not pass, as it was guarded by the barbarians; so that taking his clothes, which were neither many nor heavy, and binding them about his head, he laid his body upon the corks, and swimming with them, got over to the city. And avoiding those quarters where he perceived the enemy was awake [τοὺς ἐγρηγορότας], which he guessed at by the lights and noise, he went to the Carmental gate, where

there was greatest silence, and where the hill of the Capitol is steepest.

With the account of the Ardean victory, Pontius easily convinces the senators to name Camillus dictator; then they dismiss him and he comes back by the same route with equal success (25.4–5).

It is therefore certain and stated that the double exploit of Pontius was accomplished at night, on two successive nights.

Finally, it is again at night (*nocte sublustri*, Livy, 5.47.2) that the last, or rather the only fortunate battle for the Romans of the Capitol takes place against the besieging Gauls. Alerted to the traces of Pontius' escalade, Brennus decides to take his chance the same way. His troops agree enthusiastically. "In the dead of the night [περὶ μέσας νύκτας]," says Plutarch (27.1–5), "a good party of them together, with great silence, began to climb the rock. . . ."

But the sacred geese of Juno's temple take the place of the drowsy sentinels. Manlius, soon joined by others, throws down the first assailants who thought they had reached their goal, and the Gauls do not persist. At daybreak, ἅμ' 'ημέρᾳ, all the Romans have to do is to honor Manlius and punish the leader of the watchmen who had been on duty (27.6).

Thus, without exception, the military episodes of the second part of Camillus' exile are placed under the sign of the night, and though a nocturnal setting was requisite for the exploits of Pontius Cominius and Manlius, those of the Ardeans and the Romans of Veii might just as well have been accomplished by day. But to fulfill another social convention it was probably necessary that it be night when all that prepares Rome's deliverance is accomplished. One notes in addition that three out of four of these successes also lead progressively to the dictatorship of Camillus, the condition and means for this deliverance. These are his first victory at the head of a foreign army, the first two victories of the Roman army that waits for him and calls him, and the dangerous mission that allows him to receive a proper nomination; actually, even the last episode, that of the geese and Manlius, is related to the same group since it is only a direct consequence or even an extension of the preceding episode, the foolish enterprise and unlikely success of the messenger from the "exterior Romans." This insistence and exclusive use of the night, opposed to the auroral refrain that punctuates the rest of the biography, reinforces the explanation of the exile which we have seen. If this explanation is retained, it should be assumed that it is the very plan itself of the chronicle of Camillus, which clever authors drew from the entire theology of Aurora: not only from what the rites of her festival instruct about her *modus operandi* and her spirit, but also from what emerges of the Roman concept of day and night, namely the shaping of dawn by the preceding dark hours.

SUTRIUM LOST AND REGAINED IN A DAY

Assuming the retention of this explanation, the second problem already tends toward a hypothetical solution of the same type. In the fourth part of the chronicle two successes other than the "victories at dawn" or "with Aurora (Satricum)" appear to translate specifically Roman solar concepts[8] into dramatic form.

The first of these successes is the reconquest of the city of Sutrium. The geographic position of this faithful ally made it the first prey of the Etruscans each time they revived their war against Rome. As dictator, Camillus has just obtained his second victory over the combined Æquians and Volscians when, entrusting to his son Lucius the camp with the booty and prisoners, he hastens

[8] Unlike its illustrious, ambitious, and debatable ancestor, the limited solar interpretation that reappears here is clearly Roman, is based exclusively on verified Roman concepts and customs, not on abstract poetic and philosophical speculations; cf. note 1 of this chapter.

toward Sutrium which he knows has been attacked. But he doesn't know everything. Plutarch tells us (chapter 35):

> Having taken the city of the Æquians and reduced the Vol-
> scians to obedience, he then immediately led his army to Sutri-
> um, not having heard what had befallen the Sutrians, but
> making haste to assist them, as if they were still in danger and
> besieged by the Tuscans. They, however, had already sur-
> rendered their city to their enemies, and destitute of all things,
> with nothing left but their clothes, met Camillus on the way,
> leading their wives and children, and bewailing their misfor-
> tune. Camillus himself was struck with compassion, and per-
> ceiving the soldiers weeping, and commiserating their case,
> while the Sutrians hung about and clung to them, resolved not
> to defer revenge, but that very day to lead his army to Sutri-
> um; conjecturing that the enemy, having just taken a rich and
> plentiful city, without an enemy left within it, nor any from
> without to be expected, would be found abandoned to enjoy-
> ment and unguarded. Neither did his opinion fail him; he not
> only passed through their country without discovery, but
> came up to their very gates and possessed himself of the walls,
> not a man being left to guard them, but their whole army
> scattered about in the houses, drinking and making merry.
> Nay, when at last they did perceive that the enemy had seized
> the city, they were so overloaded with meat and wine, that few
> were able so much as to endeavor to escape, but either waited
> shamefully for their death within doors, or surrendered them-
> selves to the conqueror. Thus the city of the Sutrians was twice
> taken in one day; and they who were in possession lost it, and
> they who had lost regained it, alike by the means of Camillus.

Livy (6.3) offers the same account with some minor differences
and in a more dramatic form. Only a few lines are important for
our purposes. Moved by the lamentable cortege of exiles, Camillus
has the baggage set down, entrusts the Sutrians to a small detachment, commands the soldiers to take nothing but their weapons,
and hurries toward the city,

where he was not surprised to find everything at loose ends, as a consequence—common enough—of their success; there was no outpost before the walls; the gates were open; and the victors had dispersed and were fetching the booty out of the houses of their enemies. For the second time, therefore, on the same day, Sutrium was captured . . . and before night the town was restored to the Sutrians, unharmed and without scathe of war, because it had not been carried by assault, but had been surrendered upon terms.

The improbability of this is evident. The Etruscans were not a horde of greedy and stupid barbarians and they knew the regulations for armies in the field. What is more, having left the inhabitants free to make known their misfortune along the road, they could not have failed, even if they were not expecting Camillus, to post some lookouts on the walls and to close the gates.

There is also something singular in this account: the insistence the narrator puts on emphasizing that the occupation of the city by the enemy and its reconquest by Camillus took place "the same day," "in a single day": ἐκείνης τῆς ἡμέρας, 'εν ἡμέρᾳ μιᾷ (Plutarch), *eadem die, ante noctem* (Livy), αὐθημερόν (Dio Cassius). This is what is presented as the marvel of the affair. And yet, would the success have been less efficacious or less glorious had it occurred the next day? The Etruscans would simply have continued their drinking, would have occupied the bedrooms after the dining rooms: the damage might not have been much greater. Why then this emphasis?

The texts give a reason that once again brings to the fore an important trait of Camillus' character, compassion. Moved to tears by the misfortune of the Sutrians, Camillus and his army are anxious to lead them back to their homes. This psychological motive, however, is probably not the essential point since the accent is not placed on the Romans' emotion but on the external, objective fact, which is only introduced and justified by the psychological motive that the city, fallen into enemy hands at an unspecified moment of the day, is taken again and restored the same day, before nightfall so the Sutrians need not spend a single night away from home.

Here I suspect the utilization of another part of the Roman theory of day, the dramatization of a rule, also well illustrated in religious, civil, and political practices. The day is a unit, and diverse complex actions comprising two complementary moments —whether the second leads back to the point of departure (departure and return, going out and coming back) or completes a transformation begun by the first (preparation and accomplishment, *consecratio* and *profanatio*)—must be entirely completed during one solar revolution, between midnight and midnight and at times even between dawn and nightfall.

We have seen above the postulated ritual by which the omens taken between midnight and dawn and the corresponding act accomplished after dawn are reputed to belong to the same day. This has a negative counterpart: if the act for which the omens were taken is not accomplished before the following midnight, the omens are no longer valid and must be renewed the following day. Compensatorily, however, if the omens were unfavorable, the corresponding action is only condemned for the day, that is to say, until midnight, and it is licit to resume the consultation the following day, that is, after midnight.

In more general terms, not only is the day a unit in religious and lay practice, but, in the feriae, none of the primitive rituals can exceed one day's duration or have a continuation the following day, even though, by virtue of the rule that makes all festivals fall on uneven dates, the day after each one is empty and does not include a new festival.[9] Thus, the strong cohesion of the day, not only as a unit of calculation but as a self-enclosed unit, was one of the categories in which the Romans envisioned time and, when they were the masters, utilized it. What depends on chance, Fortuna, rather than on man, does not of course lend itself to this conceptual

[9] The series of days devoted to the same religious service (such as the Parentalia, in February, the days of Vesta in June) are subsequent revivals and do not figure as such in the feriae.

framework. Famine, pestilence, and in war a campaign, a siege, at times even a battle, imposed on those who suffered from it or took part their own measurements, which were longer and unforeseeable. This is precisely why the exploit of Camillus at Sutrium has the effect of a marvel. It imposes the familiar mold of the closed and unitary day on a type of event that by nature escapes it. Is it fortuitous that this operation is attributed to the hero protected by Aurora, whom we have already seen several times act according to the model of the star that makes the day and its laws?

THE PARDON FOR THE TUSCULANS

The second episode is that of the pardon of the Tusculans, longtime and generally faithful allies of Rome. One day, after a battle won by Camillus as consular tribune over the Volscians (Livy) or over the reunited Volscians and the Praenestians (Plutarch), a battle that allowed him to reconquer the city of Mater Matuta, Satricum,[10] the Romans discover among the prisoners several Tusculans who claim—whether falsely or truly we don't know—that they participated in the affair only under the orders of their magistrates (Livy). Immediately the Senate decides on a punitive expedition against Tusculum and Camillus commands it (Plutarch, *Camillus*, 38.4–5):

> The Tusculans, hearing of Camillus' coming against them, made a cunning attempt at revoking their act of revolt; their fields, as in times of highest peace, were full of ploughmen and shepherds; their gates stood wide open, and their children were being taught in the schools; of the people, such as were tradesmen, he found in their workshops, busied about their several employments, and the better sort of citizens walking in the public places in their ordinary dress; the magistrates hurried about to provide quarters for the Romans, as if they stood

[10] See above, chapter 2: "The Ethics of Mater Matuta."

in fear of no danger and were conscious of no fault. Which arts, though they could not dispossess Camillus of the conviction he had of their treason, yet induced some compassion for their repentance; he commanded them to go to the senate and deprecate their anger, and joined himself as an intercessor in their behalf, so that their city was acquitted of all guilt and admitted to Roman citizenship. These were the most memorable actions of his sixth tribuneship.

Livy says essentially the same thing more elaborately (6.25):

But no war was, in fact, waged with the Tusculans; by their steadfast adherence to peace they saved themselves from violation by the Romans, as they could not have done by resorting to arms. When the Romans entered their territory, they did not withdraw from the places near the line of march, nor break off their labour in the fields; the gates of their city stood wide open; the citizens, wearing the toga, came out in great numbers to meet the generals; and provisions for the army were obligingly brought into the camp from the city and the farms. Camillus set up his camp before the gates, and desirous of knowing whether the same aspect of peace prevailed within the walls that was displayed in the country, entered the city and beheld the house-doors open, the shops with their shutters off and all their wares exposed, the craftsmen all busy at their respective trades, the schools buzzing with the voices of the scholars, crowds in the streets, and women and children going about amongst the rest, this way and that, as their several occasions called them—with never anywhere an indication of surprise, much less of fear. He looked everywhere for any visible evidence that a war had been on foot; but there was no sign that anything had been either removed or brought out for the moment; everything looked so undisturbed and peaceful that it seemed scarce credible that so much as a rumour of war should have come there.

"Overcome therefore by the enemy's submissiveness" (*patientia*), Camillus sends the Tusculan senators to entreat their Roman counterparts:

When the Tusculans arrived in Rome, and the senators of a people who before had been faithful allies appeared in the vestibule of the Curia, covered with dejection, the Fathers were straightway moved, and in a spirit that had already more in it of hospitality than hostility bade them be at once admitted.

An honest discourse by the Tusculan dictator completes the arrangement of things: the supplicants first obtain peace, then, shortly thereafter, Roman citizenship.[11]

Here again, the lack of credibility is patent. How, under a sudden alarm, could an entire people, magistrates, merchants, artisans, peasants, students, men, women, children improvise and sustain without error, without faltering, this immense and coherent performance? As for the singularity that strikes us it is, here again, the way in which Livy and Plutarch stress a certain point, the detail with which they analyze the performance, enumerating, describing in a few words such a variety of activity, private, public, and economic. Plutarch's words are "tradesmen, he found in their workshops, busied about their several employments"; Livy's "the craftsmen all busy at their respective trades." On his arrival, Camillus finds himself, and we with him, before a kind of exhibition where each class of Tusculan obligingly exhibits the essence of his vocation.

Such an exhibition, as a matter of fact, is observed every day in the morning when the shops, the schools, and all the rest open, and the lines of Horace come to mind (*Satires*, 2.6.20–23):[12]

> Father who governs the morning—unless you prefer to be called Janus—thou from whom men begin the first acts of their work and their lives. . . .

[11] Dio Cassius, *Roman History*, 28.1–2, says the same thing more briefly: πάνυ πάντες ἐπί τε ταῖς δημιουργίαις καὶ ἐπί τοῖς ἄλλοις ἔργοις 'ὡς καὶ 'εν εἰρήνη κατὰ χώραν μείναντες. A kind of counterpart of the Tusculans' repentance in which the special trait that interests us here does not appear, is found in Livy, 8.37.

[12] Matutine pater, seu Jane libentius audis,
   unde homines operum primos uitaeque labores
   instituunt . . .

The daily sunrise puts all the world's *laboratores* back to work, each at his own labor, but no known rite sanctions this multiple awakening. So it is not so much the daily concept of the rising sun which must be consulted as the rituals, the theology, the ethics of its annual birth. In fact, when the chronicle of Camillus was composed it was already the day after the winter solstice that the beginning, at least one of the beginnings of the year, was situated. The nineteenth *Roman Question* of Plutarch justifies quite well this preference, which is symmetrical to the doctrine that makes each day begin in the middle of the night:

> The best computation is that which makes the year begin after the winter solstice, at the moment when, ceasing to advance, the sun turns around and comes back toward us. The choice of this date is, in a certain way and from man's point of view, in conformity with nature since it is nature that lengthens the daylight and decreases the darkness and which draws close to us the master and guide of every moving thing.

Ovid, opening the *Fasti* with January, has Janus himself say it more briefly and more elegantly (1.163–164):

> Midwinter is the beginning of the new sun and the end of the old one. Phoebus and the year take their start from the same point.

Let us examine the rites of the calends of January,[13] considered thus as a solstice slightly shifted to mesh with the lunar conventions.[14] The poet gives a list of them in the familiar dialogue he had with the god. He is first surprised to see the tribunals busy:

> "Hear the cause," quoth Janus. "I assigned the birthday of the year to business, lest from the outset idleness infect the whole.

[13] Michel Meslin, *La fête des Kalendes de janvier dans l'Empire romain, étude d'un rituel de Nouvel An* (Collection Latomus 115) (Brussels, 1970).

[14] The exposition that follows is drawn from the rich commentary on *Fasti*, 1.175, written by Sir James G. Frazer: *The Fasti of Ovid* (London, 1929), vol. 2, p. 112.

For the same reason every man just handsels his calling, nor does more than but attest his usual work."

Columella (*De Re Rustica*, 2.2.98) confirms the rule as it applies to farmers:

During these days—the first twelve in January—the especially religious farmers abstain from working the soil, with the exception that, during Calends, on the weight of the omen they start all the varieties of their work; then they wait until the Ides (the thirteenth) to till the soil.

The custom was tenacious, since at the beginning of the eleventh century, Burchard of Worms was to again denounce it as diabolic: "Certain people," he said, "during this holy night (the Calends of January) spin, weave, sew, and execute all the kinds of work they can then begin."

These gestures are certainly not done, or were not done at first, for the moral reason that Ovid gives, as an immunization against laziness. They have in the full sense of the term an inaugural intention: at the annual sunrise the country becomes, for a few instants, the scene of a demonstration of all the techniques and vocations necessary for the next twelve months of its life—exactly what the territory and the city of Tusculum ostentatiously becomes at the arrival of Camillus.

But the Tusculans, Camillus himself, and after him the Roman Senate, do more. The Tusculans welcome the Roman army with the presents that are of greatest importance to it, *commeatus*, and put themselves at the army's disposal. By their words, their actions, they annul and deny the conflict they imprudently started. Camillus accepts and plays the game, even though he is not duped. He sends them to the Senate and gives them his support. The Tusculans serve amiably, if not sincerely. Camillus pardons and instills hope; they exchange only pleasant words. Another rule of the New Year's festival comes to mind (*Fasti*, 1.71–74):

A happy morning dawns. Fair speech, fair thoughts I crave! Now must good words be spoken on a good day. Let ears be rid of suits, and banish mad disputes forthwith! Thou rancorous tongue, adjourn thy wagging!

It is thus the moment for reconciliation, genuine or simulated. And this is exactly what happens in the Senate, when the leaders of Rome receive the envoys of Tusculum as friends, accept their explanation and their prayers and not only efface their fault but give them the most enviable present, that of *civitas*—Roman citizenship.

> But why are glad words spoken on thy Calends? and why not do we give and receive good wishes? (*Fasti*, 1.175–176)

Janus responds (178–182):

> Omens are wont to wait upon beginnings. At the first word ye prick up anxious ears. . . . (On the first day) [the Calends of January] the temples and ears of the gods are open, the tongue utters no fruitless prayers, and words have weight.

On the first day of A.D. 28, Tiberius and his servants in the Senate became guilty of conduct exactly the reverse of what Camillus and the Senate did during the grand epoch as recounted in the legend of the Tusculans (Tacitus, *Annales*, 4.70). In a letter to the august assembly on the first day of January, the emperor, after the usual greetings, accused one of the members of plotting against him. Forthwith, the suspect was declared guilty and led to the execution grounds, a rope around his neck. On the way, he cried incessantly, as loud as the rope would permit, that this was truly a fine way to start the year. Wherever he passed, the people scattered, terrorized by his voice. Streets and public places emptied and the people, while fleeing, asked one another what could be expected of a year whose first day, ordinarily devoted to religious rites with profane speech prohibited, was celebrated with chains and rope. All the *dramatis personae* that day, including the people deserting the streets, behaved contrary to their Roman and Tusculan counterparts of the fourth century.

There is no reason, of course, for claiming to place this episode from the chronicle of Camillus on the New Year. No indication of day or month is given and one would more likely place it, if such is important, during the usual season for wars. Nevertheless, it seems to allude to the rites and the spirit of the festival which mark the entrance onto the scene of the "new Phoebus," the annual birth of the sun. It would thus complete, by a reference to this second theology of the light, the image of the general whom Aurora protects.

If these remarks warrant consideration, few important traits remain in the military[15] life of Camillus that cannot be justified. Whatever facts it encompasses, the military life appears, under the sign of the goddess Aurora, as a coherent whole produced by a lucid effort to transpose into an epic all that traditional knowledge taught about the births and the rhythms of the sun.

[15] I should point out that these mythologic references deal only with the military, soldierly moments in Camillus' life. His political activity has been kept entirely separate.

4

Juno and Aurora

While the relationship between Camillus and Mater Matuta is, on the whole, clear and continuous, it contains some mystery, however, which is due not to the goddess but to her protégé.

Appointed dictator for the first time, instructed by man and by fortune to end the interminable siege of Veii, Camillus is not content simply to take the "departure omens" before leaving Rome—a thing so normal and necessary that the texts don't mention it—but, as Livy specifies, binds himself by two vows, *ex senatus consulto.*[1] If the war ends successfully, he will thank the gods by celebrating *ludos magnos,* τὰς μεγάλας θέας, and will have the newly restored[2] temple of the goddess Mater Matuta dedicated (*aedem refectam dedicaturum,* νεὼν . . . καθιερώσειν; Livy 5.19.6; Plutarch, *Camillus* 5.1). The fact is that, after the victory, although Plutarch does not mention the fulfillment of the vows, Livy states (23.7) that the dedication of the temple was accomplished before the dictator abdicated. He then notes (31.2) that the Great Games were celebrated three years later by the first titulars of the consulate, which had been temporarily restored. Thus, the victorious general and his fellow citizens deemed that the gods in general and Mater Matuta in particular had fulfilled their part of the contract.

---

[1] See above, chapter 1, note 9.
[2] See above, chapter 1, note 10.

THE OTHER VOWS OF CAMILLUS

Yet historians slight these first vows of the dictator, made in Rome, in favor of two other much more famous ones, made in camp at the moment of the final assault on Veii (Livy, 5.21.1–3):

> Then the dictator, after taking the auspices, came forth and commanded the troops to arm. "Under thy leadership," he cried, "Pythian Apollo, and inspired by thy will, I advance to destroy the city of Veii, and to thee I promise a tithe of its spoils. At the same time I beseech thee, Queen Juno, that dwellest now in Veii, to come with us, when we have gotten victory, to our City—soon to be thine, too—that a temple meet for thy majesty may there receive thee."

When Camillus says to Pythian Apollo "tuo ducto tuoque numine instinctus," he is referring to the consultation at Delphi that, just prior to his dictatorship, had enabled the Romans to solve the enigma of the overflowing Alban Lake and, consequently, to conquer Veii. The god had, in fact, added an injunction to his answer (16.10): "And know that over that city which thou dost beleaguer for so many years, the fates now disclosed have given thee the victory. When thou hast ended the war with conquest, bring to my temple an ample gift."

This pledge, unfulfilled by the general after the fall of Veii, had grave consequences, as we shall see later.[3] In any case, Camillus was not at liberty to ignore it: he had taken on the responsibility with the dictatorship.

As for the promise made to Juno, that will not be forgotten. Upon his return, at the same time that he dedicates the temple of Mater Matuta, he begins the construction of Juno Regina's temple on the Aventine hill. Its dedication is accomplished three years later by the same consuls who celebrate the Great Games. But why this gratuitous appeal to Juno on the part of the general?

Legend supplies the answer: it is an *euocatio*.[4] At the end of a

---

[3] See *Mythe et épopée III* (Paris, 1973), pp. 232–235.

[4] Regarding this evocation, see the notes of R. M. Ogilvie, *A Commentary on Livy, Books I–V* (Oxford, 1965), pp. 673–675; cf. 694–695.

siege, in addition to any previously made vow or promise, the Roman general always has the right to approach the principal deity of the enemy city thus and to propose this less-than-honorable yet attractive bargain to the god: a cult in Rome in return for his treason. In this last religious act of Camillus, there is, therefore, nothing offensive to Mater Matuta, neither infidelity nor defiance. But it presupposes—this is the law of the *euocatio*—that Juno is the principal deity of Veii, the one who holds its destiny in her hands. In fact, at this point in history, according to all evidence, this is the opinion of the authors of the chronicle. Is it not in the temple of Juno, at the spot where the king is in the midst of sacrificing and consulting the haruspices (Livy, 5.21.8–10), that by design or by chance the tunnel dug by Roman engineers opens onto the very floor of the enemy citadel (19.10–11)—a theme often used by Roman fables of this period? But it is precisely here that we encounter a difficulty.

Not until the account of the end of the war, in the brief and decisive moment reserved for Camillus in this long war, does the reader of Livy hear of this eminent place that Juno supposedly occupies in Veii. Of course, if one believes a tradition that is itself unreliable, every Etruscan city supposedly had temples of Jupiter, Juno, and Minerva. But in this "triple model," supposing that it predates the Capitoline temple of the Tarquins, apart from the fact that Juno certainly does not play a dominant role, does not rank higher than Jupiter, it is clear that it is one thing to be a member of a divine triad and another to be "the" deity responsible for a particular city. But the fact is that the goddess is named neither by Livy nor by any other author at any moment during the stormy relationship between Rome and Veii, either before the siege or at any time during the siege itself. Her office as "goddess of the *polis*" is actually discovered only when the siege ends, when Camillus bribes her and wins her over to Rome's side. How does one explain this revelation or this promotion *in extremis*? In other words, if there is no reason for refusing to acknowledge that a Uni had been adored in Veii (since this is the name of the goddess that the Etruscans likened to the Greek Hera, doubtless after borrowing it from an

Italic people), why is it that Camillus, precisely at this point in time and with such display, links her and no other to an undertaking that he has already put under the tutelage of Mater Matuta?

Surely, one can assume that two variants of the Veian epic have been more or less cleverly incorporated into the makeup of the vulgate that we read. One can even speak of "strata," a word dear to those who easily invent history. But a recent discovery opens up another possibility.

JUNO AND MATER MATUTA

Some sixty kilometers northwest of Rome, at Pyrgi, in the Etruscan port that served Caere, a goddess had an important sanctuary. Its destruction by a fleet from Syracuse in 384 B.C. had a great impact, for several Greek authors mention it.[5] They give two different interpretations of the indigenous divine name connected with this event. Although Strabo (5.22.6) writes Εἰληθυία (Εἰλειθυία) "Ilithyia," three other texts have Λευκοθέα (Pseudo-Aristotle, *Economics*, 2.2.10; Polyaenus, *Strategies*, 5.2.21; Aelian, *Variae Historiae*, 1.20). There has been long-standing agreement that the first name is a translation, in fact current and justified, of the Latin "Lucina" and the second the ordinary, canonical translation of "Mater Matuta." The Greeks—historians of the fourth or third century on whom existing evidence must be based—thus followed preexisting Latin interpretations, or rather an indecisive interpretation, of the local goddess. Rarely do the components of one pantheon find exact parallels in a foreign pantheon. When scholars want to establish equivalents, they usually limit their choice to a personage in the second pantheon who has one or several traits recognized as important in the "corresponding" figure of the first, a practice that leads to distortions, sometimes of great consequence. Thus Quirinus, called "Mars *tranquillus*," "Mars *qui*

---

[5] It is daring to implicate the Gauls in this expedition, even as mercenaries (Marta Sordi).

praeest paci," was likened to the volatile Enyalios because already in the Iliad Enyalios is the doublet of Ares who was himself likened to "Mars." But by the same token, the differential term of the expression, the limiting adjective *"tranquillus,"* disappeared and the Greeks saw in Quirinus only a θεός πολεμίστης as they did in Mars. So it is again that Mater Matuta, once she was likened to Leucothea because of the second rite of her festival, came to be the mother of Portunus because, on his own and for completely different reasons, Portunus had been identified with Palemon, son of Leucothea. We can thus assume that the residing goddess of the sumptuous temple of Pyrgi had presented a problem of interpretation to the Latins. Furthermore, judging by Greek traditions, the two sacred names between which they hesitated are those of different divinities, but ones that converge at least in one area. Lucina parallels Juno insofar as she protects birth, the coming of children into the light ("Ηρα Φωσφόρος, says Dionysius of Halicarnassus, 4.15.5). Mater Matuta is the daily protectress of the most splendid of the newborn, and through the second rite of her feast, protectress also of a category of young children. But other features no less important separate them: Lucina governs the light insofar as it is perceived, the light of life, opposed to nothingness, while Matuta introduces the light as illuminant, opposed to darkness. We must assume that these differences were minimized and that in some way these diverse values were incorporated into the Etruscan goddess of Pyrgi, simultaneously "Ilithyia" and "Leucothea."

As a matter of fact, the indigenous name of the goddess of Pyrgi has recently been learned: it is Uni. In 1964 successful excavations brought to light several sheets of gold foil, two of which—one in Etruscan, the other in Punic—seem if not to bear the same text, at least to refer in similar terms to the same event, the occasion of the same dedication.[6]

The Punic text begins with with these words: "To lady Astarte ('ŠTRT), this holy place, it is what Tebarie Velianas (TBRY'

[6] This discovery is explained and the results discussed in the appendix on the religion of the Etruscans, *Archaic Roman Religion*, trans. Philip Krapp (Chicago and London, 1970), pp. 680–684.

WLNŠ), king of Kayišraie (KYŠRY, that is Cisra, Caere), made and gave."

The proper names obviously correspond to those of the beginning of the Etruscan lamina: *Unialastres . . . Θefariei Velianas.* Although *Unialastres* remains mysterious in its second element, *Uni* (*Unial* in the genitive) is clear and moreover expected, since the African Augustine already knew (*Questions on the Heptateuch,* 7.16) that "lingua Punica Juno Astarte uocatur."

But probably neither the Astarte of Carthage nor each of the two Latin goddesses, Lucina and Mater Matuta, exhausted the complex composition of the Uni of the Etruscan port. Only the Latin ones count here. Lucina, who indeed parallels Juno in one of her functions, poses no problem: she reminds us that Uni, above all, is truly this Italic Juno whose name is probably distorted. But Mater Matuta, despite her approximate likeness to Lucina through concern for children, is more surprising: was Juno Lucina not enough? Why was Aurora added and generally preferred, seeing that Mater Matuta, despite her translation into Leucothea, was first of all Aurora? After all, the chronicle of Camillus now attests that the Latins of the period when these likenesses were established, during the fourth century at the latest, had full knowledge of this equivalence.

THE ETRUSCAN AURORA

A discovery by Raymond Bloch, which is as important for the history of religion as was, five years earlier, the identification of Uni–Astarte on the first stone tablets, supplies the answer. I can do no better than to quote his demonstration, together with his footnotes (arranged a, b, c[7]).

After recalling the classic equivalents Ilithyia–Lucina and

[7] "Ilithye, Leucothée et Thesan," *Comptes rendus de l'Académie des Inscriptions et Belles-Lettres* (1968), 366-375; idem, "Un mode d'interprétation à deux

Leucothea–Matuta, and after noting what in Rome itself establishes
a link between these two sacred figures, Bloch writes:[8]

> And now this dawning light that appears to us under its two
> faces, with the dawn of the morning and the dawn of life,
> today comes to meet us directly under its Etruscan name in an
> inscription from Pyrgi probably dating from the fifth century
> B.C. It concerns an inscription, engraved on a bronze lamina,
> that has just been reproduced by M. M. Pallotino[a] with his
> usual care. Discovered in 1964 in numerous pieces scattered
> throughout the dirt near the gold-leaf basin, this lamina was
> restored through long and meticulous work. It now gives us a
> text of three lines, difficult to read in some parts and incom-
> plete at the end of each line.
>   Thus:

> eta θesan etras uniịaθi ha . . .
> hutila ṭịna etiasas acalia . . .
> θanaχvilus caθarnaia . . .

---

degrès: de l'Uni de Pyrgi à Ilithye et Leucothée," *Archaeologia classica* 21 (1969),
58–65. Bloch later read an important paper to the Academy (June 16, 1972) on
"Hera, Uni, Junon en Italie centrale," *Comptes rendus de l'Académie des Inscriptions et Belles-Lettres* (1972), 384–395 (with a brief discussion), commenting in
particular on Mario Torelli's "Il Santuario di Hera a Gravisca," *La parola del
passato* 136 (1971), 44–67 (Greek sanctuary found in 1969, explored in 1970, in the
ancient port of Tarquinia; about the inscriptions of this sanctuary—among which
are four to Hera, on potsherd, in Ionian characters—see Jeanne and Louis Robert,
Revue des études grecques 84 (1971), 534, no. 730 of the *Bulletin épigraphique*).

[8] "Ilithye," 373–374. In a paper on the "decoding of the Etruscan language"
given to the Academy (November 5, 1971: *Comptes rendus de l'Académie des
Inscriptions et Belles-Lettres* [1971], 650), the undaunted V. I. Georgiev, of course,
successfully completed and translated these three lines:
   eta θesan etras uniiaθi hu[tiś? acale?]
   hutila zina eti asas acalia [eta? mulu?]
   θanaχvilus caθarnaia . . .
ista Aurora [= statua Aurorae] data (est) Junoni matri qui[nto? Junio?]
Quinquatria fac ei in Junio. Hoc? (est) uotum?
Tanaquilis Catharniä (natae) . . .

[8a] Cf. Massimo Pallottino, *Scavi nel santuario etrusco di Pyrgi. Relazione
delle attività svolte nell'anno 1967. Un altra laminetta di bronzo con iscrizione
etrusca recuperata del materiale di Pyrgi* (Rome, 1967); Giovanni Colonna,
"L'ingressa del Santuario, la via Caere–Pyrgi ed altri problemi," *Archaeologia
classica* 19 (1967), 332–348.

Unfortunately, the inscription remains difficult to understand in many respects, as is the case with longer Etruscan texts. The gaps in the text and the syllabic punctuation, which does not separate the words, increase the difficulties. The third line gives us the name of the dedicator in the genitive. The second line is unclear despite the presence of the word *Tina*, probably the great god Tina–Jupiter, spouse of Uni-Juno,[b] but here the division of the words is questionable. We recognize in the first line the locative form *uniiaθi* which perhaps means "in Uni's temple." As M. Pallotino emphasizes, this would be like the formula *bbtj* from the Punic inscription on the gold leaf, a formula that means "in the goddess' temple." But what interests us most today is Thesan, the second word of the first line. Thesan is, as a matter of fact, the Etruscan word for dawn. An Etruscan mirror from Florence, reproduced in plate 290 of the Corpus of mirrors of E. Gerhard, depicts a scene that leaves no doubt on this subject. We see a young woman named *Thesan* tenderly kissing a young man named *Tinthun*, a name in which we immediately recognize the Greek name Tithonos. Now in Greek mythology Tithonos is the lover of Eos, Aurora, the goddess of the dawning day. The latter, herself immortal, asked of and obtained from Zeus immortality for Tithonos. But in the frenzy of her passion she forgot to ask also for eternal youth for him. The unfortunate one grew so old and ugly with the passing of time that in the end Eos herself changed him into a cricket. A sorry end for a lover who was loved too much![c]

[8b] A fragmentary Etruscan inscription, likewise found in the excavations of Pyrgi, also contains the names of both Uni and Tina. See Pallottino, "I frammenti de lamina di bronzo con inscrizione etrusca scoperti a Pyrgi," *Studi Etruschi* 34 (1966), 175–206.

[8c] The group formed by Aurora and one of her lovers frequently appears in Etruscan art. Cf. also the crater of the *Aurora painter*, in J. D. Beazley, *Etruscan Vase Painting* (Oxford, 1947), pp. 80 ff., and let us not forget the handsome acroterium found at Caere itself, dating from about 550 and depicting Aurora and Cephale; cf. G. Q. Giglioli, *L'arte etrusca* (Milan, 1935), pl. CLXIV.

Naturally, one would like to understand better the beginning of the sentence containing the words Θ*esan* and *uniiaθi*. Is Thesan another name for Uni herself? The interpretation of Mater Matuta as the mistress of the sanctuary would lead one to think so. In any case, one sure and essential fact remains. According to our attempted demonstration, Ilithyia and Leucothea, by corresponding to Juno Lucina and Mater Matuta, reveal the light that strikes the eyes of the newborn and that which accompanies the coming of morning. Now this dawn, real or symbolic, emerges before us today in its direct form, under its Etruscan name in a document contemporaneous with the realities it treats.

Obviously, it is not valid to transfer mechanically to the Veian Uni the complex theological formula revealed by the variety of Latin interpretations of her sister from Caere—implicitly Juno, explicitly Lucina and Mater Matuta. But it is safer to believe that the rendering *Juno*—even designated as *Regina*—preferred by the Romans in the case of Veii may not be any more exhaustive. Even if at Pyrgi Θesan—that is, Aurora—is not an indication of Uni, the inscription attests to the fact that there existed a close link between them. One must recognize, too, that Aurora as a divine person was well enough established in Etruria for the name Tithonos to be transcribed and that of Eos translated on the mirror depicting the Greek legend of Eos and Tithonos.

Seeing this, how can one not be struck by this coincidence: the hero that the Roman epic presents as the follower and protégé of the Latin Aurora, Mater Matuta, and who before leaving Rome to conquer Veii, has just entrusted himself to Mater Matuta; this hero once in his camp before Veii, while preparing the final assault, invokes through *euocatio* an Etruscan goddess whom nothing prior to that time prepared us to regard as the most important divinity of that city, and who in another matter of the Etruscan sphere was either likened or closely linked to Θesan, the Aurora, herself interpreted by the Latins as Mater Matuta. Is it really only a coincidence? Or did the authors of Camillus' chronicle know that the

counterpart of Mater Matuta, at Veii as well as at Pyrgi, was either
a variation of Uni–Juno or a figure in her close circle? Thus, right
after the triumph, the simultaneous execution of the vows made
successively to the two goddesses, the national one and the foreign
one, takes on a richer meaning (Livy, 5.23.7):

> He then let the contract for the temple of Queen Juno on the
> Aventine, and dedicated one to Mater Matuta.

Camillus' religious activities would thus be entirely consistent.
The vow to Juno would be the extension of the vow to Matuta and
the capture of Veii which, after his heroic conduct on Mount Algidus, is Camillus' first exploit and his first victory as dictator. This
victory, already linked to Aurora through Mater Matuta, would
also be linked to her through Uni–Juno.[9]

APOLLO

Similar remarks could be made, moreover—over and above
the consultations at Delphi, which are probably as unhistorical as

---

[9] This hypothesis is not incompatible with another. As far as its structure was
concerned (length, numerous episodes), the Romans early on thought of the siege of
Veii as a replica of the siege of Troy. Given the penetration of Etruria by the civilization and the gods of Greece, this literary replica was motivated by a feeling of
politico–religious revenge: this time the besiegers, the conquerors are the Trojans,
present through their descendants. It was thus tempting to see in Juno, and Juno
Regina, the arch persecutor of the Trojans, the most eminent protectress of Rome's
Etruscan enemies—just as another epic, moreover, made her the protectress, the
inciter of their Punic enemies. It is possible (see *Mythe et épopée III*, pp. 204–205)
that the installation of the triad Jupiter O. M., Juno Regina, and Minerva on the
Capitol by the Etruscan kings, which brings together under Jupiter the two worst
heavenly adversaries of the Trojans, was a reverse demonstration of what we would
today call this "ideological warfare." The connections between Camillus and Juno
were not limited to the *euocatio*. According to Livy, 6.4.2–3, after the affair of
Sutrium (see above, chapter 3: "Sutrium, Lost and Regained in a Day"), the sale of
the Etruscan prisoners brought such a profit that after compensating the women
who had, following the capture of Veii, given their gold for the offering due Apollo,

the marvel that supposedly occasioned it[10]—concerning the other foreign divinity whom Camillus at the moment of the assault promises to serve: Apollo. It was said that the official introduction of this god in Rome dated back to 433. In that year, following a stubborn plague, a temple on a site already named Apollinar(e) had been accorded him, and two years later the temple was dedicated (Livy, 4.25.3 and 29.7). Apollo had thus been adopted as a healing god, and for a long time he remained essentially that. But exclusively? This has been widely held and I myself readily espoused this position. Yet, it is difficult to believe that, in adopting an important and multivalent figure like this Apollo, whose complexity is fairly well illustrated by the decorations on Etruscan vases, the Romans would limit themselves to his healing facet while ignoring, eliminating everything else, in particular his connection with the light, his solar affinities.

Perhaps it is already significant that, according to the legend, the dedication of the temple of Apollo, promised two years earlier, was accomplished by Consul Julius, who stayed behind in Rome, at a time when his colleague Quinctius Cincinnatus under the dictator A. Postumius Tubertus was busy winning the first great "victory at dawn." This is the battle of Mount Algidus (Livy, 4.29.7)—in which Aurora's future protégé, Camillus, of humble birth and until then unknown, suddenly becomes famous.[11]

The second synchronism is more significant. There was little mention of Apollo or of his cult for a third of a century. While he was first to be named and associated with Latona, he appeared only in the lectisternium of 399, in yet again a medical context. Then, suddenly, at the end of the war against Veii, under his true civil

---

there was enough left over to make three gold cups. Camillus' name was engraved on them, and they were placed at Juno's feet in the tripartite temple of Capitoline Jupiter where they remained, it is said, until fire destroyed it. As dictator, Camillus' son, L. Furius Camillus, promised and dedicated (Livy, 7.28.6) another famous temple, Juno Moneta's, built on the site of the house of Manlius Capitolinus.

[10] See *Mythe et épopée III*, p. 72.

[11] See above, chapter 1: "First Battle at Dawn." The "birth date" of the temple (from the very beginning?) is September 23: zone of the autumnal equinox.

status of Greek god residing in Greece, he enters the still legendary religious history of Rome with all his importance. We read that just prior to the dictatorship of Camillus and in some way in order to push him into the career of *fatalis dux*, it is Apollo who, when consulted at Delphi, gave the Romans the answer to the enigma of the Alban Lake and the first recipe for victory. That is why at the moment of the assault Camillus addresses him as well as the Etruscan Juno, promising a tenth of the spoils. And when the general has neglected—forgotten—the debt for too long a time, it is the creditor god who provides Rome and these Roman women who once a year celebrate the cult of Aurora, with the opportunity for lavish atonement. Through the Delphic oracle, and independent of it, do we not see here the total Apollo enlisted by the authors of the chronicle of Camillus? And, in this totality—since the hero to whom he opens the way and whom he renders successful is, in other respects, protected by Aurora and is, as such, likened to the dawning Sun— is it not the solar aspect of the god which, if it did not require his conjunction with this hero at least prompted it at this moment in the Roman epic?

Of course these reflections, too, are impossible to prove. If they are judged plausible, the Veian episode of Camillus' chronicle, including the role played by Juno and Apollo, appears to be a unitary structure whose total theological framework—with the Etruscan goddess linked to Θesan and the Greek god related to Helios corroborating the action of the Latin Matuta—highlights the auroral protection and the solar affinity attributed to the hero.

5

The Travesties of the Ides of June

We have seen that the days preceding the summer solstice[1] contain rites and include traditions in which are expressed various facets or moments of the conventionalized concern that Roman society experiences in the face of the reversal of diurnal time; no longer an increase; the semblance of an arrest, in spite of the name; then an increasingly felt diminution. The outer limits of this period, at least those that we have already established, are June 11 and June 20. The eleventh contains the festival designed, through the actions of the matrons, to help the goddess of Dawn, Mater Matuta, banish darkness and dote on the infant sun.[2] The twentieth is the *dies natalis* of the temple of Summanus, the god whose activity is concentrated in the premorning hours, which already are part of the impending day.[3] Finally, two days earlier, on June 18, there is the anniversary of a legendary event important enough ideologically for Ovid to mention it with the religious festivals and dates. It has a double connection with the epic whole that culminates in Camillus, hero of Mater Matuta. The battle of Mount Algidus is

---

[1] Regarding the full significance of such an expression in connection with pre-Julian calendars, see my *Mythe et épopée III* (Paris, 1973), p. 42 n. 3, and pp. 319–322.

[2] See above, chapter 1: "The Vow to Mater Matuta," and appendices 1 and 2.

[3] See above, chapter 3: "Summanus."

the occasion of the sole wound, the first exploit, and the sudden glory of the cavalier Camillus, who was unknown until then. It is also the first "victory at dawn" in Roman history and in its structure announces the third "victory at dawn" of the dictator Camillus himself.[4]

AURORA'S SEASON

The above statement, of course, necessitates an investigation. Are these three days, between June 11 and June 20—and possibly a little before, from the Calends, or a little later, up to the solstice—the only ones that, through their theological, ritual, or epic content, express the preoccupations caused by the approaching solstice?

Legend places no other ancient event during this period. As for the festivals, by virtue of a well-known rule they can take place only on odd-numbered days—in this case June 13, 15, 17, and 19. Now, as for documentation, neither the last two days, nor for that matter June 21, 23, or 25, provide anything for the record. The second half of June (16–30)—like that of January and the first half of February and April, as well as all of September and November—is one of the long fallow periods of the feria. That leaves June 13 and 15.

The fifteenth closes the period of Vesta, begun on June 7. It is only during this time that the *aedes Vestae* is open, and only to women, who must enter barefoot. June 9 is, strictly speaking, the day of the Vestalia. On the fifteenth, the "dung," *stercus*,[5] is taken according to ritual from the *aedes* and thrown into the Tiber, an event that makes this one of the three yearly *fissi*, that is, inauspi-

---

[4] See above, chapter 1: "First Battle at Dawn."

[5] Regarding the meaning of *stercus* and the import of this archaic rite, see my *Archaic Roman Religion*, trans. Philip Krapp (Chicago and London, 1970), pp. 317–318.

cious (*nefas*) during the first part until the *stercus* is disposed of and auspicious (*fas*) afterwards. Nothing in all that seems to relate directly to a solar design. Nevertheless, the dates hold our attention. The opening of the Vestal period, June 7, is separated from the Matralia on June 11, and the Matralia themselves are separated from the closing of the Vestal times, June 15, by a three-day interval which, as Wissowa noted,[6] often attested to an ideological link between the two ceremonies that frame it. It is thus possible that the placing of the main annual cult of Vesta in a period just preceding the summer solstice and whose midpoint day was Aurora's affirms that, through both of their solar references, a close link was felt between the divinities presiding over the main sources of the heat and light necessary to man: that of fire harnessed, snatched up, eventually revitalized by the rays of the sun, and that which the sun itself forms each day. This link could also be said to exist in sacred architecture were we sure that the round temple of the Forum Boarium, today occupied by Santa Maria del Sole church and the object of a lengthy debate, was Mater Matuta's. Only Vesta, of all the other ancient indigenous divinities, had a circular *aedes*. Such a link could bring to mind above all the close association, in Vedic hymns as well as in the Brahmanic liturgy, of Uṣas and Agni, of the goddess Aurora and the god Fire—in whose cult fire, lightning, and sun are, according to usual conjecture, the three manifestations at the three stages of the universe.

These links, defying hard proof, are only probable. This is not the case of the last odd-numbered day remaining available in the period, the one immediately following the Matralia on the eleventh. June 13, the day of the Ides, contains a festival that shows a less pleasing facet of Aurora and which probably has, or had originally, the task of remedying this unpleasantness. Since it is the Vedic Uṣas who has ensured the interpretation of the two successive rites of the Matralia, let us first pursue the examination of her mythology.

[6] Georg Wissowa, *Religion und Kultus der Römer*, 2d ed. (Munich, 1912), p. 437 and n. 2.

THE CHARIOT OF THE VEDIC AURORA

Each day when Uṣas brings the rising sun, she not only lights up an enchantment in the sky, she also performs a favor on earth, valuable especially because of its far-reaching effects, because of all that it allows the Arya, individuals and societies, to do or to undergo. In a word, while illuminating, she awakens.[7]

> Uṣas (. . .) comes (. . .): (at her coming) each biped stirs, and she wakes up the birds. (*Rig Veda*, 1.48.5).
> Divine Dawns, (. . .) awake the sleeping being, whether biped or quadruped, to pursue (his functions). (4.51.5)
> Radiant Uṣas, [has brought light to the roads of men] wake us up to-day for (the acquisition of) ample riches, in like manner as thou hast awakened us (of old) [awakening the five human establishments]. . . . (7.79.1)

And she does not stop with awakening the actors of the human comedy. She suggests their action to them. She provides them with the ends and means of this action, restores them to their eyes and their memory, thus to existence (1.113.4–6):

> Uṣas gives back all the regions (that had been swallowed up by night) [awakens all creatures].
> The opulent (dawn) arouses to exertion the man bowed down in sleep—one man to enjoyments, another to (the acquirement of) wealth; she has enabled those who were almost sightless to see distinctly. The expansion Uṣas has given back all the regions [has awakened all creatures].
> The dawn rouses one man to acquire wealth, another to earn food, another to achieve greatness, another to sacrifices, another to his own (pursuits), another to activity, and lights all men to their various means of maintaining life. Uṣas has given back all the regions [has awakened all creatures].

[7] I am using the translations of Louis Renou, *Études védiques et pāṇinéenes* (Paris, 1957), vol. 3 (hymns to Aurora). [The English version is that of H. H. Wilson (see above, Note on the Translation), occasionally modified to conform to Renou, with all changes indicated by square brackets.]

Finally, being a good goddess, she herself begins by lavishing her gifts, everything that makes existence and happiness possible. The poet of 1.48, the first hymn to the Aurora of the *Rig Veda*, from the very beginning asks for the most important:

> Uṣas, daughter of heaven, dawn upon us with riches: diffuser of light, dawn upon us with abundant food: bountiful goddess, dawn upon us with wealth (of cattle).

At the beginning of the following hymn, we read likewise:

> Uṣas, come by auspicious ways from above the bright (region of the) firmament . . .

All that is reassuring, idyllic: the punctual and devoted goddess, in her brilliant chariot, *rátha*, laden with goods to distribute, performs her duty (1.49.2):

> Uṣas, in the ample and beautiful chariot in which thou ridest, come to-day, daughter of heaven, to the pious offerer of the oblation.

In other words, as Renou notes,[8] "it is in fact asked that man be favored with the riches that the chariot carries or symbolizes." That these riches which, according to custom, consist of cows, horses, and men (1.113.18, etc.), are not of a kind that in reality can easily be transported by a chariot, is of little importance. The scene of the dispenser, simultaneously spirited and overladen, takes shape as best it can.

Thus we have roughly the analysis of the duties of Aurora: they are of prime importance. Is it possible to thwart them? Indeed it is and several hymns praise Indra for having saved the goddess from sinister demons just as, according to others, he rescued the sun. But it also happens that the difficulty arises from the goddess herself, physically or mentally, if one dares say so. Either she no longer has the strength necessary for her daily rounds or she shows ill will. Of course, neither the hymns that invoke her nor most of

---

[8] *Études védiques*, vol. 3, p. 30.

the others speak of this risk: they do not depict Aurora as reluctant to get up, to "go out." And if some poets, reversing roles as they willingly do in similar cases, declare that it is their praise which wakens Aurora (thus 4.52.4, 5.81.1, and 7.76.4), this claim does not imply that in their minds the person concerned is adverse to the task: like all immortals, she simply needs the priests' chants. But the hymns to Indra, all to the glory of the god, do not have the same reason for sparing the goddess. Several times they mention a scene where she is harshly dealt with by Indra, one of whose functions is to correct (even by violent interference, which is his specialty) any breach of the order of the world, whether it concern the behavior of men or the great rhythms of nature. Precisely, Indra attacks the vehicle that carriers her and is no longer the shiny and rapid chariot, *rátha*, that she drives everywhere else. It is rather a cart, a wagon, *ánas*—the name is the same as the Latin *onus*, "burden"—which is usually pulled by oxen, *anaḍváh*, not horses.[9]

The most precise text is *Rig Veda* 4.30.8–11:[10]

Inasmuch, Indra, as thou hast displayed such manly prowess, thou hast slain [struck] the woman, the daughter of the sky, when meditating mischief.[11]

Thou, Indra, who art mighty, hast enriched the glorious dawn, the daughter of heaven [and broken her].

The terrified Uṣas descended from the broken waggon when the (showerer of benefits) had smashed it.

[9] To explain the second rite of the Matralia, I utilized this episode in another way, probably mistakenly, in my *Déesses latines et mythes védiques* (Collection Latomus 24) (Brussels, 1956), pp. 30–38. On this point I have benefited from the critique of John Brough.

[10] Except for restoring to *ánas* its proper meaning, "cart" and not "chariot," I am using Abel Bergaigne's translation, *La religion védique d'après les hymnes du Rig Véda* (Paris, 1883), vol. 2, p. 193. [Wilson's translation already uses the correct term "waggon." See above, n. 7.]

[11] Precisely "auf Unheil sinnend" (Hermann-Günther Grassmann, *Wörterbuch zum Rig-Veda* [Leipzig, 1873]), "missgünstig" (Karl-Friedrich Geldner, trans., *Der Rigveda* [Göttingen, 1923]).

Then her shattered waggon reposed (on the bank) of the Vipāś (river), and she departed from afar.[12]

More briefly, in 2.15.6, Indra shatters Uṣas' cart with his thunderbolt; in 10.73.6 he struck down the two women of Manuci as he did the cart of Uṣas; in 10.138.5 Uṣas, trembling before the thunderbolt of Indra, abandoned her cart.

How should we take this scene where the goddess is humiliated, ridiculed by Indra and the poets? Abel Bergaigne, in the remarkable study he devoted to Indra, suggested that we see in this scene a particular case within the general conflict that sets this god against the powers of darkness:[13]

In the fourth part, we will see that the gods which Indra battled are the greedy guardians of the heavenly treasures who, contrary to the basically liberal god, have characters that in some measure liken them to demons. In verses 3–6 of the hymn 4.30, we see Indra "steal" the sun from them so that he may let it appear to men. The combat against the dawn, whose description follows almost immediately in verses 8–11, must likewise be, strange as it may seem at first, a battle for light. . . . We see that here the dawn, like the gods whom Indra fights, has a quasi-demonic character. The phenomenon that announces rather than creates daylight, sometimes seems to delay it by its too lengthy duration. This idea is formally expressed in verses 5.79.9: "Shine, daughter of Heaven, do not draw out your work, lest the sun, like a lying thief, burn you with his brightness." In our myth, Indra is the one who has the role of the sun, or who at least clears the way, through the

---

[12] Here is the text of the last two stanzas:

ápośā́ ánasaḥ sarat
sámpiṣṭād áha bibhyúṣī
ní yát sīṃ śiśnáthad vŕ̥ṣā.   10
etád asyā ánaḥ śaye
súsampiṣṭaṃ vípāśy ā́
sasā́ra sīm parāvátaḥ.   11

[13] *La religion védique*, pp. 192–193.

dawn, for the daystar. In one of the very formulas that show him shattering dawn's cart with his thunderbolt, we read that "he rends with swift ones those which are not," 2.15.6. The "swift ones" are probably the prayers of the Aṅgiras or, more broadly, of the ancient sacrificers whom we will see intervene as assistance in the combats of the god. Those who are not "swift" must be the dawns themselves. . . . Thus the dawn that Indra battles is a dawn that lingers too long and whose slowness likens her to the night. The appearance of the sun is Indra's victory over her as much as over darkness.

This is most likely the direction research must take. I question only that Aurora, after arriving, was slow to leave, for this image would not be congruent with reality except in the climates of the extreme North from which Indra is far removed. Once the sun is brought forward, daybreak does not linger, cannot linger. Rather, it is a question throughout, including 5.79.9, of her slowness in coming, in dissipating darkness.

As a rule, as I have just said, she could be innocent of this delay, which prolongs night to the detriment of day. If thick clouds cover the sky, how can the sun, which she ushers in, shine? In this case the intervention of Indra as the customary cleaver of clouds would be normal. But Indra does not attack the clouds that are the enemy of Aurora and of the light. He attacks Aurora herself, and above all it is Aurora herself that the poets make fun of and insult.

The only experiential data upon which this idea of "delay in coming" can rest is seasonal. Day does not begin at the same time throughout the year on Indra's doorstep, where the Vedic hymns were composed, any more than it does in Mediterranean Europe. And for six months it continues to grow shorter—that is, Aurora is slower and slower in coming. Makers of myths may explain this decrease by positing that, from the beginning to the end of the crisis, Aurora loses strength. This is the interpretation that, as we have seen, justifies the Roman festival of Mater Matuta in June, designed to revitalize the goddess at the moment when she is going to weaken. Yet the same phenomenon may be viewed with less benevolence. Neither threatened nor debilitated, but lazy or irreverent, Aurora knowingly and willingly performs her task poorly. The intervention of Indra is again justified, but in another sense: here, as is often the case, he maintains or reestablishes the world order—that is, in the last analysis, he serves the interests of the gods, the priests, and all the Aryans, three groups among which Aurora must each day start the mechanism of the triangular distribution, salutary for all.

This culpable slowness, and only this, is expressed in the image of the "cart" or "wagon." One could indeed imagine that Aurora chose this vehicle, at the risk of being slow, rather than the chariot in order to increase her cargo of goods. This is not the case; the contents of the wagon, ordinarily a load-carrying vehicle, are not mentioned in any of the four references made to the myth. Indra is not concerned with emptying the *ánas*, no object falls from it, nothing in particular is said about anything that the hymns to Aurora say she brings and which they ask her to bring. Finally, there remains only debris scattered in a river bed,[14] while Aurora, the sole passenger, is forced to get out and flee. We must thus assume that she preferred the *ánas* in order to lose time, reluctant to take up her daily task again and to reappear before the eyes of men. This aversion can be understood and can take on a naturalistic meaning only at the coming of the summer solstice.

THE QUINQUATRUS MINUSCULAE

It is not a Latin version of this myth that provided a fundamental legend for the June 13 rites, but a myth with the same meaning, based on the same representation.

The picturesque Quinquatrus Minusculae are celebrated on the Ides of June. In March, under the auspices of Minerva, all the professions had a common festival, the Quinquatrus. However, one guild and only one held back: the flute players, the *tibicines*.

---

[14] This mention of a terrestrial place (the Vipāś River) does not permit one to interpret historically the exploit of Indra against Uṣas and, through the exploit, Indra himself (John Brough, agreeing with Jarl Charpentier).

They waited for June 13 to take over the streets. Such a privilege, made fun of, for that matter, by the disparaging label *minusculae* instead of *minores* (*Fasti*, 6.651), may seem outrageous. Why did these musicians not share the lot of the bakers, shoemakers, teachers, barbers, doctors, weavers, and all the other craftsmen? In fact, they had a good reason both for keeping to themselves and for taking over the Ides—that is, a day of Jupiter. Their corporation, economically insignificant and little esteemed in itself, was of prime importance to religious life. As Ovid says (*Fasti*, 6.657–660),

> In the times of your ancestors of yore the fluteplayer was much employed and was always held in great honour. The flute played in temples, it played at games, it played at mournful funerals.

Censorinus (12.2) says more prosaically that the *tibicines* were required for all the supplications in the temples as well as for triumphal processions;[15] and they played, Cicero specifies (*De lege agraria*, 2.13), while victims were being sacrificed. Their sounds were not purely ornamental but were an indispensable part of the ceremonies, preventing profane noises in particular from breaking the required *silentium*. In a word, without being priests, even lower than priests, they sustained all ritual activity of the Republic and its families. In intention and scope their office was comparable to that rendered by the chanting priests in the Vedic sacrificial team. These priests made use of passages taken from the *Sāma Veda*, along with the priest specialists in the *Yajur Veda*—that is, the books that prescribe and describe the rites and the formulas, the *mantra*.[16] The office of the *tibicines* was perhaps even more important in the

[15] The entire beginning of chapter 12 ("*De laudibus musicae eiusque uirtutibus*") should be read.

[16] Regarding the homologies between the Roman special sacerdotal functions and the duties of the Vedic priests, see *Archaic Roman Religion*, pp. 576 ff. Two calendars place the *natalis dies* of the temple of the Muses on the same Ides of June. Regarding one of them, the publisher does comment on this coincidence (*Corpus Inscriptionum Latinarum*, I², 1, p. 320): "natalis Musarum aperte coniunctus est cum iisdem cantorum feriis."

Roman religion where nothing corresponded to the *Rig Veda* and where sacred rhetoric certainly was not subtle. This had the result that, according to the legend, the day they went on strike—or rather, according to the local term, seceded—their withdrawal paralyzed the cult entirely and the incident took on national proportions. The priests had scruples about performing the sacred gestures without musical accompaniment, τις ἥπτετο δεισιδαιμονία τῶν ἱερέων ἄναυλα θυόντων, Plutarch says (*Roman Questions*, 55), and this scruple, this *religio* (Livy, 9.30.6), reached even as far as the Senate. Given so singular a power, it is understandable that in March they did not join the throng from the other professions. They had to have their own special day.

In exchange for their unusual service, they held a traditional privilege: that of being fed, *uesci*, on the Capitol, within the walls of Capitoline Jupiter.[17] That also is understandable. Since Jupiter is the highest guarantor of religion, the sacred being par excellence as shown by the demanding code of his *flamen*; and since, on the other hand, all the Ides belong to him, it is only natural that the day of the *tibicines* be placed at one of these monthly high points. But why the Ides of June? Why are the *tibicines* in the limelight during the short period that precedes and ritually prepares the summer solstice? The fundamental legend provides the answer.

We have four detailed versions of this legend, whose differences have no bearing on our problem: Livy, 9.30.5–10; Valerius Maximus, 6.5.4; Plutarch, *Roman Questions*, 55; Ovid, *Fasti*, 6.653–692. A few other texts refer briefly to it.

First Plutarch:

> LV. Q. Why is it that on the ides of January [sic[18]] the flute-players are permitted to walk about the City in women's clothes?
>
> A. They enjoyed, it appears, great honours which King

[17] They gathered in the temple of Minerva, the collective patroness of all the trades (Varro, *De lingua latina*, 6.17; cf. Festus, 134L[1] = 266L[2]), but *epulabantur in Capitolio* (Livy, 9.30; Censorinus, 12.2).

[18] See *Mythe et épopée III*, p. 65. An obvious error for the "Ides of June."

Numa had given them by reason of his piety towards the gods; of these they were afterwards deprived by the *decemuiri consulari potestate* [ὑπὸ τῆς ἀνθυπατικῆς δεκαδαρχίας] and so left the City. Great search was consequently made after them and certain superstitious fears were felt, by the priests, who had to sacrifice without flutes. When they would not listen to persuasion but remained in Tibur, a freedman secretly promised the government to bring them back. Preparing a sumptuous banquet under pretext of having made a sacrifice, he invited the flute-players; women were present, wine was not spared, and the feast went on noisily through the night with dancing and sporting. Then suddenly the fellow started a report that his patron [*patronus*] was coming upon him and, making a great commotion, persuaded the flute-players to get into wagons, which were screened with skins [ἀναβάντας ἐφ' ἁμάξας δέρρεσι κύκλῳ περικαλυπτομένας], and so get to Tibur. But here he befooled them; for he drove the wagons by a round-about way and, his passengers being too drunk and the night too dark for them to notice, he took them all into Rome by morning [ἕωθεν) without their being any the wiser. Now most of them, in consequence of their nocturnal drinking-bout, were in flowered garments such as women wear. So, when they had been won over by the government and a settlement reached, it became the custom for them to dress in women's clothes on that day and revel through the City.

Livy apologizes for incorporating such a puerility into the account of the serious events that fill his ninth book: C. Junius Bubulcus is consul for the third time, Q. Aemilius Barbula for the second, and Rome is involved in the difficult Samnite wars:

> I should omit, as an incident hardly worth narrating, a little thing that happened in the same year (*rem dictu paruam*), but that it seemed to concern religion. The flute-players, angry at having been forbidden by the last censors to hold their feast, according to old custom, in the temple of Jupiter, went off to Tibur in a body, so that there was no one in the City to pipe at sacrifices. Troubled by the religious aspect of the case, the senate dispatched representatives to the Tiburtines, requesting

them to use their best endeavours to restore these men to Rome. The Tiburtines courteously undertook to do so; and sending for the pipers to their senate-house, urged them to return. When they found it impossible to persuade them, they employed a ruse, not ill-adapted to the nature of the men. On a holiday various citizens invited parties of the pipers to their houses, on the pretext of celebrating the feast with music. There they plied them with wine, which people of that profession are generally greedy of, until they got them stupefied (*oneratos sopiunt*). In this condition they threw them, fast asleep, into waggons (*in plaustra somno uinctos coniciunt*) and carried them away to Rome; nor did the pipers perceive what had taken place until daylight found them—still suffering from the debauch—in the waggons, which had been left standing in the Forum (*nec prius sensere quam, plaustris in foro relictis, plenos crapulae eos lux oppressit*). The people then flocked about them and prevailed with them to remain. They were permitted on three days in every year to roam the City in festal robes, making music and enjoying the license that is now customary, and to such as should play at sacrifices was given again the privilege of banqueting in the temple. These incidents occurred while men were preoccupied with two mighty wars.

Valerius Maximus underlines in particular the rites, the disguise, and the *licentia*:

Custom has it that the guild of flute players, wearing masks and multi-colored clothes, called attention to itself on the Forum by disrupting with its music serious public as well as private business. Here is the origin of this liberty.

Having for some time been prohibited from having their meals in the temple of Jupiter, as was the ancient custom, they took offense and withdrew to Tibur. The Senate could not allow sacrifice to take place without their assistance and asked the Tiburtines to intervene in order to return them to the Roman temples. Since the flute players persisted in their refusal, the Tiburtians lured them to a so-called religious banquet and there, when they saw that they were overcome with wine and sleep, managed to bring them back to Rome in wagons. Their privilege was restored to them, and they were given the right to indulge in the amusements of which we are speaking.

The use they make of masks arises from their shame at being caught inebriated.

The most detailed account comes from the *Fasti*, where the poet does not hesitate to question the blonde Minerva:

Why does the flute-player march at large through the whole city? What mean the masks? What means the long gown?

The goddess puts down her spear and replies:

In the times of your ancestors of yore the flute player was much employed and was always held in great honour. The flute played in temples, it played at games, it played at mournful funerals. The labour was sweetened by its reward; but a time followed which of a sudden broke the practice of the pleasing art. [A likely lacuna: deletion of the Capitoline refectory, then:] . . . Moreover, the aedile had ordered that the musicians who accompanied funeral processions should be ten, no more.

The flute-players went into exile from the city and retired to Tibur: once upon a time Tibur was a place of exile! The hollow flute was missed in the theatre, missed at the altars; no dirge accompanied the bier [*supremos toros*].

At Tibur there was a certain man who had been a slave, but had long been free, a man worthy of any rank. In his country place he made ready a banquet and invited the tuneful throng; they gathered to the festal board. It was night, and their eyes and heads swam with wine [*nox erat et uinis oculique animique natabant*], when a messenger arrived with a made-up tale, and thus he spoke (to the freedman): 'Break up the banquet without delay, for see here comes the master of thy rod!' Immediately the guests bestirred their limbs, reeling with heady wine; their shaky legs or stood or slipped. But the master of the house, 'Off with you all!' says he, and when they dawdled he packed them in a wain that was well lined with rushes.

The time, the motion, and the wine allured to slumber, and the tipsy crew fancied that they were on their way back to Tibur. And now the wain had entered the city of Rome by the Esquiline, and at morn it stood in the middle of the Forum [*et mane in medio plaustra fuere foro*].

In order to deceive the Senate as to their persons and their number, Plautius commanded that their faces should be covered with masks; and he mingled others with them and ordered them to wear long garments, to the end that women flute-players might be added to the band. In that way he thought that the return of the exiles could be best concealed, lest they should be censured for having come back against the orders of his colleague.

The plan was approved, and now they are allowed to wear their new garb on the Ides and to sing merry words to the old tunes.

The similarities and differences among these narrations have been carefully pointed out. Some and not others bring in the emancipated Tiburtines. One speaks of a *triduum* of *licentia*, the others only of the day of the Ides. Only Ovid brings the censors by name, one lenient, the other harsh, into the account. But in any case it is clear that the reform that those concerned experience as intolerable victimization falls within the competence of the censorship, enemy of luxury and laxity, and bears especially the stamp of the inflexible Appius Claudius—whom Plutarch confused, erring by a century, with the decemvir of the same name.[19] The most serious divergence deals with the proximate justification of the rites: masks, disguise, feminine garb. According to Ovid, these "alterations" take place in Rome itself, are done willingly and for the good of the *tibicines*, while other authors interpret the accoutrement to be the result of a night of orgies and of a hurried flight.

[19] Regarding these two Claudii and the confusion, see Franz Bömer's commentary on the *Fasti: Ovidius Naso, Die Fasten* (Heidelberg, 1958), vol. 2, p. 381 (at 6.663).

They attribute the wearing of the mask to a sudden feeling of shame. Nothing in all that changes the objective, established constant: in order to bring back to Rome the self-exiled flute players who refused to return, a Tiburtine or a group of Tiburtines get them drunk during the night and, while it is still dark, pile them into enclosed *plaustra*, which they drive to Rome. Once there they disappear, leaving the wagons on the Forum. The first light of day reveals to the *tibicines* their situation. Costumed and masked, they get out of the wagons (or they are then costumed and masked) and, receiving their privilege again, they once more take up their duties.

DAWN'S PLAUSTRA

These carefully enclosed, heavy vehicles that make their way from Tibur to Rome during the night, arriving thus from the East, are abandoned on the Forum and at daybreak spill out their unusual cargo. They bring to mind the cart, the *ánas*, from which the goddess Aurora is forced to emerge. Without being two variants of the same account, the Roman legend and the Vedic myth took advantage of—probably independently of each other—the same picturesque symbol:

Vedic India	Rome
1. Aurora, lazy or cunning,	1. The *tibicines*, angry and on strike,
2. delays her return and her duties	2. refuse to come back from Tibur to Rome to resume their duties.
3. by traveling in a cart whose slowness prolongs the night.	3. A freed Tiburtine (or Tiburtines) intervenes (intervene)
4. Indra intervenes,	4. puts (put) them during the night in heavy, enclosed wagons
5. shatters the cart.	5. that he (they) drives (drive) through the darkness and leaves (leave) on the Forum.
6. Aurora is forced to get out,	6. The *tibicines*, at daybreak, are forced to get out,
7. looking like a fool.	7. looking like fools.

The discrepancies in the intrigue are partly a result of differences in the distribution of the roles:

The Roman account does not personify Aurora as does the Vedic myth and as the Matralia rites did implicitly two days earlier in Rome itself. As in Camillus' "victories at dawn," it is only insofar as the hour (daybreak) is concerned that she intervenes and, as in these victories, she helps a plan succeed only if it was drawn up during the night.

The Vedic Aurora, an active and reliable goddess, drives her cart herself from nightfall until "her" moment arrives, while the *tibicines* in theirs, during the night until daybreak, are only an inert load carried away by men, strangers.

The Indian myth is directed to the glory of Indra. Uṣas, uncooperative, evidently unconcerned about leaving or simply speeding up her cart, cuts a pathetic figure before the god who breaks it to pieces. There is nothing of the kind in the Roman legend. The Tiburtines driving the wagons are of good will and, if they abandon them on the Forum, they do it on purpose, for the good of the Romans.

But what do the masked and costumed *tibicines* represent? For they are indeed paramount. Just as the *ánas* of the Indian myth seem to hold nothing but the goddess, the *plaustra* of the Tiburtines have no other load but them, no other mission but to transport them.

We could assume that the colorful band, which in the morning pours out onto the Forum, represents humanity itself. Dawn indeed does not just show the luminous child—the sun—in the sky. As we said regarding the Tusculan episode,[20] she also brings back in our consciousness or in the perception of others everything that sleep and darkness had filched, so to speak—the actors and props of all life, all the farces, idylls, tragedies, epics that make up men's lives. The travesties of the Ides of June could be just that—sketches of the ridiculous and charming character-types of the Italian comedy, through which the comman man, in a simplified form, portrays

[20] See above, chapter 3: "The Pardon for the Tusculans."

himself. Another swarm of histrions also comes to mind, these Passions contemplated by the visionary while they faded into the dusk of age, "one taking his mask with him and the other his knife."

But such an interpretation would meet with two difficulties. On the one hand, it does not take into account that the flute players are wearing women's clothing. On the other hand, if those in disguise had this significance, they would have to be varied, each evoking a type, a character, a profession. Now, on the contrary, the textual phrases lead us to believe that they are indistinguishable, all wearing the same accoutrement.

We are thus led to assume that the symbolism is more purely naturalistic, that the musicians dressed as women are a sort of replica in caricature of the matrons who, two days earlier, had assumed the role and gone through the salutary actions of conscientious Auroras. These matrons too, in their travesty, are multiple figures of dawn; but they represent the Auroras who for six months are going to be reluctant to discharge their duty and thus cannot merely be encouraged to perform according to their obligations but must be forced to do so. It is easy to verify, moreover, that the transposition thus seen extends to the whole, the only things remaining unaltered, of course, are the indications of time (night, dawn).

Rites of June 11:	Legend of June 13:
1. The *matres* (representing the *conscientious dawns*)	1. The *flute players* (representing the *unwilling dawns*)
2. force a *slave woman* (representing *evil darkness*)	2. through an *emancipated* Tiburtine, *are forced*, during the night,
3. to *enter* Aurora's temple	3. to *leave* Tibur, still at night,
4. and *they* drive her *from* it	4. and he *brings* them back to Rome, at dawn,
5. *violently*.	5. by *trickery*.
6. They *are* then *able* (second rite) to perform their functions (as Auroras) by doting on their nephews (representing Suns).	6. They *are* then *supposed* to resume their regular duties, which they do, in exchange for compensation.

The festivals of June 11 and 13, which the *dies natalis* of June 20 completes, thus mark progressively three aspects of the ritual effort that the impending reversal of the solstice imposes on the Romans. During the Matralia the Roman women reenacted the proper gestures of the Auroras (to banish Darkness, to dote on Suns) and by this very reenactment claimed to strengthen them. Two days later, during the Quinquatrus Minusculae, the disguised men represent the recalcitrant Auroras, brought back through trickery to their duty despite themselves. Finally, on June 20 the god honored will be Summanus, active during the second part of the night, those nights that will begin to lengthen but will nonetheless continue to prepare the light.

THE FLUTE PLAYERS AND THE CULT

The interpretation just given raises a new question: why is the band of public *tibicines* responsible for these rites and this symbolism? In order to give support to a masquerade, itself justified by a legendary farce, more is required than saying that men, of little esteem even though free, were necessary. Instead of compromising a guild so closely linked to religion, another kind of actor could easily have been found. But perhaps it is precisely their religious importance and their general participation, necessary to the cult, that qualifies them. Here again the Vedic Aurora enlightens the Latinist.

If Uṣas again sets all human activity in motion, her first task, on which all the others depend, is to open the series of rites for the whole day, as her place in the morning liturgies shows. She puts the gods and their faithful in contact with each other. We read in the *Rig Veda*, 1.48.11–12:[21]

> Bring to the ceremony the pious . . . Uṣas, bring from the firmament all the gods, to drink the *Soma* juice.

[21] I am using the translations of Louis Renou (see above, n. 7).

In addition, we read in 1.113.9:

Uṣas, inasmuch as thou hast caused the sacred fire to be kin-
dled, inasmuch as thou hast lighted the world with the light of
the sun, inasmuch as thou hast wakened men to perform sacrifice, thou hast done good service to the gods.

The gods are not the only beneficiaries of this service. The
priests live on it; they are impatient to see the tide of honoraria rise
with the day. Thus, in 1.124.10:

Awaken, wealth-abounding Uṣas, those who delight (in holy
offerings): let the (niggard) traders, reluctant to wake (for such
a purpose), sleep on. Arise, opulent Uṣas, bearing wealth to
the liberal (worshipper): speak of truth, who art the waster
away (of living creatures) [sic], arise, bearing wealth to him
who praises thee.

In 4.51.3:

The gloom-dispelling, affluent Dawns animate the pious worshippers to offer (sacrificial) treasure: may the churlish (traf-
fickers) sleep on unawakened, in the unlovely depth of darkness.

Thus is established among the officiating priests, the gods, and
Aurora (or Auroras) a multi-meaning solidarity not always coherent. A hymn of the Vasiṣṭhas provides a good formula for this
solidarity, a formula approved through the precedent of the fabled
priests of the past (7.76.1–7):

The Dawn has made all creatures visible. The paths that lead
to the gods are beheld by me, innocuous and glorious with
light: the banner of Uṣas is displayed in the east, she comes to
the west, rising above high places.
Many are the days that have dawned before the rising of
the sun, on which thou, Uṣas, hast been beheld like a wife
repairing to an inconstant husband, and not like one deserting
him.

Those ancient sages, our ancestors, observant of truth,[22]
rejoicing together with the gods, discovered the hidden light,
and, reciters of sincere prayers, they generated the Dawn.

. . . Auspicious *Uṣas, the Vasiṣṭhas, waking at dawn, and*
praising thee, glorify thee with hymns: Uṣas, who art the con-
ductress of cattle (to pasture), the bestower of food, dawn
upon us: shine, well-born Uṣas, the first (of the gods).

Uṣas, the object of the sincere praises of the worshipper,
is glorified when dawning, by the Vasiṣṭhas bestowing upon us
far-famed riches: do you (gods), ever cherish us with blessings.

Thus, we understand that the *tibicines*, assistants to all sacrifices, and "table companions of the gods," at least of the most
important among them, are, on a socially inferior level, as concerned with Aurora, as allied with Aurora as are the *kavi*, the
Indian trustees of hymns and melodies.

THE DENARII OF L. PLAUTIUS PLANCUS

This is the convergence of data that lays the foundation for the
auroral interpretation of the Quinquatrus Minusculae. What would
the learned Romans of the closing Republic, faithful to rites but
forgetful of ancestral theologems, have thought of it? We will be
careful not to put words into their mouths. But there is proof that,
in the middle of the last century B.C., one Roman at least knew that
dawn and through it, the goddess Aurora, was essential to the
occurrence. And this witness had a good reason for knowing, even
though not understanding the full significance of his information,
since he linked himself by adoption to C. Plautius, the censor who,
according to Ovid (an obvious correction of an apparent slip of the
copyists), had in the end saved the *tibicines* from trouble two and a
half centuries earlier, by deceiving his stern colleague Appius

---

[22]   tá íd devā́nāṃ sadhamā́da āsann
ṛtā́vānaḥ kaváyaḥ pūrvyāsaḥ.

Claudius. We recall that it is he who had the shamefaced fugitives, just awakened at dawn in their enclosed wagons, put on masks and women's garb.

In 47 B.C., L. Plautius Plancus was a minter and—according to the custom of his times—it is likely, a priori, that he chose to depict, on the obverse or reverse of the coins he struck, figures evoking scenes from the real or legendary life of someone among the elder members of the family. Of his work we know only a set of denarii that contains—once the counterfeit ones are separated out —few specimens.

On the obverse side, above the name L. PLAVTIVS, is a full-face mask, more or less large, with coiled snakes on each side of the face, similar to the heads of Medusa. On the reverse side, above the name PLANCVS, the goddess of dawn is depicted, in Greek style, on foot, draped and winged, holding a palm branch encircled by a wreath in her left hand and running toward the right leading the quadriga of the sun. Here is the commentary on these coins made in his intelligent catalogue of 1910 by H. A. Grueber, then Keeper of the Department of Coins and Medals of the British Muesum:[23]

> Lucius Plautius Plancus was of the Munatia gens and a brother of L. Munatius Plancus, T. Munatius Plancus, and Cn. Munatius Plancus. He was adopted by an L. Plautius, and therefore took his praenomen as well as nomen, but retained his original cognomen. Before his adoption his praenomen was Caius. Nothing appears to be known of him in history beyond that he was included in the proscription of the triumvirs B.C. 43, and having taken refuge in the neighborhood of Salernum, was discovered and put to death. His brother Lucius Munatius, who was a praefectus Urbi in B.C. 45, was a party to his proscription.
>
> The types of the mask of Medusa and of Aurora with the horses of the Sun have been explained by Eckhel (*Doct. num. uet.*, t. V., pp. 276 f.) as referring to an event connected with

---

[23] *Coins of the Roman Republic in the British Museum* (London, 1910), vol. 1, pp. 516–517. E. A. Sydenham, *The Coinage of the Roman Republic* (London, 1952), vol. 2, p. 160 n. 959, indicates the coins without comment.

the moneyer's family, told by Ovid (*Fasti*, vi, 651 f.), who relates that during the censorship of C. Plautius Venox and Ap. Claudius Caecus, B.C. 312, the latter quarrelled with the *tibicines*, who retired to Tibur. As the people resented their loss, the other censor, Plautius, caused them to be placed in waggons at night when they were intoxicated, and conveyed back to Rome, where they arrived early in the morning, and in order that they should not be recognized their faces were covered with scenic masks. The chariot of Aurora is an allusion to the early arrival of the *tibicines*, and the mask to the concealment of their faces. In commemoration of this event the fetes called *Quinquatrus Minusculae* were celebrated yearly at Rome on June 13, at which those who took part in them wore masks.

After this rather free account, Grueber adds:

> Though Eckhel's explanation may appear fantastic, we are unable to accept that of Panofka (*Zur Erklärung des Plinius*, pp. 14 f.), who would see in the reverse type a representation of the picture of Nicomachus, which Pliny (*Hist. Nat.*, XXXV, 10, 36) relates that Plancus placed in the Capitol, showing *uictoria quadrigam in sublime rapiens*; L. Munatius Plancus, the *imperator*, who placed the picture there, did not go to Greece, where probably he obtained it, till some years after the above coins were struck. Also, at this time none of the moneyers record contemporary events connected with their families.

Is Eckhel's explanation really "fantastic"? Grueber's impression was probably based on the fact that the emphasis it puts on Aurora seemed contrived to him. The mentioning of dawn, the time of day and not the goddess, was in his opinion only a minor detail in the account. And yet as early as his era, at the beginning of our century, this skepticism was not justified. The mentioning of dawn, an incidental detail, is not any less essential since the event would not be understood if it did not link the nocturnal ruse and the early-morning surprise. To be sure, the *tibicines* are, on the one hand, certainly wary during the day, but like everyone else can weaken when faced with the temptations of night. On the other hand, if they woke up on the Forum while it was still dark, they would have the time and the means to flee. But most important, we now possess other converging facts, which confirm the idea of the old master: the shattered *ánas* of the Vedic Aurora justifies the *plaustra* abandoned at daybreak. And the masquerade of Quinquatrus Minusculae is inserted into the auroral time of the year, before the solstice and just after the mimicry of the Matralia whose interpretation has recently been confirmed, thanks again to the Vedic Aurora. The fact is, by the time of Caesar the ancient, mythical, naturalistic account that had given rise to the legend of the carts of Tibur was probably no longer known when the minter placed the mask of Medusa and the Greek Aurora on the two sides of his denarius. Thus, he did not depict a *plaustrum*, but at least he realized that the moment of daybreak was as important, as significant in this story as the travesty is in the rites.[24]

FABLIAU

I have said time and again that the Roman tale cannot be superimposed on the Vedic myth in which Indra breaks Aurora's *ánas* into pieces. It uses the striking image of the lazy goddess' heavy cart in another way, in another plot.

We do not know, we will probably never know, where the plot originated—most likely within the very ancient depths of "ingenious folklore." In any case, it is related to another, which thrived in the West to the extent of becoming the theme of numerous anecdotes that highlight the guile of women, of "good" women,

---

[24] Bömer, *Ovidius Naso, Die Fasten*, vol. 2, p. 382 (at 6.685): "Die Geschichte scheint in der Familienüberlieferung fortzuleben: Münzen des L. Plautius Plancus um d. J. 45 zeigen Maskenbilder: Babelon, *Monnaies de la République romaine*, 325 f." (But the old book by Ernest Babelon [Paris, 1886], vol. 2 also mentions, p. 326, copies that have since been judged as apocryphal.)

in their relationship with their husbands. It is the one that Stith Thompson classified under the number J.1545.4 (with bibliography), in his *Motif-Index of Folk-Literature.* Allow me to quote a short variant of it, recently collected among the Ossets of the Caucasus, that I translated on pages 42–43 of my *Livre des Héros* (1965):[25]

> One day a very angry Uryzmaeg said to his wife Satana, "For God's sake, go back to your parents. Take what you want from our home, the treasures you cherish most. But leave me alone; I can't stand you any longer!"
>
> "Very well," Satana answered. "How could I disobey you, dear husband? But allow me to ask you one thing: I shared the Narts' bread and salt; they shared mine. Have a banquet for them so that I can once again offer them a cup."
>
> Uryzmaeg agreed and prepared the banquet. Satana set a magnificent table and, without sparing anything, brought out her best food and drink. After feasting seven days and seven nights, the guests went home. When only the young men who had waited at table remained, Satana said to them, "Be very nice to my husband!"
>
> And the young men, without stopping, gave cup after cup to Uryzmaeg so that he fell into a deep drunken sleep. The young men then left.
>
> Satana yoked well-fed oxen to a cart, filled the bottom with dry grass, spread out a mattress, then a carpet. She stretched out her sleeping husband on this edifice and, without taking anything else, set out for her parents' house.
>
> As they arrived in flat, open country, Uryzmaeg awoke sober. He looks around. Satana is sitting next to him driving the oxen with a birch rod and shooing flies from his face with a burdock twig. . . .
>
> "What's happening?" Uryzmaeg asks himself. "I can't figure it out."
>
> And he asks his wife, "Where are we going?"

[25] On the subject of the Ossets and the Nart epic, see the second part of my *Mythe et épopée I* (Paris, 1968).

"Have you forgotten that you put me out of your house? I'm simply going home to my parents."

"Yes, but me. Tell me where you're taking me."

"As you sent me back to my parents, you told me, 'Take with you whatever you cherish the most. . . .' In my life I have no treasure more precious nor more beloved than you. So, leaving all the rest, I took you."

"Leave it to me to marry the devil in person!" said old Uryzmaeg smiling. He made up with his wife. They went home and lived together in mutual love.

In this story we find again the theme of the man made intoxicated and put into a wagon that takes him—ultimately for a happy reconciliation—where he did not expect to go. But of course dawn, the specified moment of day, which would be of no interest here, is missing.

Conclusion

As we bring this study to a close we will not set our findings and suggestions into rigid propositions. It is better to leave them flexible while waiting for the discovery and analysis of parallel cases. But it will be useful to consider certain orientations.

The groupings of Matralia, the Quinquatrus Minusculae, the Vestalia, and the *dies natalis* of Summanus within a brief annual period of time fixes a "season of dawn" and of what prepares or conditions it. The situating of this "season" in June, just preceding the summer solstice, sheds light on its meaning and purpose.

Above and beyond dawn and its June difficulties, representatives peculiar to the sun have appeared. This resurgence of a naturalistic interpretation is not a regression. Unlike the reverie of one hundred years ago, this takes few liberties. Linked to the calendar, to the feria, to specific religious or juridical rules, its constituent elements, its supporting auroral or solar "facts," are not reconstituted but ascertained, are not poetic but practical. We have involved only the Roman dawn and sun, conceived and adjusted to by the Romans as they themselves have described it to us.

The Roman mythology of dawn, which an early study on Mater Matuta had begun to uncover, took shape, was nuanced, enriched, and at the same time confirmed the close analogy between this mythology and the Indian myth. The linking of Mater Matuta with Fortuna and her interventions in the career of a hero like Camillus show, furthermore, that she is not just a colorless entity, the specialized executrix of a natural phenomenon. She is also a complex divine person, as superior to this phenomenon as is, for example, the solar Apollo or the lunar Artemis in Greece. We can thus better appreciate the high level of thought and imagination of the indigenous Latins before the invasion of the Olympians. We are a long way from the *mana–numen* of the primitivists.

We now also know that this mythology remained living, and was understood for several centuries after the establishment of the feria. Before becoming so many riddles—or rather uninteresting oddities—for the gentleman of classical times, the rituals of the Matralia, the masquerade of the *tibicines*, the special cakes of Matuta and Summanus were still, in the middle of the fourth and at the beginning of the third centuries, perhaps later, clear symbols that made effective action possible.

Several of the facts noted here contribute ultimately to the clarification of links between the myths and the rites in Roman observance. From this point of view, the most useful of our analyses is probably that of the Quinquatrus Minusculae. Here we do not merely have at our disposal, as for the Matralia, some rites on the one hand, and on the other some mythical conceptions that the rites clearly reveal but which must be sorted out from them. For the June 13 festival, we have both the ritual and, directly from it, an anecdote that in historical form is its justificatory myth. Comparing the anecdote with the ritual shows that the parallelism one can expect in such a case is limited. The myth is not the slavish transposition of the ritual. It is richer; and we must not conclude from certain, even important, details of the myth that corresponding behaviors exist in the ritual. It is likely that the *plaustra*—essential to the Tiburtine anecdote and, judging by the cart of the Vedic Aurora, already a part of the myth—play no role in the festival. The jocose inebriation of those in disguise wandering through the city (an inebriation mentioned moreover by Censorinus alone, "temulentis," 12.2, the other texts recording only the disguises), certainly has no common measure with the state of the dead-drunk carousers of the anecdote.

Conclusion

But it is above all the origin of Roman historiography on which the study of Camillus' chronicle will help shed light. It is no longer a question of a circumscribed episode, as was the case of the Alban Lake, of an autonomous whole that criticism easily abstracts from the account of real or imaginary events without upsetting their flow. This time a long, troubled period of Roman history and the main hero of this period come to light. They are either influenced or distorted by mythical methods based on a cohesive group of divine types, rites, controlled usages, and traditional concepts. In order to take stock of, and first of all to sort out, what has just been indicated, meticulous work will be necessary. At what period, by whom, at least in what milieu, were these continuous transpositions made? Again I say that for now I still feel that the essentials of mythology must have been organized in the period during which other reasons seem to indicate that the history of origins also took shape: the second half of the fourth century and the first quarter of the third. This does not, of course, preclude the possibility of subsequent additions or modifications, whether or not inspired by ensuing events, up to the time of the first annalists whose names we know—and later. I have nothing further to proffer. To say that the most ancient "Roman history" took shape among the pontifexes or within important *gentes* is not enough. Indeed, the rise of families like the Marcii is adequate to explain why one of the first four kings was named Ancus Marcius. But it is surely neither through the help of gentilic tradition, nor through the efforts of the Marcii that history was composed, as the very type of this fourth pre-Etruscan reign was ideologically well articulated with the three that precede it. We can naturally assume that, beginning with the fourth century, some Greeks set to work. Yet intelligent, educated Romans, knowledgeable about religion and about what remained of mythology, surely did not remain inactive.

The same admission of helplessness is called for as far as the portion of authentic events contained within this period of Roman history is concerned. Just as the sudden disappearance of Veii proves that it was really conquered by Rome at the approximate date given in the annals, so Rome was undoubtedly destroyed shortly afterwards by a Gallic band. In addition to its national tradition, a short Greek document corroborates this local misfortune that, at the time, probably was not earth-shaking. But aside from these two established points, each of us is free, too free, to give more or less credence, according to his temperament, to what he will call either embellished evidence or historicized fiction. As for me, this credence will be shortlived. In the first chapter, the comparison established between Plutarch's and Livy's accounts of Camillus' "victories at dawn" showed how difficult it is to get one's bearings from the personal equations of annalists. A philosophical repugnance on the part of the Roman to record the supernatural and gaps in general information on the part of the Greek altered in various ways the pictures they painted, and everything does not boil down to a matter of sources. If we had not had at our disposal the small spark of light that the goddess Aurora distributes, the conscientious friction of the variants would have ignited only illusory fires.

How would the doubts that are cast upon these relatively late events not extend to the centuries preceding the siege of Veii? Speaking of France alone, I relish, with an astonishment renewed with each reading, the numerous statements on the royal periods, on the beginnings of the Republic, on the war of Veii voiced by the two most faithful heirs of Jérôme Carcopino and André Piganiol, Jacques Heurgon and Jean Gagé. They are as zealous as their teachers to disentangle "the complex stratifications of Latin chronicles" to which the first accuses me of being indifferent (*Rome et la Méditerranée occidentale jusqu'aux guerres puniques = Nouvelle Clio*, 7 (1969), 230). It is not a question of indifference but of respect. I do not want to force this complexity to secrete literary history at any price, any more than any other kind of history. I refuse to invent missing documents or criteria. I would not dream of saying that "Numa lived for a long time in the memory of the sacerdotal colleges, Vestals and Salii, flamens and pontifexes," and "found fertile ground there for the preserving of his memory and the elaboration of his personality" (page 233), when "some of the features of the legend of Tullus Hostilius" (page 234) are due to *carmina conuiualia*, promoted to chansons de geste just to prove a point. Regarding the battle between the Horatii and the Curiatii and the exploit of Horatius Cocles, I look in vain for the mention of "epic hymns" in Livy, 1.25 and 2.10, where they refer me (page 234). As for the torture of Mettus Fuffetius, I cannot decide if Ennius has or has not recaptured the "barbaric tone of the original *carmen*," for which I am not given the reference (ibid.).

How I would like, too, to be able to assume that "the annalists drew their very full and detailed accounts of the Etruscan phase of the Roman monarchy from Etruscan sources" (page 236). Actually, these Etruscan sources, providentially protected from our inquisitiveness, and which Jean Bayet already used a great deal, are very useful to our contemporaries. Two years ago a historian expressed an apparent consensus when he wrote, "The problem of Livy's sources is of prime importance here, not only for the elaboration of Camillus' character and of his oration, but also for the entire Gallic episode. Above and beyond the Latin sources of the end of the third century or the beginning of the second, Livy brought together numerous echoes of Greek and Etruscan sources, the oldest of which are contemporary, or almost so, with the facts under consideration." This view led him to formulate an opinion that is challenged by the entire present work: "If the hero most probably had a historical existence and role during the fourth century B.C., we must restore them, not in Rome as the savior of the city facing the Gallic period, but in Etruria and in the context of the contentions of Veii and the Etruscan league."

Of course this exhortation to caution, which would be as easy as it is useless to support with dozens upon dozens of examples from the most recent textbooks, contains no condemnation of principle, no irreverence toward sound history. For historians, the very first mission is to establish *facts*, as many facts as possible: may they fulfill that mission. May they continue, in particular, to compare the variants of each account and try to draw up a comparative chronology among them. But so that these results, the basis of all the rest, will not be mirages, one must discard once and for all three types of reasoning which seem to have been singularly productive in the exegesis of Camillus' chronicle as in that of the legends about the first centuries of royal and republican Rome:

First: the oldest remaining source does not contain a certain element found in others? This element was, therefore, added at a later date.

Second: a certain element is attested only beginning with a certain author? Therefore, it is this author who made it up or introduced it.

Third: certain sources do not simultaneously contain elements X, Y, and Z, which form a well-articulated whole? Therefore, despite appearances, bringing them together is secondary and unimportant.

At the risk of harsh reprisals, one might add to these common paralogisms the implicit postulate that has given assurance, for lack of soundness, to so many works of every period: everything written by an established historian partakes in the honors, privileges, and franchises of history.

Appendixes

Appendix 1

Mater Matuta

In memory of Jean Hubaux

The studies on Aurora belong to the second period of the new comparative mythology. Between 1935 and 1948 all comparative studies had been concentrated on the idea of the three functions—acknowledged in 1938—which is basic to Indo-European ideology. The main concern had been to take stock of living or fossilized expressions in the religious, epic, and social life of the different peoples of the language family. Only then could the procedures established for this core material be applied to other kinds of representations: the mythology of origins, of fire, of seasons, eschatology.

In several courses at the Collège de France, as early as 1952, the comparison of the Vedic Uṣas with the Latin Mater Matuta produced results, and in 1955, in an article in the Revue des études latines 33 (1955), 140-151, entitled "Les 'enfants des soeurs' à la fête de Mater Matuta," the second and most mysterious of the two known rites of the Matralia was confirmed. Then in 1956, following a lecture given at the University of Liège, I put forth an overview of the question in my short book Déesses latines et mythes védiques (Collection Latomus 24) (Brussels, 1956), pp. 9-43, together with a supplement on another no less remarkable and in some respects similar goddess, Diva Angerona. This publication gave rise to discussions; and on November 13, 1959, in a course at the Collège de France I, taking into account a critique of John Brough, corrected the interpretation of the first rite of the Matralia and, in so doing, justified the probable sequence of the two rites. Since then the dossier has scarcely been altered. It will probably be necessary to extend the study to include other parts of the Indo-European world. Concerning this I have only to indicate Johann Knobloch's very interesting article, "Der Ursprung von nhd. Ostern, engl. Easter," Die Sprache 5 (1959), 27–45 (the relationship between dawn and springtime, between night—or early morning—and daybreak in the Christian Easter rituals of the East and the West; etymology of the Lithuanian aušrà-, the Lettish àustra "dawn," the Old Church Slavic za ustra "at daybreak").

I thank my friend Marcel Renard for allowing me to insert into this appendix the sections, improved and rearranged, from my 1956 exposé, which seem to me to retain their validity.

THE TWO RITES OF THE MATRALIA: TEXTS

On June 11, during the Matralia, the festival of the goddess Mater Matuta,[1] the Roman women—*bonae matres*[2]—who were in their first marriage—*uniuirae*[3]—performed two notable rites, which from antiquity to our day have not ceased to challenge historians of religion. On two occasions these two acts, apparently characteristic of the cult, are brought together in what has been preserved for us of Plutarch's work. They are assigned an analogy,

---

[1] The goddess was common to the people of central Italy, but we know only of her Roman ritual. The word order is always *Mater Matuta*, except in Livy, 5.23.7, where the dative, *Matutae Matri*, is used.

[2] Ovid, *Fasti*, 6.475: "ite, bonae matres, uestrum Matralia festum . . ."

[3] Tertullian, *On Monogamy*, 17.

an *interpretatio graeca*, common in antiquity, which is of no importance here. In the *Life* of Camillus, 5.2, we read:[4]

> For they [the Roman women] take a servant-maid into the secret part of the temple, and there cuff her, and drive her out again, and they embrace their brothers'[5] children in place of their own.

The sixteenth and seventeenth *Roman Questions* are worded thus:[6]

> 16. Why is the temple of Matuta forbidden to slave-women; and why do the women bring in one slave-girl only whom they slap and strike in the face?
>
> 17. Why do they not pray this deity for blessings on their own children, but only on those of their sisters?

[4] καὶ γὰρ θεράπαιναν εἰς τὸν σηκὸν εἰσάγουσαι ῥαπίζουσιν, εἶτ' ἐξελαύνουσι καὶ τὰ τῶν ἀδελφῶν τέκνα πρὸ τῶν ἰδίων ἐναγκαλίζονται. For the establishment and the meaning of this and the following texts, I refer the reader to the excellent article by Robert Flacelière, "Deux rites du culte de Mater Matuta, Plutarque, *Camille, 5,2*," *Revue des études anciennes* 52 (1950), 18–27. Except for the point indicated in the following note, I follow this translation. [The English translation is taken from the Dryden edition; see "Note on the Translation," above.]

[5] The majority of interpreters—not Flacelière—have interpreted τῶν 'ἀδελφῶν as "sisters," even though the form could also be masculine. I believe they are right. James G. Frazer, *The Fasti of Ovid* (London, 1929), vol. 4, p. 280 n. 2, summarizes the question well: "In both the passages of Plutarch [= *Roman Questions*, 17 and *Camillus*, 5.2] the work translated 'sisters' (τῶν 'ἀδελφῶν) is ambiguous; it might equally mean 'brothers' or 'brothers and sisters'. It is only the analogy of Ino and Semele [in the *interpretatio graeca*] which seems to show that it was for their sisters' children alone that women prayed in the rites of Matuta." Cf. the first explanation of the *Roman Questions*, 17: πότερον ὅτι φιλάδελφος μέν τις ἡ Ἰνὼ καὶ τὸν ἐκ τῆς ἀδελφῆς 'ἐπιθηνήσατο, ἡ δὲ περὶ τοὺς ἑαυτῆς παῖδας ἐδυστύχησεν and the introduction to the last sentence of *De fraterno amore* (cited below at n. 8): ἢ τε Λευκοθέα τῆς 'ἀδελφῆς 'ἀποθανούσης ἔθρεψε τὸ βρέφος καὶ συνεξεθείασεν· ὅθεν αἱ 'Ρωμαίων γυναῖκες. . . . The *alterius* of the *Fasti* (see below, n. 9) elucidated by its context, parallels this. But see below, "The Maternal Aurora," n. 74.

[6] 16: Διὰ τί δούλαις τὸ τῆς Λευκοθέας ἐρὸν ἄβατόν ἐστι, μίαν δὲ μόνην αἱ γυναῖκες εἰσάγουσαι παίουσιν ἐπὶ κόρρης καὶ 'ῥαπίζουσιν; 17: Διὰ τί παρὰ τῇ θεῷ ταύτῃ τοῖς μὲν ἰδίοις τέκνοις οὐκ εὔχονται τἀγαθά, τοῖς δὲ τῶν ἀδελφῶν. This text and those quoted in footnotes 8 and 9 alone prevent translating (Deubner, etc.) πρό τῶν ἰδίων of *Camillus*, 5.2 (see above, n. 4) as "*before* their own." It is, of course, "*instead of* [in place of] their own."

Elsewhere there is no mention of the first rite. In the *Fasti*,[7] Ovid contents himself with pointing out the prohibition made to the slave women without mentioning the exception. The second rite is noted in a third text of Plutarch, in the final lines of the treatise *De fraterno amore* (*Moralia*, 492D):[8]

> Whereupon the Roman dames even at this day, when they celebrate the feast of Leucothea (whom they name Matuta), carry in their arms and cherish tenderly their sisters' children, and not their own.

and in book 6 of the *Fasti*, 559 and 561:[9]

> Nevertheless let not an affectionate mother pray to her on behalf of her own offspring. . . . You will do better to commend to her care the progeny of another.

Everyone seems to agree that Ino–Leucothea[10] should be ruled out of the problem of origin. The moral reason for the second rite put forth in the seventeenth *Roman Question*[11] is no more binding. But the attempts at interpretation are very divergent. They have in common only the fact that they are linked to only one, or possibly two, of the elements of the dossier, as if each one could be inde-

---

[7] *Fasti*, 6.551–558.

[8] 'ὅθεν αἱ 'Ρωμαίων γυναῖκες ἐν ταῖς τῆς Λευκοθέας 'εορταῖς, 'ήν Ματοῦταν ὀνομάζουσιν, οὐ τοὺς 'εαυτῶν παῖδας, ἀλλὰ τοὺς τῶν ἀδελφῶν 'εναγκαλίζονται καὶ τιμῶσιν.

[9] non tamen hanc pro stirpe sua pia mater adoret:
  ipsa [= Leucothea] parum felix uisa fuisse parens.
 alterius prolem melius mandabitis illi:
  utilior Baccho quam fuit illa suis.

[10] Ino–Leucothea and Semele, daughters of Cadmos, were sisters. It is said that after the death of Semele, Ino nursed her son Dionysius. On the contrary, among her own sons one, Learchos, was killed by his father in a fit of madness and the other, Melicertes, escaped from the paternal fury only to fall into the ocean and drown. According to a variant, his mother, who also went mad, plunged him into a cauldron of boiling water, then threw herself with the cadaver into the ocean. The link made between Matuta and Portunus is the result of a no less artificial assimilation between Portunus and Palemon–Melicertes and is not based on a Roman concept (Ovid, *Fasti*, 6.545–574).

[11] ἢ καὶ ἄλλως ἠθικὸν καὶ καλὸν τὸ ἔθος, καὶ πολλὴν παρασκεύαζον εὔνοιαν ταῖς οἰκειότησι;

pendent of the others. There are four elements: the goddess' name, the date of her festival, and the two rites that are mentioned and that probably followed each other in the order in which Plutarch and Ovid describe them.

Actually, commentators have been interested above all in the rites, and in the second one more than the first, the former being indeed more notable in the religions of classical peoples taken as a whole. Let us briefly outline these comments, beginning with the second rite.

THE CHILDREN OF THEIR SISTERS

The exclusive privilege enjoyed by the children of the sisters during this festival has been explained in five ways, three of which do not need much refutation despite the eminence of the scholars who formulated them. The first is a ritualization of the concern, verified in several historical cases, of the Roman aunts for their orphan nephews and nieces (J. A. Hild).[12] The second would be the remains of an archaic "system of kinship" (Georg Wissowa).[13] Finally, the third would be a nurses' rite, comparable to the Laconian Τιθηνίδια (M. Halberstadt).[14] There are solid objections to these attempts at an explanation, for the beneficiaries of the rite are not actually orphans (Halberstadt);[15] no known system of kinship, matrilineal or patrilineal, brings a woman closer to her sisters' children than to her own (H. J. Rose; James G. Frazer),[16] and the

[12] See "Mater Matuta" in Charles Victor Daremberg and Edmond Saglio, *Dictionnaire des antiquités grecques et romaines* (Paris, 1904), vol. 3, col. 1626a n. 7.

[13] *Religion und Kultus der Römer* (Munich, 1902), p. 98 (= 2d ed. [Munich 1912], p. 111).

[14] *Mater Matuta* (= Frankfurter Studien zur Religion und Kultur der Antike 8) (Frankfurt, 1934), pp. 58–59.

[15] Ibid., pp. 60–61.

[16] H. J. Rose, *The Roman Questions of Plutarch* (Oxford, 1924), p. 176; Frazer, *The Fasti of Ovid*, pp. 280–281.

Matralia rite does not involve the relationships between nurses and their nurslings, but between aunts and their nephews.[17] The other two explanations must be discussed more carefully.

Frazer, without shutting his eyes to the dubiousness of the interpretation, assumed[18] that during the Matralia Roman women were scrupulously forbidden to utter the names of their children and that, consequently, they were prevented from recommending them to the goddess. The rite would thus fit into a well-documented category of ethnographic facts. Here are the objections: (1) The ancients knew well what an "onomastic taboo" was and, when necessary, pointed it out in clear language.[19] Plutarch would not, therefore, be mistaken in his seventeenth *Roman Question*. (2) An "onomastic taboo" prevents only the uttering of a name, but in prayer it is easy to indicate the unnameable one with paraphrases. Yet here one's "own children" are excluded from both prayers and embraces. (3) Frazer himself recognized that, in his ethnographic dossiers, onomastic taboos generally apply to relationships by marriage (husband, wife, husband's father, wife's mother), rarely to blood relations (from children to parents, between brothers and sisters), and that they are uncommon from parents to children. In fact, the few examples he gives are all explained by special circumstances which have nothing to do with the Matralia.[20] (4) Frazer

[17] "Les 'enfants des soeurs' à la fête de Mater Matuta," *Revue des études latines* 33 (1955), 142.

[18] Frazer, *The Fasti of Ovid*, pp. 281–283, developing a suggestion by Lewis R. Farnell, "Sociological Hypotheses Concerning the Position of Women in Ancient Religion," *Archiv für Religionswissenschaft* 7 (1904), p. 84.

[19] For example: Servius, *Commentary on the Aeneid*, 4.58: "Romae cum Cereis sacra fiunt, obseruatur ne quis patrem aut filiam nominet," quoted by Frazer himself, *The Fasti of Ovid*, p. 281 n. 1.

[20] Frazer, *The Fasti of Ovid*, pp. 282–283. In certain northern regions of New Guinea, *if a child bears the name of the deceased paternal grandfather*, his mother must call him by another name. But this is only a particular instance of the general rule that forbids any woman from mentioning her in-laws by name. In northern Nigeria and elsewhere, parents avoid pronouncing the name of their *firstborn* child, pretending to despise it and to treat it like a stranger. This is because the firstborn is especially vulnerable to the ventures of evil spirits. Among the Halbas of central India, the child's name must not be pronounced *during the night* because if an owl hears and repeats it, the child is liable to die.

likewise recognized that in any case his proposition would not explain the positive part of the rite, that is, why the Roman women treated with consideration, carried in their arms, and recommended to the goddess their sisters' children.[21]

H. J. Rose proposed a more daring solution, one that aims no less at doing away with the problem, and which has the advantage of revealing it to its fullest.[22]

All that we know of Rome [he wrote in 1934] forbids us to suppose that each woman present at the rite prayed for blessings on the offspring of any sisters she might have in such words as she chose to use. The worship of the goddess is old, belonging to the 'calendar of Numa,' and so not later than the end of the regal period and probably much earlier. In such a rite, old and obsolete Latin words may be confidently assumed, and I believe one of them can be, not indeed certainly restored, but guessed at with a tolerably high degree of probability. I suggest that the goddess was addressed in some such terms as these: *Mater Matuta, te precor quaesoque uti uolens propitia sies pueris sororiis.*

The whole explanation rests on the *pueri sororii.* This expression—which is fictitious—of the archaic prayer did not mean "sisters' children" but "adolescents." In fact Rose, after consulting Joshua Whatmough, distinguishes *sororius* from *soror* and sees in it

---

[21] Ibid., p. 283: "Similarly we may perhaps suppose that for certain reasons now unknown it was deemed unlucky for women to pronounce the names of their own children in the rites of Mother Matuta, and that they were thus precluded from praying for their offspring to the goddess. Still this would not explain why they might pray for their sisters' children instead. No satisfactory solution of this problem has yet been found."

[22] This interpretation is found in three studies by H. J. Rose: "De religionibus antiquis quaestiunculae tres," *Mnemosyne,* n.s. 53 (1925), 407–410 and 413–414 (summary of a personal communication from Joshua Whatmough); "Two Roman Rites," *The Classical Quarterly* 28 (1934), 156–157; *Ancient Roman Religion* (London, 1948) [see my note on this book in *Revue de l'histoire des religions* 139 (1951), 209], pp. 78–79 (see below, n. 77.1). In a prior work, *The Roman Questions of Plutarch,* p. 176, Rose had put forth another explanation (ethnographic facts where the maternal aunts, not the mothers, take care of young girls at the time of puberty), which he later retracted ("Two Roman Rites," 156 n. 5).

the derivative of a *soros* theme—taken from an unconfirmed Indo-European root, *swer-*, doublet of *swel*, "to swell up," which is known with certainty only in the Germanic (Ger., *schwellen*, Eng., *to swell*). Now are not puberty and adolescence, like the ripening of grain, characterized by various "swellings"—and most especially in the case of young girls?[23] We thus arrive at a plausible meaning for this rite which, Rose says, would otherwise be absurd. During the festival of a goddess whose name, furthermore, is related to *maturescere*[24] the *bonae matres* simply asked her to bless the growth of the adolescents. In a word, from Ovid to Halber-

---

[23] "Two Roman Rites," p. 157: "As regards the adjective which I have conjectured was used, I had occasion some years ago [= the article in *Mnemosyne*, 1925] to discuss it in another context, with the aid of Mr., now Professor, J. Whatmough. As a title of Iuno, I believe it to be connected with the verb *sororiare* [see below], not with the noun *soror*; this verb presupposes an adjective *sororius*, corresponding to it as *uarius* to *uariare*, and the adjective again a substantive *soros*, which, following Professor Whatmough, I would derive from a rt. *swer*, identical with that which gives rise to Germ., *schwellen* and Eng. *swell*; hence, applied to Iuno, the adjective means the goddess of swelling, ripening or maturing, in other words of adolescence or puberty, presumably that of girls. That epithets appropriate to worshippers of deities are often applied to the deities themselves is well enough known; for Rome, Fortuna Virgo may serve as an example, or Pudicitia Plebeia. Hence, there is nothing in the least unlikely in the supposition that this rare adjective, which if derived from *soror* makes no reasonable sense, witness the attempts of the Romans themselves to explain it by the aetiological story of Horatius and his sister, was applied, not only to Iuno, but to those for whom her protection, or that of any other goddess of fertility, was especially desirable, the younger generation, and especially the growing girls. However, *puer* being epicene, and Mater Matuta having apparently some connection with boys also, since she was identified with the nurse of Dionysos, and mother of Melikertes–Palaimon, it seems best to suppose that the *pueri sororii* on whose behalf I believe her to have been addressed were the adolescents of both sexes." I do not believe that any likely result can come from as loose a method as this, and as frivolous a reasoning. Rose alludes to an interpretation of the legend of the Horatii and the Curiatii which he also expounded several times, especially in his article "Mana in Greece and Rome," *Harvard Theological Review* 42 (1949), 165–169, with on p. 167 the most detailed presentation of the etymology of *sororius–sororiare* based on the alleged root *swer-* "to swell." The entry for *soror* in Alois Walde, *Lateinisches etymologisches Wörterbuch*, 3rd ed., rev. J. B. Hofmann (Heidelberg, 1954) does not even mention the etymology of *sororius*, *sororiare* put forth by Rose.

[24] See below, n. 45.

stadt, Romans and Latinists have based their speculations and labor on a misconception.

Rose has put forth this explanation no less than three times and rightly so. It provides a good example of the calm daring of the school of which he is the most articulate representative. But what a lot of unfounded claims! (1) The basic assumption is that the Roman women no longer understood at all the meaning and the purpose of what they did or said and that, thanks to the *Wald- und Feldkulte* and the *Golden Bough*, and especially to the Melanesian *mana*, modern scholars are able, in retrospect, to enlighten them. Nothing is more dangerous than taking such liberty. The primitivists compete in being arbitrary with the works of epigones who, three quarters of a century ago, discredited naturalistic mythology. (2) The expression *pueri sororii*, like the whole formula of this prayer, is no more than a fabrication of the English philologist who neglected to provide the reasons which confer on him "a tolerably high degree of probability." (3) Despite what Whatmough says, a Roman doublet *$suer$- of *$suel$-, is difficult to accept. The adjective *sororius*,[25] where it is authenticated, like the slang verb *sororiare*,[26] can be well enough explained by "the sister" so we need not have recourse to the monster *$soros$, "swelling" (which for inanimate things, furthermore, would be rather *$sorus$, *$soreris$). (4) In the ritual formula, what reason is there to devise the substitution of Rose's *$sororii$ for the ordinary and ancient expression *adolescen-*

---

[25] In the name of *Juno Sororia*, linked to the legend of Horace killing his sister.

[26] Festus, p. 381L¹ = p. 396L²: "sororiare mammae dicuntur puellarum, cum primum tumescunt, ut fraterculare puerorum." Slang willingly enlivens the parts of the body where the energy or the appeal of the sex organs is evident (cf. the refrain of a song sung at the front in 1918: "Oh, how much pleasure he gives me / Fernand's little brother!"). In an incomplete fragment of *Frivolaria* preserved by Festus, Plautus must have played with these expressions in speaking of a young girl barely in her puberty: "[tunc] papillae pri[mulum] fraterculabant, ——[illud] uolui dicere, so[roriabant]," "It was precisely at the moment when her points began to 'become brothers'—excuse me, that is not what I meant to say: 'become sisters.' " The other gloss on *fratrare* (p. 80L¹ = p. 209L², with Lindsay's note; cf. *fratrescunt* in another glossary) does seem to prove that *sororiare* was created from verbs derived from "brother."

tes, together with the highlighting of the glandular "swelling" of puberty? (5) Two of Plutarch's three texts specify that the Roman women "take" the children for whom they pray "in their arms," ἐναγκαλίζονται. That is fine for babies, much less so for grown boys and girls.[27] It is true that the apt philologist has no trouble doing away with so imprudent a statement: "I suggest that Plutarch got his information in the *Q.R.* [in which there is no troublesome verb] from Verrius, that in the *de frat. amor.* [where the said verb is found] from hearsay, inaccurate memory, or some other inferior source, unless indeed ἐναγκαλίζονται is corrupt."[28] This liberty is enviable.

THE EXPULSION OF THE INTRUDING SLAVE WOMAN

The other rite of the Matralia—probably the first chronologically—has raised controversies.

Plutarch suggests that the poor treatment inflicted on a woman slave is no more than the illustration of the prohibition made against all of them, σύμβολόν ἐστι ποῦ μὴ ἐξεῖναι,[29] the only ban

[27] Rose's hypothesis is furthermore discredited by the large number of ex-voto having the form of a diapered baby which were found in the non-Roman sanctuaries of Mater Matuta and which are sufficiently and naturally explained by the Matralia rite. Regarding the relationship between Mater Matuta and Ilithyia at Caere, see above, chapter 4: "Juno and Mater Matuta."

[28] Cf. Flacelière, "Deux rites": "Concerning the text of *De fraterno amore*, *Moralia* 492 D, H. J. Rose, *Classical Quarterly* 28 (1934), 156 n. 1, notes that Plutarch is the sole author who says that, during the Matralia, children were carried in the arms of the matrons, and he wonders if ἐναγκαλίζονται is not corrupted. He forgets, though, that this word is verified by the parallel passage in the *Life* of Camillus where it is also found. Indeed, it is very likely that Plutarch made mistakes when speaking of institutions or rites that he learned of through Latin writers whose language he didn't know well. I think that is what happened, for example, regarding the statue of Juno Quiritus, *Romulus*, 29. But it is important, first of all, here as well as there, to determine exactly what he meant and to be careful not to correct or interpret his text in a way which would arbitrarily bring it into line with the other statements." See in Halberstadt, *Mater Matuta*, p. 56, the references establishing that ἐναγκαλίζεσθαι is used especially with regard to love and maternal care.

[29] *Roman Questions*, 16: ἢ τὸ μὲν ταύτῃ ῥαπίζεσθαι σύμβολόν ἐστι τοῦ μὴ ἐξεῖναι, κωλύουσι δὲ τὰς ἄλλας διὰ τὸν μῦθον.

from then on that there is reason to justify. He justifies it by the *interpretatio graeca* of Matuta as Ino and by the legitimate complaint that this latter had against a slave woman. Until recent times, ancients and moderns were happy with this explanation by way of "symbol." In the *Fasti*[30] Ovid, already pointing out the prohibition that excludes women slaves, does not even mention the scenario of the expulsion, obviously because he, too, sees in it only a tangible expression, a dramatization, which adds nothing either essential or different to the prohibition. Frazer, his most recent annotator (1929), does not seem to hold a different opinion. What is important in his eyes is the general prohibition. As for the sole slave, admitted in, struck, and driven out, he simply notes that she is "a curious exception to the rule"[31]—an exception that dramatically reinforces the rule.

The general prohibition itself poses no difficulty. Greek and Roman antiquity, and on the whole civilizations based on slavery, offer analogous cases. It simply proves that Matuta's cult was a noble cult and that Roman society, in the strict sense, alone benefited from it.[32] But it is not so obvious that the expulsion scenario is tied to this prohibition. Rose (1924) and Halberstadt (1934) are the first to have expressed doubts, for which the latter gave strong grounds.[33] Among the well-documented records of cases where access to a sacred place is forbidden to beings considered impure or unworthy, Halberstadt notes that one would be at a loss to find such a staging having illustrative and pedagogic value. He thus formulates two objections. First, for this type of prohibition to be clear and effective there is no need of expression, of a symbolic ritual incorporated into the cult. It is enough to notify those concerned by word or in writing. Second, the symbolic ritual would result in the defilement that the prohibition is precisely designed to avoid. If indeed it is only a matter of a stronger warning to the

---

[30] *Fasti*, 6.481–482.

[31] *The Fasti of Ovid*, vol. 4, p. 279.

[32] "Les 'enfants des soeurs,' " 150.

[33] *Mater Matuta*, p. 15.

servant class, the introduction of one of its representatives into the temple is jumping out of the frying pan into the fire. The two philologists thus looked for other interpretations.

The first[34] proposed that the thrashing of the slave resembles a fertility ritual more than a warning. Let us consider the well-known collection of facts—"das Schlagen mit der Lebensrute," as has been said since the *Wald- und Feldkulte*—where women are in fact struck, thrashed, and whipped with the purpose of encouraging the mysterious processes of maternity within them. Ten years later, Halberstadt proved that the Mannhardtian exegesis was not satisfactory.[35] In such scenarios it is the persons struck, not the floggers, whose flesh benefits from the violence done to them. Therefore, during the festival of Matuta, the matrons would have wanted, at best, to promote the fecundity of their slaves, which is improbable. Are we to surmise that the woman slave was there only as a substitute for the matrons, the latter feeling it inappropriate to allow themselves to be whipped, but reserving the benefit of the rite for themselves through a mystical transference? The example of the Lupercalia, when Roman women willingly gave themselves over to goat-whips,[36] is enough to prove that the supposed impropriety was not felt. We could add that the Romans, if through no more than the Lupercalia, were very familiar with these fertility rituals. Further: if, during the Matralia, it had been a question of such a ritual, they would not have made a mistake and would not have looked for another justification.

Halberstadt was less fortunate in developing his own theories than he was in critiquing those of others. Pushing aside the temptation of another analogy—the rituals of the Scapegoat, such as "the expulsion of Hunger," βουλίμου ἐξέλασις, described succinctly but clearly for Chaeronea[37] by Plutarch—he interpreted, explained the

---

[34] *The Roman Questions of Plutarch*, p. 175.

[35] *Mater Matuta*, p. 16.

[36] Plutarch, *Romulus*, 21.12: αἱ δ' ἐν ἡλικίᾳ γυναῖκες οὐ φεύγουσι τὸ παίεσθαι, νομίζουσαι πρὸς εὐτοκίαν καὶ κύησιν συνεργεῖν.

[37] Plutarch, *Convivial Questions*, 6.8.1.

first rite of the Matralia in the same way as the second, looking for a link between it and the nurses. He thus compared Greek rituals— the Charila of Delphi[38] and the festival of Dionysus at Alea in Arcadia[39]—in which the nurses of Dionysus intervene, though indirectly and only occasionally. We need only to read with an open mind the descriptions of the two rituals to see all that separates them from the Roman facts. At Alea women are whipped, as are the Spartan ephebi during the festival of Artemis Orthia, but there is no expulsion rite.[40] At Chaeronea the ruling king presides over a novenial atonement ceremony in expiation for a sin committed in the past, during a great famine, by the king of the country, against a little girl named Charila. He distributes flour and vegetables to all those who present themselves. When the distribution is finished, he throws his shoe on a statuette representing Charila. Then the leader of the Thyiades—the sole link in all this with Dionysus—takes the statuette to the ravine where the little girl was buried after having choked to death, puts a rope around its neck, and buries it.

For the first as well as for the second rite, each of the proposals we have looked at contains at least one artifice that makes it lack credibility. Moreover, although many try hard to reconcile the interpretations of the two rites—Rose through life-producing whippings, Halberstadt through the nurses of Dionysus—the unity that they offer is no less obviously artificial. Finally, none of the proposals takes into account the significance of the other two facts: Mater Matuta's name and the date of the Matralia. When Halberstadt says that Mater Matuta is the goddess of nurses, he is forcing a role on her designed to fit his explanation of the second rite. He does not even try to match this function with the name. When Rose makes Matuta a goddess of fertility, this, too, is a result of his astonishing translation of the expression *pueri sororii*, that he

---

[38] Plutarch, *Greek Questions*, 12.

[39] Pausanias, 8.23.1.

[40] καὶ ἐν Διονύσου τῇ ἑορτῇ κατὰ μάντευμα ἐκ Δελφῶν μαστιγοῦνται γυναῖκες, καθὰ καὶ οἱ Σπαρτιατῶν ἔφηβοι παρὰ τῇ Ὀρθίᾳ.

began by inventing. From Hild to Rose everything takes place as if
the exegetes had implicitly acknowledged that the gesture of the
bonae matres in the second rite was self-sufficient, Mater Matuta
being there only to preside over it without guiding it, without con-
tributing a special meaning to the marks of affectionate attention
showered on the children or to the specification of these children as
"nephews."

As always we must work backwards and obtain an overall
view that, bringing together all the facts, reveals what makes them
equally useful or necessary, with each one having a different
purpose. Let us look at what has been most misused or neglected in
the dossier: the name and the date. First the name: what does *Mater
Matuta* signify?

MATER MATUTA, GODDESS OF DAWN

In Roman observance, for the "ordinary Roman" of the period
with which we are familiar, Mater Matuta is the goddess of dawn
or Dawn personified. The very classical derivative, *mātūtīnus*,
means absolutely nothing other than "pertaining to early morning," just as *uespertīnus* refers only to the evening. Now none of the
numerous Latin adjectives ending in *-īnus* (*diuinus*, *libertinus*,
equinus, *Latinus*, and so on) changes anything in the concept to
which it simply makes reference.[41] Were not *matutinus* and *uesper-
tinus* accepted prior to Cicero? It was certainly not he who invented
them. He used them with an ease that presupposes an accepted
usage. The construction of the second term, analogical to that of
the first, must on the whole have originated with the people. The
first mention in literature of the goddess Matuta herself comes in
the fifth book of Lucretius (650).[42] Here she is no more than a poetic

---

[41] *Mythe et épopée III* (Paris, 1973), p. 42 n. 1.
[42] Tempore item certo roseam Matuta per oras
aetheris aurora refert et lumina pandit
aut quia . . .
aut quia . . .

designation of early morning, which seems "old hat," as much as a cliché in this passage as does "Aurora's chariot" in French writers of the age of Louis XIV. The atheistic poet Lucretius probably used her name only in conformity with the accepted meaning.

Why and how has this unquestionable meaning been contested for three quarters of a century by a certain number of authors? The reason appears to be simple. Matuta–Aurora has suffered from the general disrepute of naturalistic mythology. She had to be something else, something more acceptable to the new directions of the science of religions. An intemperate use of linguistics has provided not one, but at least two means of effecting this distortion.

The family of words to which *Mātūta* and *mātūtīnus* belong is vast. In addition to the archaic adjective *mānus*, "good," with its opposite *immānis* and the name of the *Mānes*, the ancient neuter form turned adverb *māne* "early," it includes the adjective *mātūrus* "ripe" and its derivatives. At the end of the last century, the linguist M. Pokrovskij studied it thoroughly[43] and showed that the meaning one must give to the root *mā*—which has given rise to these various concepts—is that of "passen, angemessen sein," to be ready: a "ready" plant or organism, a favorable season, and so on, are *maturus, -a, -um*. Something that happens "in the nick of time," a being adapted to its intended purpose, and so on, is *manus, -a, -um* (the general meaning of "good" has come from that). The awaited time in which one can again take up activities suspended during the night, "daybreak," is *mane*, presided over by *Matuta*.

But once we have acknowledged these relationships radiating out from a common central point, we do not have the right to establish arbitrarily other cross-filiations, and still less exchanges between the meanings of one and another of the terms in the family. Each one of these terms has taken on a precise and fixed meaning and cannot, on the pretext of an etymological relationship, be given the meaning of any of the others. In French *pommade*

---

[43] "Beiträge zur lateinischen Etymologie," *Zeitschrift für vergleichende Sprachforschung* 35 (1897), 233–237: "8. Maturus, Matuta, matutinus, manus (manis), manes, mane" quoting, other than ὡραῖος, ἀκμαῖος, semantic families of the same type, in particular in the Slavic languages (roots *dob-*, *god-*).

[pomade], *pommeau* [pommel], and *pommette* [cheekbone] are all derivatives of *pomme* [apple]. The cosmetic called "pomade" was originally prepared from the pulp of the apple. The pommel of a saddle and the cheekbones of the face call to mind in two different ways the shape of the apple. But who would dream of making a direct progression from *pommeau* to *pommade* or from *pommade* to *pommette*? However, the etymologists of antiquity sometimes did make just this kind of mistake, which the moderns have repeated. The former can be pardoned; the latter less. In the family of the *mā-* derivatives, *maturus* is "ripe,"[44] and not "good," in spite of the term *mānus*. Despite Saint Augustine[45] or his sources, and despite Rose,[46] *Matuta* has no need to take its meaning from *maturescere*, a secondary derivative of the primary one **matu-*. There are three ambiguous accounts found in Paulus Diaconus under *"Matrem Matutam," "mane,"* and *"Mater Matuta,"* which go back to Verrius Flaccus.[47] Furthermore, in spite of these, *Matuta* does

[44] With numerous derived nuances: see for example Gellius, 10.11.1.

[45] *City of God,* 4.8: "florentibus frumentis deam Floram, maturescentibus Matutam, cum runcantur, id est e terra auferunter, deam Runcinam. . . ." The text is ambiguous; certain manuscripts have *Maturam.* Perhaps, therefore, it is not even a matter of an approximation of *Matuta.* In the glosses of Pseudo-Placidus (Georg Goetz, *Corpus glossariorum latinorum* [Leipzig and Berlin, 1894], vol. 5, p. 221) this Matura reappears, but it carries, because of an inverted confusion, the personality of *Matuta*: "Matura dea paganorum quam Greci Leucotea[m] dixerunt." See below, n. 47.

[46] See above, "The Children of Their Sisters."

[47] Pp. 109, 112, 154L¹ = pp. 248–249, 253, 278L²; (1) Matrem Matutam "antiqui ob bonitatem appellabant, et *maturum* idoneum usuri, et *mane* principium diei, et inferi dii *manes,* ut suppliciter appellati bono essent et in carmine Saliari Cerus *manus* intelligitur creator bonus; (2) *mane* a diis *manibus* dixerunt, nam *mana* bona dicitur, unde et *Mater Matuta* et poma *matura*"; (3) Mater Matuta, manes, mane, matrimonium, materfamiliae, matertera, matrices, materiae "dictae, uidentur, ut ait Verrius, quia sint bona, qualia scilicet sint quae sunt *matura,* uel potius a *matre,* quae est orginis graecae." We see that Paulus (Festus, Verrius), having put together the accurate dossier of related words, goes too far and tries artificially to set up relationships (2: *mane* does not come from *di manes*). The first gloss (M. M. "ob bonitatem") is obviously only the same kind of hypothesis, having no more importance than many others of the *De significatione uerborum* (*genus* from γῆν, *gloria* from κλέος, *obliteratum* from *obliuio* or from *litus,* etc.). Priscian,

not, because of the adjective *manus* and still less because of the related Celtic adjectives with the same meaning,[48] have to exchange its own meaning for that of "Good Goddess, Good Mother."

On the other hand, it seems to me that scholars allow a little too much leeway to religious facts and cults when they coldly write that Mater Matuta was first the equivalent of "Bona Dea" and that once her name was no longer understood, she was "transformed" into a goddess of Dawn. A goddess of Dawn is not so easily invented by using as a model another divine type. Stylus or pencil in hand, Verrius Flaccus and his modern emulators can very well establish evolutionary diagrams—which, incidentally, they refrain from sharing with us. The concrete realities of religion—the traditional devotion of the faithful, the routine of the festival, the religious conservatism of these Romans who let so many cults and priesthoods weaken and die—would not have facilitated such a metamorphosis. From the beginnings to the principate, apart from the likenesses with the Greeks, the true Roman pantheon offers less evidence of change than impatient philologists would like to see or are willing to admit.

Strictly speaking, relatively few authors have pursued this path to the end. W. Warde Fowler, whose mind was strongly marked by Mannhardtism, in 1899 contented himself with voicing a doubt about the traditional, auroral meaning of Matuta.[49] In his

---

Institutiones grammaticae, 2.53 (= vol. 2, p. 76, of Henrich Keil, *Grammatici Latini* [Leipzig, 1855–1870]): matutinus "a *Matuta*, quae significat Auroram uel, ut quidam," Λευκοθέαν; but later (4.34) he gets caught in an incorrect derivation. He says that we should have **manumine*, from *mane*, and we have *matutine*! At the beginning of an account by Nonius Marcellus (see *manum*, pp. 66–67 of Quicherat), which is little less ambiguous than those of Paulus Diaconus, the adjective *manus* is incorrectly translated as "clarus" and thus made to explain *mane* and *Matuta*. We sense everywhere that this well-known family of words caused problems for the "prelinguists" of antiquity which were beyond their means: cf. above, n. 45. The definition of *Matuta* in the etymological dictionary of [Walde-] Hoffman, vol. 2, p. 53) strangely continues this confusion.

[48] Gaulish *Mati-*, *Mato-* (*-matos*) in proper names, Irish *maith*, Gallic *mad* "good."

[49] *The Roman Festivals of the Period of the Republic* (London, 1899), p. 156, after quoting Lucretius, 5.654: "We should, however, be glad to be more certain that

commentary on the *Fasti* (1929), Frazer did not even go that far[50] and, with noticeable reluctance, followed the "good modern authorities," K. O. Müller, Theodor Mommsen, Ludwig Preller, Georg Wissowa, and even Alfred von Domaszewski, who agree that our goddess is Aurora. J. A. Hild, in Daremberg and Saglio, *Dictionnaire des Antiquités*,[51] Link in Pauly–Wissowa, *Real-Encyklopädie der classischen Altertumswissenschaft* (Stuttgart, 1928),[52] Carl Koch in his *Gestirnverehrung*,[53] Halberstadt in his monograph (1934),[54] did not think differently. But the French textbooks published recently (Albert Grenier, 1948; Paul Fabre, 1955) are less careful and even altogether careless.[55] In addition, Matuta has found a particularly determined restorer in the person of Rose. "That Mater Matuta was a dawn-goddess, as has been often enough asserted,[56] I may believe when I see some reason to suppose

---

Matuta was originally a substantive meaning dawn or morning. Verrius Flaccus [= Paulus, p. 109] seems to have believed that the words *mane, maturus, matuta, manes,* and *manus,* all had the meaning of 'good' contained in them; so that Mater Matuta might after all be only another form of the Bona Dea, who is also specially a woman's deity. But this cult was not preserved, like that of Vesta, by being taken up into the essential life of the State, and we are no longer able to discern its meaning with any approach to certainty." Strange logic. Having confidence in the etymological games of Verrius Flaccus, the philologist gratuitously bestows a prehistoric meaning on the cult, anterior and foreign to the known and clear historical meaning. He then states that no document informs us of this prehistoric meaning and concludes that we can never be certain of its "true meaning." One has only to eliminate these artificial detours to avoid difficulty. The "true meaning" of the cult is its historical meaning. There is no objective reason for finding its prehistoric meaning. Warde Fowler (with a bad translation of Plutarch's πρό, *Camillus*, 5.2: see Halberstadt, *Mater Matuta*, p. 56) writes wisely about the "sisters' children" rites (p. 155 n. 2): "I cannot explain the rule that a woman prayed for nephews and nieces before her own children, which is peculiar to this cult."

[50] *The Fasti of Ovid*, p. 273.

[51] Vol. 3, col. 1625a: see *Mater Matuta, Matralia.*

[52] See *Matuta*, 14, col. 2326, refusing to follow Walter Otto, who had suggested the meaning "gute Göttin" in "Iuno," *Philologus*, n.s. 18 (1905), 212.

[53] *Gestirnverehrung im alten Italien* (= Frankfurter Studien zur Religion und Kultur der Antike 3) (Frankfurt, 1933), p. 99.

[54] *Mater Matuta*, p. 63.

[55] See below, n. 77 (2) and (3).

[56] "Two Roman Rites," 157. "Often enough" is tendentious: it is by far the most widely held opinion.

a cult of a dawn-goddess, not a mere appearance of an Eos or Aurora in mythology, in either Italy or Greece."

Here we are again in the midst of a philology of convenience. The adjective *matutinus*, the *Matuta* of Lucretius do not have any bearing, are no longer facts, but "suppositions" that should be supported by "reasons." We find ourselves above all at the very root of the fundamental illusion that harsh truth must confront: in its social structure and its religion ancient Rome did not have the affinity and special solidarity with neighboring Greece that Rose and many other experts of Greek and Latin imagine. Humanistic tradition and our academic formation, which closely link—and rightly so regarding the Golden Age—the two civilizations we call "classical," are poor teachers for the understanding of origins. Great progress was definitely made during the past century when the translations of Homer or of Euripedes no longer contained "Jupiter," "Minerva," and "Diana." Still today we must not think "Eos" when we study Matuta. In compensation young generations of Latinists must strive to place the ideas and things of most ancient Rome into the comparative structure indicated by linguists as early as 1918[57] and outlined by a half century of study. In religious matters especially, Vedic India, through striking, numerous, and well-structured analogies, provides the key to many of the most important Roman facts. Thus one of the most notable feminine figures of the *Rig Veda*, if not of the *Atharva Veda*,[58] is precisely the goddess

[57] Joseph Vendryes, "Les correspondances de vocabulaire entre l'indo-iranien et l'italo-celtique," *Mémoires de la société de linguistique* 20 (1918), 265–285, specifying the meaning of a summary of the *Einleitung in die Geschichte der griechischen Sprache* of Paul Kretschmer (Göttingen, 1896).

[58] N. J. Shende, "The foundations of the Atharvanic Religion," *Bulletin of the Deccan College Research Institute* 9 (1949), 235: "On the whole, the Atharvanic poets do not attach much importance to this deity. She has been neglected. There is not that charm and beauty of Uṣas as they are found in the *Rig Veda*. She is also not employed for magical purpose by the poet. It thus seems that in the Atharvanic mythology Uṣas is totally neglected." Is this loss of importance explained in part by the increasing importance of the god Savitar, "the Energizer" who, among other things, presides at sunrise? Cf. Giancarlo Montesi, "Il valore cosmico dell' Aurora nel pensiero mitologico del Rig-Veda," *Studi e materiali per la storia delle religioni* 24–25 (1953–1954), 111–132; and F. B. J. Kuiper, "The Ancient Aryan Verbal

Aurora, Uṣas. Likened to a mother for us mortals (7.81.4), compared also to the mother of the gods *mātá devánām* (1.119.19), she is very often invoked or celebrated. We must not, therefore, take the inconsistency of Eos as a pretext for rejecting a priori the authenticity of a goddess Aurora in Latium.

SIGNIFICANCE OF THE MATRALIA

If Matuta is the goddess responsible for opening the "matutinal" hours, her festival date takes on great importance. June 11 falls a few days before the summer solstice, the day on which the balance between daytime and nighttime—in what is for us a "twenty-four hour day"—will shift. Ever since the winter solstice, through the spring equinox, diurnal time has unceasingly taken the advantage; dawn has continued to nibble away at the darkness, to come earlier. But then in June this daily gain dwindles, becomes unnoticeable, until the summer solstice. It then becomes a daily loss, a withdrawing of dawn, also unnoticeable at first, then more and more marked, through the autumn equinox, until the winter solstice.

Of course the summer solstice, which for us falls on June 21, does not have a fixed day in the poorly regulated luniscolar calendars of the days prior to Julius Caesar. The summation of months merely tallied was far from producing a total of "twenty-four hour days" coinciding with the exact, astronomical duration of one revolution of the sun. In order to reestablish a parallel or at least to prevent the scandal, for example, of a calendar summer encroaching on a natural winter, it was necessary to make adjustments from time to time—that is, to insert periods of time of varying length depending on the number of years that had passed since the prior adjustment. Have these intercalations always been periodic? Have

Contest," *Indo-Iranian Journal* 4 (1960), 217–281 at 217–242 (in particular, 223–242, "Uṣas and the New Year").

they taken the form of supplementary days or months? Surely not, but they must have tended to become so in order to delimit accurately the section of the calendar within which the highlights of the sun's annual career—equinoxes and solstices—could reasonably vary. Finally, they did become cyclic while waiting for the Julian reform to reduce to its extreme limit the zone of mobility.[59]

In historical reality how did this system function? A reference by Livy to an eclipse in 191 B.C. bears witness to a discrepancy, readily cited, of nearly four months. He places it on July 11, while calculations show that it should have been recorded on March 14.[60] But this is probably a grossly extreme case caused by an extended malfunction of a generally better controlled mechanism. Obviously, it would be unwarranted to conclude that the Republican calendar did not relate to the seasons when many facts testify to the contrary. The war season framed by the war rituals of March and October could not have fallen normally in another season even if, through negligence or superstition, the pontifexes by way of exception had let the calendar drift for too many consecutive years. Festivals like the Consualia and the Opiconsivia which concern the gathering in of the harvest, the Volcanalia which turns aside the fires caused by the hot season, and many others that have fixed dates, *statae, statiuae*, in the calendar, are of necessity linked to the actual course of the seasons. Janus, who gave his name to January, is the god of beginnings, of transitions. Only exceptionally could his month, therefore, stray far from the "transition," from the beginning—the winter solstice. We must thus assume that during the first centuries of the Republic, when religious observance was certainly more demanding than it was during the last, competent

[59] The few known facts are analyzed and discussed, moving back from the first to the fifth century, in the second part of Agnes Kirsopp Michels' book, *The Calendar of the Roman Republic* (Princeton, 1967). See in particular the discussion of the supposed change of the beginning of the year (from March 1 to January 1) in 153 B.C., pp. 97–101; p. 99: "It seems to me more probable that the republican calendar had always begun its year on the Kalends of January. The calendar which it supplanted must, however, have begun on the Kalends of March."

[60] Ibid., p. 102.

authority was watchful. By the rather frequent insertion of cush-
ions of time, it sought to keep within reasonable, thus conservative, limits the discrepancy between the unfolding of the calendar
and the course of the sun, between the dates of seasonal festivals
and seasonal realities.

That is particularly true of the solstices, which are, moreover,
easy to situate through observation.[61] That the shortest days of the
year, *angusti dies*, fall right at the time of the actual winter solstice,
breuissima dies, *bruma*, does not depend on calendars. The goddess who steps in on this occasion, Diva Angerona, and who gives
her name to these days has her festival, the Divalia, during the
period in which, as a matter of fact, we await December 21. In
ancient times, when theological definitions were still obvious to
everyone, how could the Romans with their common sense have
accepted for long the drifting of this festival with its goddess
toward the springtime?

Let us thus be careful not to exaggerate the freedom of movement of the Republican calendar just because of the peculiarity of
191 B.C. From the beginning, the calendar by its very purpose was
filled with festivals that were essentially seasonal, linked to the
beginnings, heights, limitations, and characteristics of the real
seasons. We can trust the Latin peasants; corrections perhaps by
trial and error, perhaps more or less periodic, kept enough order to
it all. Therefore, modern scholars should not be shocked when, to
make a long story short, it is said that Angerona was "the goddess
of the winter solstice," or that the festival of Aurora preceded the
summer solstice only by a few days. In thus verbally assigning the
ancient solstices to their proper place within the structure of
Republican time, the inaccuracy is certainly less serious than in
attributing to them mad deviations from their mark. Rome had
common sense.[62]

[61] Ibid., p. 100.

[62] See the discussion of the texts on the intercalation in ibid., pp. 160–172; in
particular p. 169 (with n. 18): "It seems to me more probable that the pontifices followed the much simpler course of omitting an intercalation or two when they
observed that the calendar was inconveniently behind the seasons. This would have
kept the calendar in an approximately correct relation to the solar year, and it is

It is certainly no accident that Aurora's festival is thus fixed—
no more than that a festival consecrated to the Sun[63] precedes, in
the same way, the winter solstice on December 11—that is, six
months later to the day. We know beforehand how to interpret this
fixing of the festival. In Rome more than elsewhere, a festival,
feriae, festus dies, cannot be without purpose. Through it, through
what takes place, the celebrants try to obtain a result, to influence
the course of the hoped for or dreaded events that either depend on
the current dispositions of a divinity or obey gestures or words formerly taught or exercised by a divinity or an august ancestor. On
the occasion of the Matralia, during the slowing down and on the
eve of Aurora's lengthy withdrawal, what can society hope for if
not to help the goddess with a task that is becoming increasingly
difficult for her? The scenes reenacted by the celebrants should tend
toward this end. They accomplish in the temple what the goddess
does in the sky. Just as each morning the duty of the goddess
breaks down into two actions, so the celebrants "act out" two
scenes. The first action, a negative one, consists of banishing the
darkness that at one and the same time unduly and of necessity has
invaded the sky; the other consists of receiving and revealing the
young sun who has matured below the horizon. In the two corresponding scenes, the celebrants violently drive from the temple a
slave woman whom they first unduly ushered in, and they show
affection, concern, and respect for children. The symbolism is
immediately clear and easily extends to two characteristic details of
the festival. If the celebrants in the two rites are multiple, probably
numerous, it is most likely because they represent not "Aurora per
se," but the throng of individual dawns that begin in succession the
days of the year or the days of an indefinite period of time. If in the
second rite the celebrants dote on and recommend to the goddess
not their own children but "those of another," precisely those of

---

clear that, until Caesar spoiled them, the Romans were quite satisfied with an
approximate relation."

[63] To "Forefather Sun": Ἀγωνάλια δαφνηφόρῳ γενάρχῃ Ἡλίῳ, Lydus, *Months,
fragm. Caseol.,* p. 118 Beck. This correlation was emphasized by Koch, *Gestirnverehrung,* p. 99.

their sisters (or brothers?), it is probably in order to signify on the one hand that Aurora, having only a brief moment at her disposal, cannot herself produce the Sun. She can only receive it after another entity, having the same nature as she, has prepared him. The action probably signifies, on the other hand, that Aurora and the Sun's real mother, whoever she be, work in harmonious collaboration.

This is and can only be a hypothesis since the mythology of Matuta as such has disappeared with the whole of Roman mythology. But it is a reasonable hypothesis, since it limits itself to deciphering the imprint that mythology has left on the rites, and to throwing light on this imprint both by the definition, in fact, by the very name of the goddess, and by the precise necessity that the date of her annual festival reveals.

THE VEDIC AURORA

This reconstitution is completely and coherently supported if, beyond the Greek Eos, we consider the Vedic Aurora. This is the Uṣas whom we called to mind earlier and of whom much is said in the hymns[64]—more in the hymns than in the rituals because Uṣas has no cult of her own. She does receive invocations or offerings under various circumstances, in morning liturgies or in marriage rituals, but always along with other divinities. The twenty hymns that are addressed to her, without mention of the numerous references to her in the rest of the collection, give reason, nevertheless, to think that this was not always the case.

In the hymns themselves, contrary to custom, no "myth of Aurora" as such is recounted. The daily service that she ensures gives rise to numerous vivid expressions, most of which do not seem to allude to connected narratives or even to consistent repre-

[64] See the personal ideas of Kuiper about Uṣas in "Aryan Verbal Contest."

sentations. They are simply rhetorical "games" among which the authors, even within a poem, do not worry, have no need to worry about maintaining coherence. For example, in regard to her appearance, if she is generally a woman, and a young woman, she is at times represented by a mare and more often by a cow. Still, a few representations statistically command attention.

First, we are struck by the frequency of the plural. Auroras are spoken of as well as Aurora, Daughters of heaven (4.51.1 and 10) as well as Daughter of heaven—and sometimes in consecutive stanzas of the same hymn. Louis Renou writes:[65]

> She is invoked at times in the singular—it is either a question of the present Uṣas, the last born, or of Uṣas generally conceived—at times in the plural. These are the "continually successive" Uṣas (śáśvatī), which group forms an entity that is simultaneously young and yet dates from time immemorial. . . . Nowhere does the Uṣas invoked seem to have a privileged position except for that resulting from the invocation itself.

"The Auroras" thus constitute a group equivalent to Aurora and are invoked collectively in the prayer of day as if all participated in the action of each one. We have seen that in Rome the multiple celebrants who act together and together mime the tasks of the unique Mater Matuta behave in like manner.

Another very natural expression recurs often. Since one of the aspects of the auroral phenomenon is to dissipate the darkness, which for several hours had been filling the sky, the poets speak often of hostility—but not of an equal contest. Aurora (or the Auroras) limit themselves to driving back darkness, *támas*, barely personified, but willingly laden with disagreeable epithets. Uṣas, for example, "chases away the mass of unshaped blackness" (*bā́dhate kṛṣṇám ábhvam, Rig Veda*, 1.92.5). "Driving back hostility and darkness, Aurora, Daughter of heaven, arrived with the light" (*ápa dvéṣo bā́dhamānā támāṃsi*, 5.80.5). "As a valiant archer (chases) the enemies, she drives back the darkness (*ápa . . . bā́dhate*

---

[65] *Études védiques et paninéennes* (Paris, 1957), vol. 3, p. 6.

támaḥ), like a swift driver (of a battle chariot)" (6.64.3); "The Auroras, leading the high sacrifice, repel the darkness of night by casting it aside" (*ví tā́ bā́dhante táma ū́rmyāyāḥ*, 6.65.2); "Aurora marches on, goddess, driving back (*bā́dhamānā*) with the light all the darkness, the dangers; here the brilliant Auroras appear, . . . the darkness, the unpleasant one, goes away toward the west (*apā́cínaṃ támo agād ájuṣṭam*, 7.78.2 and 3)." Thus the obscurity is likened to the enemy, monstrousness (*á-bhva*), danger, and is repelled, pushed far away (one will note the frequency of the root *bādh*, which carries this meaning) by Aurora or by the troop of Auroras themselves described as *aryápatnīḥ* (7.6.5), *supátnīḥ* (6.44.21).[66] This is exactly what the *bonae matres* of Rome "perform" in the first rite of June 11 when they expel a slave woman who, unduly present in the temple of Aurora, must represent, in opposition to them, the bad, low-born element of society as well as the cosmic "enemy" of the goddess.

As for the other, positive, aspect of Aurora's work, her relationship with the Sun and the light, the Vedic poets express it as mentioned above through numerous images, in particular in terms of kinship that would be useless to attempt to reconcile. Most of these images, used only once or twice, certain of them also in enigmatic formulas, probably do not refer to a mythological tradition. Thus, one text signifies perhaps that she is the daughter of the night (3.55.12), another that "the great sun fathers her" (2.23.2); elsewhere she is called wife or lover of Agni, of the Sun. These isolated, banal images do not give evidence of stable representations. Certain more frequent texts are also too natural to be significant. Thus, she is consistently called *divó duhitā́* "daughter of heaven" (and not, in spite of what has been said, "daughter of the sun"). She is mother (4.2.15; 5.47.6), mother of prayer (5.47.1), as on occasion, mother of the sun or light, and even according to Louis Renou, "a type of universal mother, an Aditi, mistress of the world, called *mahī́*, 5.45.3."[67] This is probably explained by the same analogous

[66] Ibid., p. 10.
[67] Ibid., p. 9.

reason that makes the Roman Aurora *Mater* Matuta, honored at the *Mat*ralia.

But at least one expression, more original, exists whose usage statistically would suffice to prove the importance of Uṣas in the Vedic concept: *she is the sister goddess par excellence.* In the *Rig Veda*, the word *svásṛ* "sister" appears thirteen times applied to a divinity. Eleven times it is in reference to Uṣas or of a divinity called the sister of Uṣas.

It is with Rātrī, the Night, a divinity of the same style as Uṣas, that she forms a "sisterly couple," one that is particularly close and important. Of the eleven texts just mentioned, six concern Uṣas as sister of Rātrī or vice-versa. As for the binary form, in five examples the expression "the two sisters" designates Uṣas and Rātrī three times, the Heaven and the Earth two times. Moreover, whether in the composites of the couple (*náktoṣásā*, five examples; *uṣásānaktā*, ten examples), in the two joined but separated pairs (*uṣásā . . . náktā*, two examples), or in the dual form with one of the names equaling in itself the entire couple (dual form of *uṣás*, four examples; dual form of *nákta*, two examples), the link between the two "sisters" Night–Aurora is strongly emphasized.

This is not a matter of language artifice or of poetic cliché. Regardless of how fundamental the antithesis of dark and light may be, the Vedic Night and Aurora function mythically toward one another like respectful and devoted sisters, as has been brought out innumerable times. Abel Bergaigne very subtly says:[68]

> Nevertheless, this black cow (= Night) who comes among the bright cows (10.61.4) is considered the sister of dawn, a sister whom the latter thrusts aside and from whom she moves away (10.172.4; cf. 4.52.1), but who also moves away from her sister (7.71.1) by voluntarily relinquishing her place (1.124.8;

---

[68] *La religion védique d'après les hymnes du Ṛig Véda* (Paris, 1878), vol. 1, p. 248. Cf. John Muir, *Original Sanskrit Texts* (London, 1870), vol. 5, p. 191; Alfred Hillebrandt, *Vedische Mythologie* (Breslau, 1899), vol. 2, pp. 44–47 (= 2d ed., 1927, vol. 1, pp. 45–49), and especially A. K. Coomaraswamy, "The Darker Side of Dawn," *Smithsonian Miscellaneous Collections* 94 (1935).

cf. 113.1 and 2). These two sisters, *samānábandhū* (1.113.2), though they reciprocally efface their color (ibid.), no more quarrel than do they stop in the common path they follow one after the other (ibid., 3); though of opposite forms, they have only one and the same thought (ibid.). It is probably still dawn and night which are designated in verse 3.55.11 as those who take on their twin forms differently, one shining and the other dark and who, one being dark and one bright (cf. 1.17.1), are nevertheless sisters.

We may be surprised that, as darkness constantly belongs to the demoniacal and dangerous world, Night as a divinity is on the contrary a favorable goddess, the sister of the good Aurora, and that both are jointly called "the mothers of *r̥tá*," of ritual and moral cosmic Order (1.142.7; 5.5.6; 9.102.7). Certain individuals believed there was reason to distinguish here between starlit Night and dark nights, but Abel Bergaigne has aptly remarked that Night associated with Aurora, either explicitly or implicitly, in the pairs such as *uṣásā*, *náktā*, does not appear to include this nuance.[69] The explanation is elsewhere, in a trait that is strongly indicated by the hymnal and which throws light on the ritual rule of the Matralia: from the human point of view, Night and Aurora have a maternal work in common, a work more important than that which separates them. These sisters are mothers, and collaborating mothers at that. Either *they are, by a physiological wonder, the two mothers of the same child*, the Sun or the celestial Fire, *or Aurora takes delivery of the son from the Night alone and in turn cares for him.* Here are a few examples of these mythic presentations of one and the same cosmic act:

1.96 (hymn to Agni):

5. Night and Aurora, changing entirely their color, nurse in common (samícī) a single child. Between Heaven and Earth he shines afar (like) a golden jewel.

1.146 (hymn to Agni):

[69] Contrary opinion again in Hillebrandt, *Vedische Mythologie*, p. 44 (= 2d ed., p. 46).

3. Both moving toward their common calf (*samānáṃ vatsám*) the two milk cows make their way separately, measuring carefully the distance so as not to cross. . . .[70]

On occasion the calf also changes color when passing from Night to Aurora:

1.9 (hymn to Agni):

1. Two cows of different colors, making their way straight to the objective, one after the other, nurse the calf (*anāynyā vatsám úpa dhapayete*). He becomes yellow near one according to his own will; beside the other he is brilliant, adorned with a beautiful luster.

3.55 (enigmatic hymn concerning various gods, where the stanzas 11–14 all seem to apply to the couple Night–Aurora). As happens in Vedic poetry, here incompatible conceptions are seen united: Night and Aurora as sisters (stanza 11), but also as mother and daughter (?stanza 12); a calf, probably their common calf, which they nurse together (stanza 12), but also the calf of one, which is licked by the other (stanza 13):[71]

---

[70] Renou, *Études védiques*, vol. 12, translates: "measuring interminable journeys." The meaning of *samānám*, "common," has been contested, although it is clear: see Renou, p. 42.

[71] The commentator Sāyaṇa thinks that, if the eleventh stanza concerns "day and night," the following three concern "heaven and earth," and the fifteenth stanza one or the other of these pairs. This division is probably faulty. In the introduction and the notes of Karl Friedrich Geldner's translation, good reason is found to attribute the twelfth and fourteenth stanzas, like the eleventh stanza, to Night and to Aurora, and the fifteenth stanza to the neighboring couple Night and Day, but this interpretation must be extended to the thirteenth stanza. Not only does the presence of the calf, surely the same one, in twelve, thirteen, and fourteen advise against separating these three stanzas in the exegesis, but the poetic form itself, the *r̥tá* mentioned in the genitive at the beginning of the last verse of each (*r̥tásya . . . sádasi; r̥tásya . . . páyasā; r̥tásya . . . sádma*), proves that it is a unit, and a unit that the couple Night–Aurora fits very well since Night and Aurora are the two "mothers of *r̥tá*" (see above at n. 69). Bergaigne's objections to this unitary interpretation (*La religion védique*, vol. 2, p. 11 n. 2) are weak, and the principal one is erroneous. He says that Night and Aurora are never presented in the *Rig Veda* as mother and daughter; indeed, the "sisters" concept is predominant, and by a great deal (even here, stanza 11), but in 10.3.2 for example, "the dark" with which Agni fathers the "young woman" (*yóṣām*) is likely Night in the capacity of mother of Aurora.

11. The two twin (*yamíā*) sisters have put on different colors, one shines, the other is dark. The dark one and the pink one are two sisters (*svásārau*).[72]

12. There where the two good milk cows, mother and daughter, nurse together (their calf), I invoke them both to the seat of *ṛtá.*

13. Licking the calf of the other, she mooed (*anyásayā vatsáṃ rihatī́ mimāya*). Through what world has the cow hidden her udder? The *iḷā* (or *Iḷā* personified) swelled from the milk of *ṛtá.*

14. The multiform entity dresses in beautiful colors . . .[73] she remains upright, licking the calf of eighteen months. I glance over, I who know, the sojourn of *ṛtá.*

Throughout these variants we see that a key idea remains: Aurora nurses, licks the child who is either hers in common with her sister, Night, or is the child of the latter only, thanks to which this child, the sun (for whom can be substituted in the sacerdotal speculations, the fire of offerings), born first from the womb of the night, reaches the day's maturity for the good of mankind. This myth, which forms the notions of "mothers," of "sisters," and of "child of the sister," tangibly expresses the theologem that defines the essential kindness of the short-lived Aurora, the reappearance of the sun or of a fire that nevertheless precedes her, which was already formed when she came on the scene.

It is probably this same theologem, in the form most acceptable to positive minds—Aurora receiving, doting on the child of her sister the Night, and not in the enigmatic and monstrous form preferred by the *Rig Veda* in which the two sisters Aurora and Night are mothers of the same child—which intervened in the conception of Mater Matuta, of Mother Aurora, at the time when the exposure to the Greek gods had not yet led the Romans to disdain and forget their own theology. If the myth corresponding to the

[72] I leave out the refrain common to twenty-four stanzas of the hymn, as it is not significant.

[73] I refrain from choosing among all the artificial translations proposed for *pádyā*; Renou, *Études védiques*, vol. 5, p. 16: "(Aurora) placed at the feet (of the cosmos) . . ."

theologem has disappeared, the latter is nonetheless recalled, attested to by a ritual rule that transposes to men, or rather to women here, the very behavior of the divinity: at the Matralia when Mother Aurora is honored, the mothers do with the children of their sisters[74] what this sister of the Night does with the Sun, the child of the Night.

THE MATERNAL AURORA

The agreement of Rome and Vedic India even to the point of making Night the *sister* of Dawn—which is found virtually throughout Roman ritual and explicitly in the Indian myths—is remarkable. It is reinforced by the fact that, in the two mythologies, the dark sister exists only in terms of the luminous sister. Nothing supports the idea that Rome ever knew a practical personification, a cult of the night (Summanus is something else), and Rātrī, according to Renou's expression, is "only a pale reflection of Uṣas, without her own individuality."

In fact, despite this precise connection between Rome and Vedic India, the important element of the theologem is less the "sorority" of the two "mothers of the Sun"—she who ripens him in her bosom and she who receives him and rears him—than the principle of this "duality." We have proof of this in India itself. It has been shown elsewhere, in the wake of the memorable discovery of Stig Wikander, that not only the central group of heroes of the *Mahābhārata*—the five Pāṇḍava brothers—but also many other characters of the poem reproduce in their character, their behavior, and their lives the essential traits of the gods of whom they are the

---

[74] If the broadest meaning of "brothers and sisters" is given to the ἀδελφῶν of Plutarch's texts (see above, n. 5), we will acknowledge an extension, a generalization that is not improbable in a ritual. It can also be advanced that the deity who presides over certain phenomena in the second part of the night is masculine, Summanus; see above, chapter 3: "Summanus."

declared sons or incarnations. Further, just as the Pāṇḍavas, sons
of canonical gods of the three functions, spread themselves among
these functions, so their half-brother Karṇa, offspring of the Sun,
took on two mythical representations of the Vedic Sun. His chariot, in combat, loses a wheel (and this accident is fatal to him);
but before that he himself had two mothers: one according to
nature, Kuntī, who abandons him at his birth and who much later
will be the mother of the first three Pāṇḍavas, the other by adoption after this abandonment. It is this second one alone, Rādhā,
whom he considers his mother. Kuntī and Rādhā are not sisters but
successive mothers of the solar hero.[75]

What we have here is a representation of a myth that dates
back at least to the Indo-Iranian period. This is borne out by the
solar hero of the European Iranians, the Ossets in the Caucasus,
who are the latest descendants of the ancient Scythians. Soslan
(Sosryko), in several situations, presents very clear solar traits, in
particular at the time of his death, which was provoked by a wheel
—the mythic representation of a kind of Saint John's wheel ("the
wheel of Father John"). He also has two mothers. He was formed,
an embryo, in a rock from which he was taken after nine months
by her who would rear him, who would then constantly call him
"my son whom I did not beget" and who, like the *bonae matres* of
the Matralia, would show even more attention, more affection to
him than to her own children. In this Caucasian tradition, the rock
and Satana are not sisters either, but only collaborating and successive mothers.[76] These variants only make more noteworthy the fact
that the *alterius proles*, "the child of another," whom the second
"mother" takes in and cares for, should have been specified as "the
child of the sister" in the myth put forth by the Matralia as in the
Rig Veda.

[75] *Mythe et épopée I*, pp. 123–144 (concerning the two mothers, pp. 126–135).
[76] See my *Légendes sur les Nartes, suivies de cinq notes mythologiques* (Biblio-
thèque de l'Institut Français de Léningrad 11) (Paris, 1930), pp. 75–77 (birth of
Soslan) and 190–199 (solar elements of Soslan); *Loki* (Paris, 1948), pp. 227–246; *Le
livre des héros* (Paris, 1965), pp. 69–71 (with the current bibliography).

Thus we have the four principal elements of the case of Mater Matuta completely and coherently explained, and her festival understood. The Roman ladies encourage, stimulate, and strengthen Aurora the night before the crisis that the summer solstice is about to open; they do so by sympathetic magic, by reproducing on earth the mythical acts that she accomplishes in heaven and which are expressed for us in the birth of successive days. But one must assume of course that this cosmic intention has a dual function. While they mime the solicitude of Aurora for her mythic *alterius proles*, the Sun, they themselves express an equal solicitude toward the little "extras" in this scene, their nephews, whom they hold in their arms; and, since they celebrate the festival of a goddess and can hope for her attention, they recommend them to this goddess who, beyond her concern for the celestial child, cannot fail to be interested in terrestrial children. Thus, in another connection, the maternal ex-voto found on the site of the sanctuaries that she possessed outside Rome are explained, as is the assimilation Matuta–Lucina that occurred in at least one of them.[77]

[77] See above, chapter 4: "Juno and Mater Matuta," and, more generally, all of that chapter, on the relationship between Mater Matuta and Juno (cf. Uṣas and Aditi); on Mater Matuta and Fortuna (cf. Uṣas and Bhaga), above, chapter 2; on Mater Matuta and Janus (cf. Uṣas and Savitṛ), above, chapter 3: "Summanus" and "The Pardon for the Tusculans." The need for the celebrants of the Matralia to be married in a first marriage recalls the mention of the Auroras in the hymns and the Vedic marriage ritual (*Atharva Veda*, 14.2; 31.43, 44), where, moreover, Sūryā, daughter of Sūrya (the Sun), the prototype of every newly married girl, is perhaps only a variation of Uṣas. In order to measure the difference that separates the concepts and processes of the present study from those of recent manuals on Roman religion, I reproduce the lines that the three principal ones devote to Mater Matuta.

(1) H. J. Rose, *Ancient Roman Religion*, pp. 78–79: "In passing, a minor deity of the field should be mentioned, because her name has been much misinterpreted in ancient and modern times. This is Mater Matuta, who had a festival, the Matralia, on June 11, and a temple in the Cattle Market. A perfectly satisfactory explanation of her name has come down to us, and is due to Varro; she looked after the ripening (*maturescentia*) grains. This fits the time of her festival, not very long before harvest, also the fact that her feast was in the hands of free married women, for clearly her share in the provision of *numen* for the fields was important enough to demand the attention of these traditional practitioners of farm magic and doers of the lighter farm work. It equally explains why no slave-women might take part;

slaves are foreigners, and what should they know of the way to approach the native goddess? Equally, it makes it clear why some Greek theologians thought she was the same person as their own Eileithyia, the goddess of birth; if she can ripen the fruit of the ground, why not that of the womb, seeing that the equation between Mother Earth and human mothers runs through all ancient religion and magic? But the same root which gives Latin its word for 'ripen', produces several words which signify 'early', especially early in the day. So the notion came about and is not yet quite departed that she was a dawn–goddess. It is refuted by the fact that she had a cult. Dawn—Eos in Greek, Aurora in Latin—is a pretty figure of mythology and folk-tales, whom no one is known to have worshipped in the whole ancient world." (This explanation of H. J. Rose was unfortunately adopted unreservedly in R. M. Ogilvie, *A Commentary on Livy, Books I–V* [Oxford, 1965], p. 680.)

(2) Albert Grenier, *Les religions étrusque et romaine* (= *Mana* 2.3 [1948]), pp. 116–117: "The Matralia, on June 11, is the festival of *Mater Matuta*, the goddess of happy beginnings and of the birth of beings. In this she singularly resembles Juno, and by virtue of this the matrons invoke her. As an attribute she has a key, because she facilitates deliveries, as *Juno Lucina* does later. The epithet Matuta that means "good, favorable" links her with Bona Dea, occasionally named *Fauna*, the favorable, and related to *Faunus*, the genie of fertility. . . . *Mater Matuta* had a temple in the Forum Boarium which probably was built by Camillus in 396 on the site of the old sanctuary whose foundation was attributed to Servius Tullius. Honored throughout Italy, she was one of the principal goddesses of Caere (Cervetri), the Etruscan port of Rome, and had a very ornate sanctuary there which was pillaged by Dionysus of Syracuse. Recent excavations have furnished numerous ex voto representing children in swaddling clothes. The findings had been the same at the temple of *Satricum* in Latium. *Bona Dea* and *Mater Matuta* were obviously Mother-Goddesses closely related to Juno and quite similar to the Gaulish Mother-Goddesses. Later assimilations made *Bona Dea* a *Hygie* and *Mater Matuta* the companion of *Portunus* or a relative of *Janus matutinus*." P. 132: "The epithet of *Matuta* means 'good, favorable': J. Vendryes, *Teutomatos* in *Comptes rendus Acad. Inscr.* (1939), pp. 466–480. The same root *matu* formed the word *matutinus* because morning is the favorable moment par excellence. *Mater Matuta* is 'the Good Mother'; her name has the same meaning as that of *Bona Dea*. Not understood, it transformed her into the goddess Aurora, associated with *Janus matutinus*, Hor., *Sat.*, 2.6.20. Mythologic speculation then assimilated her into the Greek Ino–Leucothea."

(3) Paul Fabre, *La religion romaine* in *L'histoire des religions* by Maurice Brillant and René Aigrain (Paris, 1955), vol. 3, p. 338: "Mater Matuta—again a nutritive *numen*; Matuta means 'good', favorable' [cf. Vendryes, *Teutomatos*, pp. 466–480]; *Mater Matuta* is thus the 'Good Mother'. She was honored on June 11, the day of the *Matralia*, which was the festival of matrons, and only of those who had been married but once. The goddess received cakes baked in terra-cotta containers. At the time she was linked to Janus and was made a deity of beginnings who presided at the coming of dawn, probably through bringing together the epithets of

Matuta and *Matutinus*. It is possible moreover that this coming together was not fortuitous. In any case, she presided, like Juno, with whom she seems to have more than one trait in common, at the birth of children. In short, she appears to be very much like a fertility goddess, very close to the other goddesses we have already encountered, but specialized above all it seems in the protection of the family. Her cult seems to have extended over all of central Italy."

It is remarkable that neither of the two specific and original rites of the Matralia that we have studied is mentioned in these presentations. Grenier and Fabre are wrong to quote Vendryes, *Teutomatos* to support their interpretation as "Bona Dea." Vendryes limited himself to noting correctly, as Porkrovskij had done, that the name of the Roman goddess of dawn, the derivative in *tu-ta* from the root *ma-*, rests on the concept of the type "of favorable hour"; he did not insinuate that *Matuta* ever specified "good" in general.

Appendix 2

Matralia, N or NP

To Agnes K. Michels

The study of Roman calendars, carried to a high degree of interest by Theodor Mommsen, has become, it is often said, one of the most promising areas of humanism. The publication of new inscriptions, in particular the discovery of the pre-Julian calendar of Antium—the only evidence of the computation of time before Julius Caesar—an enormous amount of analysis, thought, hypothesis, and debate, make in any case an area capable of commandeering a scholar's activity. It is necessary, however, to remain calm. Despite this documentation, these repeated efforts, despite much hope and some aspiration, most of the problems that Mommsen had not resolved remain, and several that he thought he had resolved appear anew. This occurs because the data, even at Antium, are late. There are no good documents on the methods of computation, which were probably diverse, prior to the first century. Already in Varro's day, Roman scholars could make nothing more than suppositions and constructions, so that lowly common sense, little enough appreciated in the world of erudition, remains the best guide on many points.

A few examples have just been cited. Even though we devise methods of correction and practical intercalation between the

*origins and the first century, the following must indeed be estab-
lished: the Roman calendar is shot through with seasonal festivals
that are devoid of sense unless they are celebrated during the
season, at the point of the season for which they are created. Consequently, the ferial was conceived from the beginning in terms of
moments of solar revolution. Finally, in normal time, the corrections must have been such that the mobility, and thus the inaccuracy in the annual dating of the festivals, were reduced to a
minimum.*[1]

*Among the other problems still pending, we can cite the
extremely unequal distribution of festivals over the months, the
extreme case being that of September and November, which are
entirely empty in the calendar of Antium as well as in the Julian
calendar. On the one hand, the customs of rural life and, on the
other hand, an unknowable history—perhaps for September, that
which followed the abolition of the throne—are probably responsible for this imbalance.*

*Above all, we can cite the system formed by the notations
attached to each day of the year and expressed on the calendar by
the letters or groups of letters: F (= fastus), C (= comitialis), N
(= nefastus), EN (= intercisus), NP (= nefastus + ?), and FP
(= fastus + ?). The question still remains as to what exactly a
"fastus" day and a "nefastus" day are. Conditioned by the meaning
retained for these notations, we face the problems posed by their
distribution in the course of the days. And along the same line of
thought, there is the problem of the mechanism of the nundinal
letters, each one assigned to a day, which go from A to H, and on
whose meaning no ancient text enlightens us.*

In 1967, under the title The Calendar of the Roman Republic,
*Agnes Kirsopp Michels published a very well-focused restatement
of the problem. She does not refrain from proposing some new
interpretations, but deserves considerable merit for never presenting them as positive solutions. Her principal concern is to enable
students to see the insufficiency of the documentation. Thus, the*

---

[1] See above, appendix 1: "Significance of the Matralia."

analysis of the dossier on intercalation begins with these excellent lines (pp. 167–168):

> For the historian it is perhaps less important to determine the precise length of the intercalary month, or the existence of an intercalatory day, than to find out how often intercalation took place and whether it followed a regular pattern. Modern scholars have expended enormous efforts on this problem, winding their way through intricate and detailed calculation to establish systems of intercalation. Unfortunately no two of these systems agree, and historians have had to accept one or another as the basis of a chronology. This lack of agreement in a field that has been studied for centuries suggests that the evidence now available is inadequate for a solution. Indeed, since the late nineteenth century no major effort has been made to solve the problem. All I hope to do in this discussion is to point out the reasons why the problem is difficult.

Such a tone characterizes the faultless inquiry of this entire book.

It is into the dossier of characteristic letters that the Matralia propel us—and into two superimposed circles of this little inferno. Why is their day, June 11, like the majority of the feriae, nefastus? *And why is it that this is almost the only one of these* nefasti *marked simply N, not NP, on certain calendars? I hope some glimmer of light can be shed on the first point, starting, moreover, from a proposition contested, wrongly so I believe, by Mrs. Michels. For the second point, the meager facts we have at our disposal compel us to set aside the explanations that have been proposed rather than to construct a more probable one.*

THE CHARACTERISTICS OF THE DAYS

On pages 550 to 551 of my *Archaic Roman Religion* I defined the overall problem in a few words, which to me still seem valid, while avoiding any discussion and without concern for shades of meaning. Here they are, with a few changes:

The days are classified into two categories, *dies festi* and *profesti*, *dies fasti* and *nefasti*, from which the ideas of *feriae* and of *fas*, respectively, were set in motion.

The second, *fas*, is metaphysical. **The *dies fasti* are those which give to man's secular activity the mystical basis, *fas*, which assures him of the chance to succeed; the *dies nefasti* are those which do not give him this basis.**

The word *feriae* is only descriptive and was originally negative. In a broad sense, it is a fragment of time which man reserves for the gods, with or without a distinct cultic act. Consequently, the *dies festi* are assigned to the gods and the *profesti* left to men for conducting private and public business (Macrobius, *Saturnalia*, 1.16.2). That is the oldest teaching, which was altered later and in different ways, *feriae* often being given a positive ritual character of the "festival" type, from which the *dies festus* remained exempt. Occasionally the opposite occurred; but that concerned only the theorists. For all practical purposes the quasi-totality of the *feriae*, and with them the *dies festi*, had a religious, a ceremonial character.

The two categories are thus very different in principle. One (*fasti, nefasti*) defines the days from the point of view of human activity, the direct concept being favorable to this activity. The other (*festi, profesti*) defines them from the point of view of divine ownership, the direct concept affirming this ownership. Thus, **if all the *festi* days are *nefasti*,** the converse is not true. Mystical reasons other than respect for divine ownership may advise man against acting on certain days.

The principal objections dealt with the two propositions that are printed in bold face.

FASTI DAYS AND NEFASTI DAYS

Provided we do not revert to the etymological play on words that derives *fas* and *fastus* from the root of the verb *fari*, the articulation *fastus* or *nefastus* remains a type within which one may prefer various definitions—that of Mrs. Michels, for example, as well as mine.

I, myself, continue to think that the adjectives *fastus* and *nefastus* originally had the same intention and extension as the noun from which they are derived. *Fas*[2] (not declined, without plural; only *fas est*) is the solid, undifferentiated mystical basis on which all human activity (private, public, diplomatic, and so on) can rely for support with assurance, not only from the point of view of human justice (*ius*, declined with its plural *iura*, meaning natural or acquired rights) but also of unknown divine plans or, more generally, the mysterious forces of the invisible. A day, and probably originally also a place, an occasion, could be *fastus* or *nefastus* depending on whether or not it furnished this basis.

Keeping in mind Varro's definitions—but are these not merely to justify the etymology by *fari*?—Mrs. Michels restricts the extension of the *fastus* and *nefastus* concepts solely to the acts of civil law, and restricts the usage of these concepts at all times to characterize the days; a *fastus* day is a day on which the Romans had the right *lege agere*, that is, to enforce or to promulgate a *ius*. A *nefastus* day is one that does not assure the litigant or the *iudex* this solid basis and during which, consequently, *non licet lege agere* (Caius).[3] This definition is, in sum, a particular instance of the general meaning I prefer, limiting it but, within this limited area, confirming it.

FESTI DAYS AND NEFASTI DAYS

On the second point, the relationship between *festi* and *nefasti* days, my disagreement with Mrs. Michels is unfortunately difficult to pinpoint. At the most I would replace the expression "all the *festi*

[2] See my *Archaic Roman Religion*, trans. Philip Krapp (Chicago and London, 1970), pp. 131–132 and 562; *Idées romaines* (Paris, 1969), pp. 61–69. I cannot follow Michels, *Calendar*, pp. 52–53.

[3] Michels, *Calendar*, pp. 48–50 and 61–62.

days are *nefasti*" with "the *festi* days are, generally speaking and in principle, *nefasti* (N or NP)." In addition, the rare cases to the contrary ought to be considered exceptions to the rule and justified as such.

Statistics provide the first indication: (1) *nefasti*: the twelve days of the Ides,[4] the one day of the Calends (or two, the Calends of August being a variable sign), and thirty-six days, each named after a festival, are marked NP in the pre-Julian calendar; five days of the Calends and six named days are marked N; let us say, sixty (or sixty-one) *feriae statiuae* in all; (2) *fasti*: the five (or six with those of August) remaining Calends and one named day (Feralia, February 21) are marked F (with the mysterious variant FP for the Feralia); let us say six (or seven) *feriae statiuae* in all; (3) for two named days (the two Vinalia, April 23 and August 19), the calendars do not agree, but the pre-Julian calendar marks them F (April) and FP (August).

This proportion of F days to N (NP) days—about one or ten—cannot be fortuitous.

On the other hand, whether one gives the limited (judicial) meaning or the broad meaning to *(ne)fastus*, it is natural that the *dies festi (feriae)*, inasmuch as they are consecrated to divinities, would be at the same time closed to human activity; that is, N or NP. This is indeed the normal situation resulting from the statistics, so it is the few *feriae* marked F or FP that pose a problem—or rather different problems, for each of which an independent solution is foreseen.

First: for the Calends, we can understand that the creators of the calendar might have been nonplussed. By virtue of the general rule, the Calends, being *feriae*, must all have been *dies nefasti*. But they are *feriae* of a particular type. The Calends mark the beginning of the month, and as such—especially the first ones, those of January—are charged with an "ominal" function. Consequently,

---

[4] For the sake of simplification, I am not taking into consideration the "intercalary month."

not only is human activity not to be set aside, but such activity is actually necessary for the day to fulfill this function. The following remark seems to explain this division in part (five or six F, six or seven N or NP). If, in principle, all the Calends, in their capacity of representing beginnings, are *in dicione Junonis*—the explicit cults of Juno under the distinctive patronage of her name, cults either very old or more recent, but in any case well anterior to the calendars we know—they are indicated only at the Calends of February (J. Sospita), March (Lucina), June (Moneta), and October (Sororia). Now, these four Calends belong to the six that are marked NP. Thus, everything occurs as if the name of the most august goddess prevailed each time over the ominal meaning of the day. The F characteristic, irregular for the *feriae* but expected for the "beginnings," would be maintained, except for the Calends where Juno received special attention through a particular religious act which was foreign to her function as protectress of beginnings. Perhaps, at the moment of the founding of the cult, these Calends returned to the common law of the *feriae*; that is, again became the NP type of *dies nefasti*. But this sort of explanation does not work for the Calends of July or December, both marked N and both devoid of special cults.

Second: for the Feralia of February 21 (F or FP), the last and only public day of the Parentalia series, the following consideration can be put forth. Only two days or series of named days put the living in touch with the dead: on February 21 in an orderly, amicable, and trusting manner, on May 9, 11, and 13 (Lemuria) in a dramatic way. The purpose of the Feralia is to maintain, through offerings on the tombs, good familial relations with the dead that manifest comparable good will, in particular those who do not leave the ground, do not visit their heirs, and do not haunt the houses where they lived. At the Lemuria, on the contrary, the anonymous phantoms of the dead circulate among the living in such multitudes that the living, by ruse, try to force them to leave. Thus, it is natural that the two times have different characteristics: everything is suspect during Lemuria, everything is reassuring during the Feralia. Regardless of the breadth or the intention given to the concepts of *fastus* and *nefastus*, we can understand that the days in May do not give a sure "basis" for the activity (juridic or broader) of the living who, on the contrary, can function in complete security on February 21.

Third: for the Vinalia, contradictions in the calendar probably do not result from errors: why would these festivals have incurred the carelessness of the copyists? Rather, it is a matter of theories, of different schools of thought, some maintaining the rule, others extracting from the rule those *feriae* that concern a very particular substance—wine.[5]

Thus, the exceptions seem to confirm the rule and we are justified in writing that, in principle, except for the particular cases, which we must attempt to justify, any *dies festus* is *nefastus*—the converse, of course, not being true.

N AND NP DAYS

The second question, which concerns essentially the Matralia, is no longer relative to the opposition N ~ F, but to the division of N into simple N and the enigmatic NP.

One fact dominates everything. While there are many days in the calendar marked N which do not contain *feriae*, all the days marked NP do contain them and are *festi*. Reciprocally, with very few exceptions, all the *dies festi* (fifty-four out of sixty) that are *nefasti* have the NP mark and not the N mark. These six exceptions are: the Regifugium of February 24 (or possibly the 23rd of the intercalary month); the three days of the Lemuria (May 9, 11, and 13); the Vestalia of June 9; and the Matralia of June 11.

---

[5] Concerning the singularity of wine among the secondary products of agriculture, see Robert Schilling, *La religion romaine de Vénus, depuis les origines jusqu'au temps d'Auguste* (Paris, 1954), pp. 91–155; and my "Quaestiunculae indo-italicae, 11–16," *Revue des études latines* 39 (1961), 261–274 ("Juppiter et les Vinalia," "le mythe des Vinalia priora," and *"inter exta caesa et porrecta"*).

Still, uncertainty exists for the Matralia, which are N in the Fasti Venusini and Maffeiani, but NP in the pre-Julian calendar of Antium (Fasti Antiates Maiores). Mrs. Michels comments appropriately (p. 184):

The date before the Ides suggests that *N* may be correct as does the position within a series of *N* days which includes a named day, the Vestalia, marked *N*. One might argue that the copyist of Ant. Mai. had made a natural mistake in giving the Matralia the character commonest for named days. One could equally well say that the fact that the Matralia was in a series of *N* days had led to a mistake in Maff. I am, on the whole, inclined to accept *N*. Degrassi (p. 468) accepts *NP*.

The day of the Vestalia warrants no remark other than that it is "included" in the same series of N days as the Matralia (June 5–12).

As for the Regifugium and the Lemuria, we can see that these are particular days, irregular in other respects. The first is the only one of the ferial to occupy an even day in the month; the second represents the only festival that is repeated three times under its name on three consecutive uneven days: the other repeated festivals are only twice repeated (Carmentalia, January 11 and 15; Lucaria, July 19 and 21).

It is impossible to interpret these exceptions until the meaning of the abbreviation NP has been determined. The attempts have been numerous, but none is convincing. From Festus (162L[1] = 283L[2]), the only ancient text that expresses an opinion on this point but which is irreparably mutilated,[6] we can merely conclude that diverse activities, probably prohibited along with many others on N days, were licit on NP days.[7] The most recent of the propositions

[6] Summary of previous propositions in Michels, *Calendar*, pp. 74–76. The attempts to restore the Festus text are not constraining, of course.

[7] This favors, to my way of thinking, the reading (*nefasti*) pu]*riores* (Festus, 1.4), since *purus* is defined willingly in the negative, as if excluding an impurity, a motif of hindrance: Paulus Diaconus (293L[1] = 354L[2]), *pura uestimenta* = "not worn out, not struck by thunder, not marked by mourning, having no spot"; (297L[1] = 356L[2]) *puri auri* = "(made) of a gold that had not previously been used for impure purposes."

is that of Mrs. Michels: the P element of the abbreviation would, according to her, refer to *populus (publicus)* and the NP days would contain the *feriae publicae statiuae uniuersi populi communes* in contrast to the N days, which would contain the *feraie statiuae* "but not on behalf of the people as a whole." Unfortunately, once we examine the particular cases, we encounter the arbitrary element. To justify that the Lupercalia of February 15 are NP and not N, we would say that this picturesque festival, though celebrated only around the Palatine and by two groups of *Luperci* with names derived from the gentility, attracted all the Romans as spectators and by its purpose and results, interested the entire community. But to justify that the Matralia and the Vestalia are N and not NP it is argued that one of these festivals is celebrated only by part of the *matronae (uniuirae)*, the other by women, neglecting the fact that the festival of Aurora at this moment of the year, and everything concerning the national fulcrum of Rome, are "on behalf of the people as a whole." To justify that the Regifugium of February 24 is N, it becomes necessary to explain it with Julian, as a ceremony peculiar to *rex sacrorum* rather than a public festival. The fact is the *rex sacrorum* was maintained, under *libertas*, only to accomplish the *sacra publica*; and, moreover, it is unclear how the personal festival of an individual could be registered in the public ferial.

It is thus wise to acknowledge our ignorance: NP retains its mystery.

Appendix 3[1]

Camillus and Jupiter

The good relationship of Marcus Furius Camillus, the last hero of Rome's legendary history, with the goddess Aurora was not limited to what is explicit at the very beginning of his great glory: taking command of the army that had laid siege to Veii for so many years and determined to end the war, he put his fate in the hands of this protectress, promising her that following the victory he would dedicate to her her recently restored temple. Indeed, all of Camillus' subsequent life, at least his military life, is a development of this theme, "Camillus, Aurora's protégé," and in some way, as a natural consequence, "Camillus, solar hero."[2] In each of the three wartime dictatorships of which he was in charge, even into his old age, he won a decisive victory from the very beginning of the operations. Now each battle, all but won from the outset,[3] even

---

[1] This appendix and the following are taken from my *Fêtes romaines d'été et d'automne* (Paris, 1975), pp. 255–283.

[2] I ask the reader to interpret this short expression in the precise and limited meaning I give it: a hero whose mutual relationship with the goddess Aurora renders him suitable for attracting solar traits and symbols to himself.

[3] I mean begun at dawn under conditions such that victory is certain from the outset and that, even if combat is prolonged, no incident threatens to turn fortune back (cf. *Mythe et épopée III* [Paris, 1973], p. 105, lines 6–5 from the bottom; = chap. 1 above: The Victories of the Dictator Camillus at Dawn). It is thus that these expressions, for which I have been reproached, must be understood,

though prolonged by the enemy's relentlessness, was always begun at dawn. Twice it was begun under conditions that highlighted this time of day. In the second battle Camillus, in order to set fire to the enemy entrenchment, took advantage of a natural phenomenon, a wind that came up only at dawn. In the first battle, Camillus appeared at dawn before Brennus and the retreating Gauls and, through this unexpected apparition, took on epic stature. Before continuing I would like to stress this point, for certain critics do not seem to have understood it.

How does Plutarch describe Rome's revenge? The previous day Camillus, unexpectedly arriving at the Forum with his swiftest troops, put Brennus in his place. He had the gold removed from the scales, and a brief skirmish ensued. The layout of the locale, a city in ruins, did not lend itself to a real battle, so Brennus withdrew and returned to his camp located in Rome itself. But he did not stay there (*Camillus*, 29):

> But Brennus, presently recollecting himself, called off his men, and, with the loss of a few only, brought them to their camp; and rising in the night with all his forces, left the city, and, advancing about eight miles, encamped upon the way to Gabii. As soon as day appeared [ἅμ' ἡμέρᾳ] Camillus came up with him, splendidly armed himself, and his soldiers full of courage and confidence.

A long and violent battle followed, but it was without setbacks. In the end Camillus routed the enemy, spilled much blood, and took their camp. The deserters who were caught perished on the spot. Most of them scattered, but the inhabitants of the villages and towns in the area attacked them and slew them.

I commented on this account in this way (above, chapter 1: "The Victories of the Dictator Camillus at Dawn"):

---

in particular the one I used several times in an attempt to be brief: "victory at dawn." I do not know how else to express this: victory of dawn? through dawn? These would not be better. Therefore, consider "victory at dawn" as a technical term with the nuance specified by this note.

The Greek expression stresses the suddenness of the attack, the disarray of the Gauls: "As soon as day appeared, Camillus was there, upon him" (ἅμα ἡμέρα παρῆν ὁ Κάμιλλος ἐπ' αὐτόν). And what a Camillus! ὡπλισμένος λαμπρῶς, "clothed in brilliant armor." Why this detail? It is never mentioned again and even here, it is surprising, since Camillus, drawn out of exile, must have had greater worries than obtaining rich armor. Why, if not to add an almost supernatural note of the military genius of the character? His surging apparition before Brennus is a luminous epiphany, at dawn.

To me, the crux of the matter is the indication of the moment of time "with the day," which returns like a refrain in the dictator's other victorious battles. The circumstance "clothed in brilliant armor" is secondary but not unimportant. I am not forgetting, as I have been reproached for doing, that λαμπρός, as applied to armor, can express beauty and richness as well as brilliance. But I reiterate that, even understood thus, this extra detail is unusual here and must have a purpose. Camillus did not leave for this campaign from his home, the house of the Furii. He left Ardea where he was living in exile, having no military project in mind. The army he commanded was composed of Roman deserters gathered in Veii after the disaster of the Allia. Since, upon arriving in Rome, he hurried with his advance units to the Forum where he found himself involved in the first skirmish, he certainly did not take the time during the night to dress up or to put on an expensive breastplate which, moreover, he would not have found in his ransacked and burned house. He lay in wait, pursued, and revealed himself to the enemy "with the day." Thus, once more, why this detail "clothed in brilliant armor" if not because Plutarch, or rather the tradition he observed, intended that in this Roman battle won by Camillus, in his first victory since the taking of Veii, the hero appear at dawn— albeit contary to probability—in a kind of splendor? In addition, there is a reason, decisive I believe, to assume that the splendor thus attributed to Camillus by the authors of his *Life* was not just beautiful, but was luminous, brilliant.

This ingenious chronicle is filled with symmetries that act as an organizing principle. If we look only at the beginning and end of the account, we see that the authors arranged events so that the revenge of the Romans was a complete replica, or rather an exact reversal of their misfortune. At the beginning of the Gallic episode, the Romans were basically wrong, and Brennus had the right to demand justice in the name of the international law that had been violated: a Roman ambassador, having come to Clusium to negotiate with the Gauls, fought in a battle against them. Brennus thus demanded satisfaction, and it was only after the Romans refused to grant it that he led a devastating march on Rome. This march, barely slowed by Brennus' victory at the Allia, was justified in every respect—from the religious point of view, as well as for military reasons. At the end of the Gallic war, on the other hand, Rome, purified by the ordeal, returned to its common sense. Although Camillus was not in Rome, his condemnation was legally rescinded, and he was made dictator. Meanwhile, Brennus committed serious religious and moral crimes by slaying the consuls, setting fire to the temples, and throwing his sword on the scales. In addition, he misjudged the situation juridically: since Camillus had legitimately been made dictator, no other official was entitled to commit Rome to a truce or a treaty. Thus in the Forum, when Camillus had the gold removed and haughtily requested the Gauls to take back their scales, Brennus protested and called on the gods in vain. He was wrong and Camillus, the sole authorized negotiator, was right. All that had been done without his order or consent was null and void.

Now the same intention of inverse symmetry is noted with regard to the "brilliant armor" in which Camillus, the defender of honor and law, accomplished—at the very last moment—the Roman revenge. On the occasion of the first mistake which triggered the misfortune, the ambassador Fabius, who forgot his duty and became a combatant, also appeared before Brennus in unusual armor (Plutarch, *Camillus*, 17.6–9):

By this answer the Romans, perceiving that Brennus was not to be treated with, went into Clusium, and encouraged and stirred up the inhabitants to make a sally with them upon the barbarians, which they did either to try their strength or to show their own. The sally being made, and the fight growing hot about the walls, one of the Fabii, Quintus Ambustus, being well mounted, and setting spurs to his horse, made full against a Gaul, a man of huge bulk and stature, whom he saw riding out at a distance from the rest. At the first he was not recognized, through the quickness of the conflict and the glittering of his armour, that precluded any view of him, but when he had overthrown the Gaul, and was going to gather the spoils, Brennus knew him; and, invoking the gods to be witness, that, contrary to the known and common law of nations, which is holily observed by all mankind, he who had come as an ambassador had now engaged in hostility against him, he drew off his men, and bidding Clusium farewell, led his army directly to Rome.

In this well-ordered ballet of images the avenging arms of the irreproachable Camillus responded to the aggressive arms of the sacrilegious Fabius. And the brilliance that emanated from the justice-loving Roman was called upon to demoralize Brennus, just as the brilliiance emanating from the guilty Roman, after the initial dazzlement, had thrown Camillus into the great adventure. Under these circumstances, how can one fail to gloss the ὡπλισμένος λαμπρῶς of the last battle with the τὰ ὅπλα περιλάμποντα of the first? Nevertheless, in the surprise that initiated the victory, what suddenly gave Camillus' armor its brilliance was the time of the apparition, at the lightening of the sky, ἅμ' ἡμέρᾳ.

In appendix 1 I improved my observations of 1956. I called to mind how close the archaic mythology of the Roman Aurora, Mater Matuta—as it must be reconstructed to give meaning to the rites of her festival—was to the mythology of the Vedic Aurora,

Uṣas, and how far from Greece, which has nothing comparable.[4] In addition, I spoke of one of the most famous episodes in the chronicle of Camillus, that of the young Faliscan boys honored by Camillus and of their wicked teacher sent back, under the blows of rods, from the Roman camp to the gates of the city. I showed how this episode transposed into the masculine mode the two ritual mimes of the Matralia by linking them through a unitary Roman plot.[5] Can one extend this method of inquiry to other scenes or characters of the mythology of the Vedic Aurora and the Vedic Sun and to other aspects or episodes of the chronicle of Camillus, which until now I have disregarded?

Despite the abundance of praise bestowed on him, the Vedic Sun, Sūrya, does not have many myths. John Muir wisely noted this more than a century ago, at a time when the massive, blind, and calm interpretation of the hymns and images of the *Rig Veda* as solar allegories triumphed. Wikander's exegesis of the *Mahābhārata* seconded this impression and allowed for its elucidation.[6] In this great epic most of the heroes, together with their characters and their adventures, are transpositions, often sons of Vedic gods or demons, having their functions and their myths. Here the hero offspring of the Sun, Karṇa, has a unique status where two features with multiple manifestations and consequences dominate. Just as the Vedic Sun, the offspring of Night, is taken at his birth and cared for by Uṣas, so Karṇa has two mothers, his natural mother who abandons him the very night of his birth, and his adoptive mother, the only one he henceforth acknowledges. On the other hand, just as the Vedic Sun is at odds with Indra, the god of storms and thunderbolts—in particular in a myth where Indra causes a wheel to fall off the Sun's chariot—so the hero Karṇa is set against the hero-son of Indra, Arjuna. In *Mythe et épopée I* I quoted some of the manifestations of this hostility for which the poem, of course, offers justifications of another kind from the realm of literature.

[4] See above, appendix 1, "Mater Matuta."
[5] See above, chapter 2: "The Faliscan Pedagogue."
[6] *Mythe et épopée I*, 2d ed. (Paris, 1974), pp. 125–144.

But the hostility is founded on a basic idea forced on the human imagination by the spectacle of nature: the shining sun and the storm cloud do not make good bedfellows. Thus at the very moment during a tournament when Karna and Arjuna seem ready to clash, the gods, their fathers, perceptibly intervene (*Mahābhā-rata* 1.134.5401–5403 Calc.):

> Then the sky covered over with flashing and thundering clouds, preceded by Indra's weapon [= a thunderbolt] and through which flocks of herons, like smiles, passed.
>
> Seeing the god with the bay horses [= Indra] look down lovingly, the Sun destroyed the clouds which had drawn near to one another.
>
> So that one saw on one side Arjuna, protected under the shadow of the clouds, and on the other Karna, enfolded in the sun's brilliance.

After showing itself time and again during the long battle, the hostility of the two heroes culminates in the eighth canto, in the scene of Karna's death, a transposition from the Vedic myth of the wheel that drops off the chariot of Sūrya. Karna sees a wheel from his chariot suddenly sink into the ground, and all his efforts to extract it are vain. One last arrow from Arjuna beheads him, and at this juncture the poet exploits at length the symbolism of the setting sun.

That is the situation of the characters in the Indian epic. We see that it carries on, with the necessary adaptations, the Vedic and probably pre-Vedic situation of the god of the thunderbolt and the god of the sun. We have acknowledged in Camillus a hero accorded solar characteristics because of his link with a goddess Aurora who is related to the Vedic goddess. Is it possible, in Rome, to find reworked traces of this part of solar mythology, of an incipient or brutal conflict between Camillus and the mythical personnel of storms and thunderbolts? I think so, but in order to become aware of this we must take into account some considerations.

Jupiter—since it can be no one but he—remains the god of thunderbolts and storms throughout every phase of Roman religion. But that is—and probably has always been—only a part of his definition.[7] He is above all the supreme god of Rome. He is the functional equivalent of the great Āditya, Mitra and Varuṇa, rather than of Indra whose Roman counterpart, deprived of wielding a thunderbolt, is Mars. Now in India the conflict has always been and still is naturalistic: even though he was made "king of the gods" in the epic, Indra is set against Sūrya—or his son against Sūrya's son—but they are characterized solely as the Thunderbolt and the Sun. In the hymns there is no conflict between Mitra-Varuṇa and Sūrya. Although the plot of the *Mahābhārata* has Karṇa, the sworn enemy of Arjuna, as also the enemy of Arjuna's brothers—and thus of the eldest, Yudhiṣṭhira, the king, in whom we acknowledge an epic transposition of Mitra—this hostility is not personal. It is not shown in the duel scenes, and it sets tight limits on itself.

At first glance we can expect to find in Rome only an unequal struggle between the "solar zone" and the "fulgurating (and sovereign) Zone." This is because Camillus, on the one hand, representing the former, is a mere man, and the divinity who backs him up is not the barely deified Sun, but a goddess Aurora without much significance. On the other hand, in the "fulgurating zone" the sole representative is a god, and what a god: Jupiter himself. The historicizing, or the doubling of theology and mythology through "history," has indeed situated the "solar hero" and the "sovereign (if not fulgurating) heroes" at points too different in the flow of "events" for them to clash. Romulus and Numa, on whom hinges a double model of sovereignty comparable to that of Mitra and Varuṇa,[8] are placed at the very origins of Rome, in the eighth

[7] *Archaic Roman Religion*, trans. Philip Krapp (Chicago and London, 1970), pp. 151–154 and 176–204.

[8] Most recently in *Mythe et épopée I*, pp. 274–279; summarizing *Mitre-Varuṇa: Essai sur deux représentations indo-européennes de la souveraineté*, 2d ed. (Paris, 1948), pp. 58–65 (and *L'héritage indo-européen à Rome* [Paris, 1948], pp. 147–152).

century. The solar Camillus lights up the first half of the fourth century.

Finally, we can expect from Camillus nothing that resembles provocation of a god, nothing of rebellion or resistance. Piety in its most Roman form, the recognition of the divine *maiestas*, is one of the constants of his character.

If we keep in mind these reservations, the study to which the Indian example invites us results in some thoughts which perhaps elucidate certain unexplained points of the Camillus chronicle.

Perhaps we should, in a section entitled *"Solisque, 3,"* study further from this point of view the first meeting between Camillus and Jupiter. For it gives rise to a situation that the Romans consider insulting to the god because of a chariot. The scene occurs precisely when the relationship between Camillus and the goddess Aurora has just begun. In taking up his command before Veii, the dictator promised to have the temple of the goddess dedicated after the victory. Once Veii was destroyed, he reentered Rome. Forthwith, before fulfilling his promise, still being *uoti reus*, he celebrated his triumph. It is on this occasion, because of the form this triumph took, that Camillus, everywhere else so pious, is supposed to have provoked Jupiter, usurped the rank of Jupiter (Plutarch, *Camillus*, 7.1–2):

> Camillus, however, whether puffed up with the greatness of his achievement in conquering a city that was the rival of Rome, and had held out a ten years' siege, or exalted with the felicitations of those that were about him, assumed to himself more than became a civil and legal magistrate; among other things, in the pride and haughtiness of his triumph, driving through Rome in a chariot drawn with four white horses, which no general either before or since ever did; for the Romans consider such a mode of conveyance to be sacred, and specially set apart to the king, and father of the gods.

The improbability, the logical impossibility of the complaint are of little importance. Camillus is blamed for having accomplished what was, on the contrary, one of the intentions and one of the *raisons d'être* of any triumph: the ephemeral assimilation of the victorious general with the Capitoline god. I, following others, dealt with this in *Mythe et épopée III* (pp. 232 and 293). Clearly we are not witnessing here a scene of embellished history, but the dramatization of an ideological conflict between the character, Camillus, such as he is presented at that time, and the meaning of Jupiter in theology. What does this little drama involve? The hero, who owes his very recent success to the goddess Aurora, reenters Rome in a *chariot* theoretically reserved for Jupiter. For Jupiter alone? It remains to be seen. Here Livy introduces a few words in which he reduces to the utmost, probably as a result of his repugnance for the supernatural, the auroral character of the hero (5.23.5-6; cf. above, Chapter 1: *"Solisque,* 1" and *"Solisque,* 2"):

> Moreover, as the dictator drew near, all sorts and conditions of men ran forth to meet him in such numbers as had never welcomed a general before, and the triumph far exceeded the measure of honour usual on that day. He was himself the most conspicuous object in it, as he rode into the City on a chariot drawn by white horses, an act which struck men as being not only undemocratic, but irreverent, for they were troubled at the thought that in respect to his steeds the dictator was made equal to Jupiter and the sun-god; and the triumph, chiefly for this one reason, was more brilliant than popular.

In fact, once we have become aware—thanks to Plutarch who, moreover, does not seem to understand it—of the title "protégé of Aurora" which remained Camillus' prerogative, this *Jouis Solisque* and the charge of sacrilege take on meaning. As he is conqueror of Veii thanks to the goddess, and about to dedicate to her the promised temple (which he quickly does after the ceremony, ibid., 7), it is not unusual that historians have him reenter in triumph in the "Sun's chariot." He had a right to it; he acted his part, played his character, expressed his very thanks to the Aurora who had helped him. But, given the latent conflict between the Sun and Jupiter probably inherited from Indo-European mythology, this expression of "solar" piety was at the same time an insult to Jupiter, the "fulgurating sovereign."

Perhaps we should go further. Taking into account what Vedic India teaches (that the fulgurating god attacks the chariot of the Sun god) and what we learn from epic India (that the son of the fulgurating god kills the son of the Sun god when his chariot meets with an accident), it could not be by chance that the motif and the means of this opposition between Jupiter and Camillus is a chariot. The moral is surely very different in both cases, but Jupiter is supposedly insulted by Camillus' *vehicular* audacity. That is also the primary grievance of men ready to avenge the god—the first of three grievances that forced the hero into a civic death: exile.

We can assume, as does Jean Hubaux, that the error that, in the midst of the triumph over Veii, began Camillus' ruin is an excessively rationalized form of a scene having several variants: the Capitoline god of Rome is set against the Veians themselves with regard to a quadriga assigned to his temple or against a Veian driver regarding a legendary quadriga. Now some special facts, which change with the variants, here point also toward solar symbolism. According to one variant the terra-cotta quadriga, fired by the Veians, instead of contracting as it dried, swelled; it formed a mass so large, strong, and hard that, after the roof and walls of the oven were demolished, it was very difficult to take it out (Plutarch, *Publicola*, 13). In another variant the quadriga mounted by the Etruscan Ratumena sped away, arrived at the foot of the Capitol, and threw its driver to the ground. In spite of obstacles along the way, it stopped only after having circled the Capitoline temple three times from left to right (Solinus, 46). Are these Jupiter's mystical victories over solar chariots? Or solar homages of Veian quadrigas to Jupiter?

Whatever its complex origins may be, the charge of usurping divine attributes represents the only instance in which the character Camillus, through the will of the writers who fashioned him, seems to sin against Jupiter. But apprised as we are, we cannot help but be struck by another comparison, this time negative. In the important circumstances of his life, Camillus does not often look to Jupiter.[9] When he routed the Gauls from Rome and appeared on the Forum, did he so much as go up to the Capitol? That would have been an appropriate "scene to write," but the authors of the chronicle did not do it. Later, following another triumph over the Etruscans when Sutrium was delivered, Camillus auctioned the prisoners. They brought in so sizable a sum of money that, first, the matrons were reimbursed for the prior gifts they had made to the State. Then "the surplus sufficed to make three golden bowls, which were inscribed, as is well known, with the name of Camillus, and kept, until the burning of the Capitol, in the chapel of Jupiter, at Juno's feet." (Livy, 6.4.2–3).[10] Thus when Camillus made an offering in the temple of Jupiter, he brought in a goddess, Aurora, the one on whom he had called at Veii and who—in Etruria—is thought to have close ties with Θesan.[11] During Camillus' very lifetime, a

[9] In Livy, 5.50.1–4, the reparative senatus consultum that was published through Camillus' initiative (*diligentissimus religionum cultor*) did provide for the foundation of the Ludi Capitolini (attributed by others to Tarquin the Elder). It contained the specification that the dictator M. Furius constitute for this purpose a *collegium* composed of inhabitants of the Capitol and the Citadel. But this was only one article within a whole where all the gods were dealt with according to their role or their fate in the Gallic crisis. All the temples destroyed and occupied by the enemy would be rebuilt and purified. The L. C. would serve to thank Jupiter for having protected his residence and the citadel of the Roman people. The unknown god who had in vain announced the misfortune would receive a cult under the name of Aius Locutius. In addition (5.50.6), all the gold and other goods that had been brought hurriedly from the other temples into Jupiter's sanctuary would be held sacred and kept *sub Jovis sella* since they could not be properly redistributed. Nothing in all that implies a gesture of personal piety on Camillus' part, no more than do the references to Jupiter contained in the famous speech (5.51–54) intended to prevent the Romans from abandoning Rome in ruins for an intact Veii. These references did no more than remind the Romans of the promises and demands of the god, as of, moreover, those of Vesta and of the other gods (the Salians) who insured the continuance of the city.

[10] The expression is not clear. Juno was not in the *cella* of Jupiter but in one of the lateral *cellae*. We presume that in Jupiter's there was a "reminder" of the goddess.

[11] See above, chapter 4: 'The Etruscan Aurora."

contrast was established between his attitude and that of another dictator, T. Quinctius. After a great victory over the Praenestines (Livy, 6.29.8–9):

> He returned to Rome bringing with him from Praeneste the image of Jupiter Imperator. This he bore in triumph to the Capitol, where he dedicated it, between the shrine of Jupiter and that of Minerva. Below it he placed a tablet, in commemoration of his deeds, with an inscription to the following effect: "Jupiter and all the gods granted Titus Quinctius the dictator that he should take nine towns."

Although there was no hostility toward Camillus on Jupiter's part, there was a kind of indifference about the progress of a nevertheless extraordinary career. In any event, the god took only a general interest in it. When he punished the Romans for the ingratitude shown to a benefactor, it was as a representative or under the auspices of δίκη, of Justice, which does not tolerate an ἀδικία. Again it is only in Plutarch (*Camillus*, 12.4) that Camillus, leaving for exile, "stretched out his hands toward the Capitol" while pronouncing his Achillean curse (ibid., 13.1), while Livy (5.32.9) limits himself to having Camillus, without being specific, put his reinstatement into the hands "of the immortal gods." Moreover, the religious causes of the disaster at the Allia and the grievances of the gods against the Romans are far from being confined to this sin against an individual. The Romans provoked Jupiter much more directly, first by scorning a clear warning (Plutarch, *Camillus*, 14.2–3; Livy, 5.32.7); then by violating the rules of law through their ambassador (Plutarch, 17.7–8; Livy, 5.35 and 36); yet again by refusing justice to Brennus' legitimate complaint (Plutarch, 18.1–3; Livy, 5.36.10–11); and finally by beginning the battle of the Allia without observing the religious rites, τὰ τῶν θεῶν, and without heeding unfavorable auspices and entrails (Plutarch, 18.5; *nec auspicato nec litato*, Livy, 5.38.1). Camillus' strength, which Jupiter could not fail to take into account, lay, on the contrary, in his faithfulness in complying with the religious and political rules that governed the making of Roman magistrates, even under circumstances that required a real *tour de force* from him. But in all that there was no special, no personal relationship. Camillus the citizen and the celestial insurer of justice and Camillus the general and the great god of the State did no more than conform, without fail, to their respective duties, which of course dovetailed.

The only time that Camillus had dealings with Jupiter on a battlefield—near Satricum, the city of the goddess Aurora, his protectress—there was neither favor nor hostility manifested on the part of the god. If the result of Jupiter's intervention went contrary to Camillus' plan, it was simply because the god saw more than the hero and that, as *Latiaris*, he had also to save the Latins from a massacre for which the Romans were only too eager. Here are the facts. In this encounter Camillus was only one of six military tribunes having consular power, but his colleagues spontaneously awarded him supreme command. In addition to a new generation of Volscians, the adversary was made up of an enormous throng of Latins and Hernicii that the Antiates, unrepentant enemies of Rome, had succeeded in stirring up. The battle, which was difficult at first, turned into a total victory thanks to Camillus' stupendous action (Livy, 6.8.6–9).

> For nothing so daunted the spirits of the Volscians as the sight of Camillus himself, when they happened to encounter him— so surely, wherever he went, did he carry victory with him. This was especially apparent on the left. That wing had already nearly given way, when Camillus suddenly threw himself upon a horse, and, armed with an infantry-shield, rode up and by his presence retrieved the battle, calling out that the rest of the army was conquering. The fortune of the day had now turned, but the enemy's numbers were an obstacle even to their flight, and a great multitude remained for the weary soldiers to dispatch with long-drawn massacre, when suddenly great gusts of wind brought on a downpour of rain, which broke off what was rather a certain victory than a battle. Thereupon the recall was sounded, and the night that followed finished the campaign for the Romans, while they slept. For

the Latins and Hernicii abandoned the Volscians and marched off to their homes, their evil counsels rewarded with as evil an outcome.

As for the Volscians, they wanted to take refuge in Satricum, but the Roman army on their heels scaled the wall, and they capitulated.

Thus, the god of celestial tempests did not deprive Camillus of a deserved victory which, moreover, terminated in the "liberation" of Aurora's city.[12] But he saved the Latins, his other protégés and future associates of Rome, from an irreparable destruction. He thus limited the hero's military glory.

We must probably interpret along the same lines another important episode in Camillus' life: his conflict with M. Manlius Capitolinus and the Tarpeian execution of the Capitol's savior. Here Plutarch more than Livy endows his hero with fierce actions and a relentlessness that astonishes us.

The moral remains constant, but varying doses of psychological causes are involved: Manlius' hate-filled jealousy of Camillus? Exaggerated pride produced by his victory? Political amibition? As for Camillus, we are free to endow him with whatever feelings we choose: annoyance before a disloyal rival? A strict notion of duty? No text ever puts him in the wrong. The story is too well known for us to insist on analyzing it in detail.

During the war with the Gauls, M. Manlius, alerted by Juno's geese, prevented a nocturnal surprise attack on the Capitol and in return received, in addition to immediate and exceptional honors, the enduring *cognomen* of Capitolinus. Little by little he convinced himself that not only Rome but also Jupiter was indebted to him, or he at least felt himself to be on familiar terms with the god. He very quickly set himself against Camillus and, since the latter then

---

[12] The theme has been taken up again several times, in particular in the first lines of Livy's eighth book, and again on the occasion of a "battle of Satricum"; a theme repeated on two consecutive days, in book 26, chapter 11 (Hannibal before Rome).

belonged to the most conservative part of the patriciate, he sided, not without demagogy, with the plebs. Indeed, he was very popular. Only the accusation of *affectatio regni*, of claims to kingship, would divide the united front of his supporters.

Jupiter did not support this proud man, but he did not discourage him, did not repudiate him with any sign whatsoever. In fact, the Jupiter of the fourth-century accounts had not yet emerged from the ambiguity, from the fragile equilibrium in which the establishment of *libertas* had placed him. The crux of his status and policy was that, throughout the changes in the social order, he remained the god of the Roman State. When the city was ruled by kings, there was complete harmony. As the annals have Romulus say while pledging to Jupiter Feretrius the spoils of Acron of Caenina, everything then took place between kings, the king of heaven protecting the earthly king who honored him. Again under the Tarquins, even though the god for whom the tremendous temple under construction on the Capitol was intended was not exactly the god of the Jupiter–Mars–Quirinus triad, he remained in essence the King, just as Juno whom he was to shelter would be Queen. The expulsion of the Tarquins, on the contrary, posed the first difficulty. But legal stratagems, a bold theory of the lawfulness of the auspices, allowed the necessary affinity between the leaders and the State god to be transferred to the "usurping" magistrates and in the end to the consuls chosen each year. Briefly, the word *rex*, always used with reverence where a god was concerned, was spurned, put out of political usage, and remained only in the name of a *rex sacrificulus* whose duties were purely religious.[13] The essential thing was that Jupiter accepted this distinction: the auspices belonged to the *Patres*, the heirs and administrators of the wealth of promises bequeathed by the founding king. The claims of the plebs posed a new problem to Jupiter or his theologians. The appearance of this new term challenged the linear pact between the god and the *Patres*, for Jupiter, the god of the State, must be that of

[13] *Archaic Roman Religion*, pp. 152 ff., 191 ff., and 585 ff.

the total society. Throughout the numerous episodes of the conflict that was beginning, Jupiter remained officially neutral in the plebs' gradual and slow drive for equality, while indicating from time to time that the patricians were not wrong in resisting.

This was the theological situation at the time in which history places the "crisis" of Manlius. But the fact remains that Manlius, as he himself stressed, had in common with Jupiter the title *Capitolinus*, which was filled with political meaning. That he did not share it depended neither on Jupiter nor anyone since his alertness and valor on the citadel hill had earned it for him: a human caricature of Jupiter, if you will. But in his illusion of grandeur, it was the image of the god, the keen feeling of this *maiestas* to which his exploit linked him, which supported his claims. The origin of his confrontation with Camillus, beyond the psychological motivations, probably stems from this. The final scene in Manlius' trial indicates both a kind of solidarity between the accused and the Capitoline god and the limitations of the god's aid. Summarized by Plutarch (*Camillus*, 36.4-8), here is the scene which, I repeat, assigns to Camillus a crucial role—watered down by Livy—within the group of the six military tribunes holding consular power.

> He, however, when set at liberty, changed not his course, but was rather the more insolent in his proceedings, filling the whole city with faction and sedition. They chose, therefore, Camillus again military tribune; and a day being appointed for Manlius to answer to his charge, the prospect from the place where his trial was held proved a great impediment to his accusers, for the very spot where Manlius by night fought with the Gauls overlooked the Forum from the Capitol, so that, stretching forth his hands that way, and weeping, he called to their remembrance his past actions, raising compassion in all that beheld him. Insomuch that the judges were at a loss what to do, and several times adjourned the trial, unwilling to acquit him of the crime, which was sufficiently proved, and yet unable to execute the law while his noble action remained, as it were, before their eyes. Camillus, considering this, transferred the court outside the gate to the Peteline Grove, from

whence there is no prospect of the Capitol. Here his accuser went on with his charge, and his judges were capable of remembering and duly resenting his guilty deeds. He was convicted, carried to the Capitol, and flung headlong from the rock; so that one and the same spot was thus the witness of his greatest glory, and the monument of his most unfortunate end.

The confrontation had nothing supernatural in it. Everything took place between men, even more between the accuser and the judges than between him or them and the accused. But the accused was there with, as is said today, an almost superhuman dimension because of his cognomial fellowship with the greatest god and because of his assertion, to which a neutral Jupiter did not object, that he saved him at the same time as he saved Rome. As a result, although Camillus did not attack the god, Manlius had nevertheless the remembrance of an exploit and the view of a setting dominated by Jupiter as his best defense. This was a sacred evocation to which Camillus, unlike the judges and the people, was insensitive. So much so that his relentlessness, the extraordinary means he took to move the tribune in order to cut Manlius off from his Capitoline support and to extract a *triste iudicium inuisumque etiam iudicibus* (Livy, 6.20.11), bordered on excess. The authors of the chronicle, within the limits allowed by the faultless piety they celebrated in Camillus in other respects, thus succeeded in showing that he did not come under the greatest god's sphere of influence.

A final manifestation of this separation of the man from the god is furnished by the unexpected role that history assigns to Camillus, at the end of his long life, in the decision to open the consulate to the plebs. The grandson of the terrible decemvir Appius Claudius—in the speech to the Senate that Livy composed for him—perfectly defined the general obstacle to the aspiration of the plebs. It was a question of an impossibility that was religious in nature. It was not men, by human decision, who could assign the right of the auspices to new social categories. The auspices came from Jupiter, and from generation to generation since the pact was made between the founder and the god, the taking of the auspices had been reserved for the patricians. Such was the impasse. Yet it was the patrician, the dictator Camillus, until then opposed to the idea, who commanded the abrogation of his order and the compromise by which one of the two consuls should henceforth be plebeian.[14] How did Jupiter accept this? As always, although he ended by acknowledging the reform which had become the law of the State, it was not without punishment and ill humor. The initial battle undertaken by the first plebeian consul was ill fated, and the patrician consul had difficulty righting the situation. But before that, the god expressed his discontent more directly. A terrible epidemic struck Rome, from the lowly people to the highest personages. The most notable death was that of Camillus, who had so often governed in Rome without himself ever having been consul.

No contrary evidence exists to disrupt the pattern of these convergent facts. They give the impression that the authors of the chronicle, who still knew a great deal about the theology of Aurora and the Sun, knew in particular that "Mater Matuta's hero," the "solar hero," no matter what his moral virtues and religious propriety, was not on familiar terms, epically speaking, with the fulgurating and sovereign god. He did not, by his comportment, pay any particular attention to him.

These facts also allow us to join two of the chronicle's main nonmilitary episodes to the unitary explanation that his relationship with Mater Matuta suggested for the war episodes.

---

[14] Camillus entrusted this work not to the ancient Fides of Jupiter's circle who maintained the traditional, originally trifunctional, order. He rather committed it to Concordia, a new and independent goddess, who henceforth would preside over the compromises in the political confrontations of the two great parties.

Appendix 4

The Nonae Caprotinae

Since the earliest calendars, aside from the *feriae Jouis* of the Ides, a long hiatus has followed the two *feriae publicae* of June, the Vestalia on the ninth and the Matralia on the eleventh. There are no more public festivals during the last weeks of June, and not until July 5 and 7, when the Poplifugia and the Nonae Caprotinae occur respectively, do we encounter any again. Such "holes" are not uncommon in the distribution of religious moments of the period and it is not certain that they all must be interpreted in the same way. Some appear to be actual breaks between two series, each one more or less homogeneous. For example, the festivals of January, all grouped in the first fortnight, are separated from the festivals of February, all grouped in the second fortnight, not only by this long interval, but also by the profound difference in their purposes, inaugural in one case, lustral in the other. Likewise, the long time that elapses between the Tubilustrium of March 23 and the Fordicidia of April 15 underscores perhaps the opposition between martial or social festivals (Anna Parenna, Liberalia) and agrarian festivals.

In other instances, contrariwise, it seems that the first holiday, but only that day, which follows a long break, seems still to be linked to those feasts that preceded it. In short, it is a matter of a parenthesis, which closes as it opens. This is the case with the

Portunalia of August 17, the first festival after the Neptunalia of July 23 which opened the dog–days, with their complement, the Furrinalia of July 25.

To which of these types does the twenty-four day interval that separates the Matralia from the Poplifugia and the Nonae Caprotinae belong? To hazard a guess, we would need to know the meaning of these last two festivals. But they have remained enigmas until now, for lack of documentation for the first festival and in spite of rather abundant detail for the second. No progress has been made since Georg Wissowa wrote (*Religion und Kultus der Römer*, 2d ed. [Munich, 1912], p. 116 n. 1):

> The Poplifugia are designated as *feriae Jovis* by the Fasti Amiternini (cf. Dio Cassius, 47.18.5, with Merkel's explanation, *Proleg. zu Ovid, Fast.*, p. clix). The "flight of the people" implied in the name had occurred, according to some (Dionysius of Halicarnassus, 2.56.5; Plutarch, *Romulus*, 29, cf. *Camillus*, 33) at the abduction of Romulus. According to others it happened at the time of an attack launched against Rome, after the departure of the Gauls, by neighboring peoples, either Etruscans (Macrobius, *Saturnalia*, 3.2.14) or Latins (Varro, *De lingua latina*, 6.18; Plutarch, *Romulus*)—an attack which was also linked to the equally enigmatic festival of the Nonae Caprotinae of July 7.

The Nonae Caprotinae seem very complex; fertility rites are not the only rites to be found there. The fact that the slave women offer themselves, according to one of the founding myths, to save the honor of the free women, or that the slave Tutula engages in an acrobatic exercise in a tree prove that more is involved. But what?

As for the Poplifugia, they are for us only a name, notable in that, unlike the singular *regifugium*, the form is plural. This is also the only festival of the year to be placed in that part of the month which precedes the Nones. The first point urges an interpretation of *-fugia*, following that of the ancient writers, as "multiple flights, disorderly and in confusion." The second invites the scholar to see in the Poplifugia a prelude to the festival that immediately follows them, the Nonae Caprotinae, which are themselves exceptional if not anomalous, as they are the only festival during the year attached to a day of Nones.

Under these conditions, a relationship between the two festivals can be considered probable. After admitting this in his *Real-Encyklopädie*, Wissowa recanted in *Religion und Kultus der Römer*. The strongest arguments remain (1) the opinion of several ancient writers and (2) the association, in the etiological account of Plutarch, of elements relating to both of the days. But these arguments are not decisive. However, just recently new information, the discovery of a purpose to the Nonae Caprotinae, one that is obvious as soon as it is formulated, has advanced the whole problem. In the following pages I will outline the present status.

In the opening chapters, I have shown that some of the sacred acts and sacred times of the month of June have a common purpose, if judged by the rites and legends linked to them. That purpose is to resist symbolically through every possible way the increasingly pressing "peril" that before the end of the month results in the halt, then the retreat of the sun. The solstice makes the curve of the duration of diurnal light turn back. Having increased for six months, triumphant after the spring equinox, this duration of daylight continues to diminish for the other six. This decrease will continue until the stylized horrors of the winter solstice, the *dies angusti* that the goddess Angerona is responsible for stopping, to achieve a turnaround in the best interests of humanity. At the Matralia of June 11, the festival of the goddess Aurora, the Roman ladies, imitating the two aspects of Mater Matuta's daily service, encourage and strengthen the willing dawns. The Vestalia of the ninth, then the care given to the national homeland from the ninth to the fifteenth, probably have the effect, among others, of maintaining and cleaning, through sympathetic action, the great homeland of the world. At the Quinquatrus Minusculae of the fifteenth, the sacred flute players, disguised as women, if they are interpreted according to the etiological legend, represent the dawns again, but this time they are reluctant and must be brought back to their service by force. Finally, the *natalis dies* of the temple of Summanus, which occurs on the twentieth, thus closest to the solstice, bears witness to a change, not in the meaning but in the application of the ritual effort: Summanus is active during the second part of the night, the part that already belongs to the following day and during which the sun that the dawn receives is formed (cf. the round cakes characteristic of this god).

In the chapters above it was also shown—I referred to it in the preceding appendix—that the authors of the chronicle of Camillus made of this character, whether he was legendary or merely laden with legends, a hero of Aurora in the fullest sense of the word. He is a devotee of Mater Matuta to whom he entrusts himself by a vow at the beginning of his career, and is favored by her at the diurnal moment that is her domain, each time he, as dictator, enters into battle. One of the most original episodes of the chronicle, the one of the Faliscan schoolmaster, even seems to have been composed only of an ingenious transposition of the two ritual scenes that constitute the essential part of the Matralia. And yet none of these events from Camillus' life is linked to this "season of the dawns" that comprises the month of June; none is even attached to a date, to a point of the ferial; none serves as a founding myth or as an explanation of a festival or a rite. We can certainly assume that most of the wars and the numerous battles occurred during the usual season between March and October: the interval is long. We can also note that the overflowing of the Alban Lake, the prelude to the capture of Veii, is placed at the beginning of the dog–days: this is not sufficient to locate the final action on the calendar. But above all, neither the story of the Faliscan schoolmaster, nor the brilliant deliverance of Satricum, nor the Tusculan display of all kinds of work, nor the exile of Camillus itself has an anniversary. In particular, June 11, the day of the Matralia, was not used by "history." Inversely, it is other events, actual or fictitious, which provided the founding legends for the *dies natalis* of Summanus and for the Quinquatrus Minusculae.

The *Life* of Camillus, however, contains an episode in which, curiously enough, the hero is not involved, and which has no object other than to explain the joint origin of the Poplifugia and the Nonae Caprotinae. Now, the second festival of the two marks the first quarter of the lunation of July—such was the former meaning of the Nones. For the first time since the summer solstice, when nocturnal time began to eat away at diurnal time, a new moon reaches the first stage of its growth and will develop, as is normal, into a full moon—will begin again the monthly liturgical life that had been suspended, as was also required, since the Calends. The Nones of July are thus a particularly important moment in the annual course of the celestial luminaries. In fact, of the twelve days of Nones in the calendar, these are the only ones that have their own festival.

Relying on these conventions, Professor Paul Drossart of the University of Lille pondered the rites of the Nonae Caprotinae and made a genuine discovery. Just after the "season of the dawns," precisely the menaced dawns driven back by the solstice, the ritual effort of the Romans was directed toward the moon and the night, the only possible substitute for sunlight and daylight. Professor Drossart informed me of his discovery in January 1974 and developed it in an article entitled "Nonae Caprotinae: la fausse capture des Aurores," published in the *Revue de l'histoire des religions* (1974), 129–139. I am pleased to include here, with the permission of the author and the editor of the journal, most of this skillful extension of my "Camillus."[1]

At the beginning of the third dictatorship of Camillus, tradition places a "victory *at dawn*," prepared and won by the dictator himself,[2] in competition with a *"nocturnal"* victory won *in his absence* (Plutarch, *Camillus*, 33.2–6). Plutarch insists on this duality, which imposes a choice on the historian:

---

[1] The following notes, numbered 2–18, are also by Paul Drossart.

[2] See above, chapter 1: "The Victories of the Dictator Camillus at Dawn," on Plutarch, *Camillus*, 34.1–5.

περὶ τούτου τοῦ πολέμου διττοὶ λόγοι λέγονται. The two reported episodes, however, are not incompatible and could very well have constituted two phases of the war; but here we are shunted toward a *symmetry*: the nocturnal victory is presented as a fabulous answer (μυθώδης) to the victory at dawn—not because the story invokes the supernatural, but because it served as the etiological legend for the festival of the Nonae Caprotinae on July 7, accessorily also to the ritual gallop of the Poplifugia of July 5. Plutarch has told this story twice (*Camillus*, 33 and *Romulus*, 29). In a similar form, it can be read also in Macrobius (*Saturnalia*, 1.11.35–40).

The Latins camp by the walls of the city, and demand of the Romans that they deliver to them the young girls and women of free birth. Not anxious to accede to that demand, but incapable of sustaining a siege, the magistrates tergiversate. A female slave named by some Philotis and by others Tutula (or Tutela) then proposes to them to give herself with a certain number of her companions in the flower of youth as hostage in place of the free women. Dressed and adorned like the ladies, they go to the camp of the besiegers, under the guidance of Philotis. Macrobius states precisely here that the pseudo matrons, distributed in the camp, uiros plurimo uino prouocauerunt. During the night (νύκτωρ), once the men fall asleep, they steal their swords. Philotis climbs up into a wild fig tree and brandishes a torch whose light (these specifics are found only in Plutarch) she conceals from the enemies by deploying her cloak on their side ('ιμάτιον, Camillus, 33.5), or perhaps even using a screen and cloth (προκαλύμματι καὶ παραπετάσμασιν, Romulus, 29.8). This is the signal agreed upon with the magistrates, without the knowledge of the other citizens. Aroused from sleep, the Romans make a disorderly sortie (etiology of the Poplifugia) and without glory go to massacre the still sleeping enemy. The festival of the nones of July commemorates the event. "For in it, first, they run out of the city in great crowds, and call out aloud several familiar and common names . . . in representation of the way in which they called to one another when they went out in such haste. In the next place, the maid-servants, gaily dressed, run

*about, playing and jesting upon all they meet, and amongst them-
selves, also, use a kind of skirmishing, to show they helped in the
conflict against the Latins; and while eating and drinking, they sit
shaded over with boughs of wild fig-tree, and the day they call
Nonae Caprotinae, as some think from that wild fig-tree on
which the maid-servant held up her torch, the Roman name for a
wild fig-tree being caprificus."* (Camillus, 33)

We see that the Greek author does not separate the day of
Poplifugia from that of the Nonae Caprotinae. Besides Plutarch and Macrobius, a brief notice in the calendar of Polemius
Silvius (*C.I.L.*, 1.2, p. 269) and an allusion of Ovid, who
speaks here moreover of a Gallic horde,[3] establish the etiological function of the story. Varro speaks only of the rite: "Nonae
Caprotinae quod eo die in Latio Iunoni Caprotinae mulieres
sacrificant et sub caprifico faciunt: e caprifico adhibent uir-
gam"; but he afterwards immediately attests to the existence of
an etiological *praetexta* played at the Appollinian Games.[4] In
addition, in the lines that precede this passage he presented the
Poplifugia as the commemoration of a tumultuous sortie by
the Romans against the besieging Latins (*De lingua latina*,
6.18).

The fertilization of the fig tree by caprification, linked to
the practices mimicking more or less realistically the fecunda-
tion of women, once inspired James G. Frazer to make numerous comparisons with African rites.[5] We know, moreover,
that the fruits, the milky sap, the leaves, the branches of the fig
tree and even the protuberances of its branches represent so
many essentially feminine sexual symbols.[6] In addition we

---

[3] *Ars amatoria*, 2.257-258 (regarding gifts to give on July 7): "Porrige et
ancillae, qua poenas luce pependit / lusa maritali gallica ueste manus": "Offer some
of them also to the female servant, on this day when the Gallic horde was punished,
duped by the nuptial gown."

[4] See "Le théâtre aux Nones Caprotines (with respect to Varro, *De lingua
latina*, 6, 18)," *Revue de philologie* 48 (1974), 54-64.

[5] *The Fasti of Ovid* (London, 1929), vol. 2, pp. 343 ff.; *Les origines magiques
de la royauté*, trans. P. H. Loyson (Paris, 1920), pp. 301 ff.

[6] Stefan Weinstock, in Pauly-Wissowa, *Real-Encyklopädie der classischen
Altertumswissenschaft* (Stuttgart, 1937), vol. 17, col. 852 (see *Nonae Caprotinae*)
which cites Plutarch, *Isis and Osiris*, 36; Athenaeus, 3.74d-76d. Regarding the inter-

know that the she-goat and the he-goat, present also in the rite (*Caprotina, caprificus*) sometimes have an identical significance.[7] This sexual dominance of the rite is also present in the *aition* where the servants play a role of *meretrices* and represent in some way the third function, debasing the warlike function, exactly as in an etiological story of the *Fasti* in which another benefactress of the Roman people, Anna Parenna, scoffed at the god Mars by not fulfilling his sexual appetites (3.675–696). But that is only one aspect of the story by Plutarch and Macrobius. We will not follow L. L. Bachofen, who wanted to see in this the prostitution of the Babylonian Sacaeca, to establish a tenuous relationship between Tutula and the Lydian Tydo with the priapic Tutunus Mutunus as intermediary.[8] The Τουτούλα (or Τουτόλα) of Plutarch[9] is indeed the Protectress, like Macrobius' *Tutela*, like that *Tutulina* who is more modestly placed in charge of the protection of the harvests (Tertullian, *De Spectaculis*, 8.3) and the *Tutilina* about whom a fragment by Varro (*Satirae Menippeae*, 216) tells us that one could invoke her during a siege.

Let us therefore treat the story as a coherent whole in order to extricate the strong points. The central theme is the *substitution* of female slaves for the Roman ladies. Likewise, in the rite, if *all* the women make sacrifices under the fig tree (Macrobius, 1.11.36) or feast under the fig tree (Plutarch,

---

pretations of the protuberances, see Jean Gagé, *Matronalia* (Collection Latomus 60) (Brussels, 1963), p. 89 (with respect to the Ruminal fig tree). Cf. *Real-Encyklopädie*, vol. 6, col. 2146, see *Feige* (Olck).

[7] Michel Lejeune, "Notes de linguistique italique," sect. 22: "Caprotina," *Revue des études latines* 45 (1967), 194–202; Frazer, *The Fasti of Ovid*, vol. 2, pp. 347 ff.; Einer Gjerstad, *Legends and Facts of Early Roman History* (Lund, 1962), p. 12.

[8] *Die Sage von Tanaquil*, 1870, in J. J. Bachofen, *Gesammelte Werke*, (Basel, 1951) vol. 6, pp. 222–230; cf. K. Vahlert, *Real-Encyklopädie*, vol. 16, col. 979–987, see *Mutunus*. Concerning the courtesan in religion and legend in Rome, see my "Meretrices et Virgines dans quelques légendes politiques de Rome et des peuples celtiques," *Ogam* 6 (1954), 3–8. Concerning Anna Parenna, *Mythe et épopée I* (Paris, 1968), pp. 544 ff. ("La fausse fiancée").

[9] See *Vies*, ed. Robert Flacelière, Émile Chambry, and Marcel Juneaux (Guillaume Budé collection), vol. 2, p. 192 n. 1.

Romulus, 29.9—but *Camillus*, 33.8, only speaks of servants here), only the slaves participate in the joyous procession and in the simulated combat, essential moments from which the matrons find themselves thus excluded. The situation is the inverse of that of the Matralia, where it is the intruding slave who is expelled from the temple.[10] Here, nevertheless, there is no hostile relationship between the two groups, but rather, on the servants' part, help and taking over, taking charge of a function normally exercised by the free women.

The comparison with the Vedic Indian mythology of dawn has led Dumézil to interpret the rites of Mater Matuta as a dramatization of the antagonism between the dawns menaced on the eve of the summer solstice (the matrons) and the invading darkness (the slaves). It is a dramatization that does not limit itself to mimicking the phenomenon but whose intention is "to encourage the dawn, the daily dawns, against the offensive, the imminent increase of the nocturnal time, or to reinforce them against their own lassitude."[11]

Now, the nones of July coincide in principle (and coincide in effect in the lunar calendar that predates the calendar called "pre-Julian") *with the first quarter that follows the summer solstice.* We find ourselves at the beginning of the first of the six monthly reascensions of the lunar light, called to supplement more and more generously, just at the crucial period of the winter solstice (the domain of Angerona), the increasingly lazy or waning dawns. From what we know of the ritual of the Nonae Caprotinae, the female slaves partially took charge of the privileges of the matrons and became the spokespersons for the community of women whose fertility must be insured. Limited to the ritual, the analogy with the Matralia does provide enough evidence to permit us to infer a drama transposing and representing the relief of the dawns by the nightly moons. The etiological myth is going to furnish us a more precise clue.

[10] Ovid, *Fasti*, 6.481–482, and 551–558; Plutarch, *Camillus*, 5.2; *Roman Questions*, 16 and 17.

[11] Cf. above, chapter 1: "The Vow to Mater Matuta," and chapter 5: "Dawn's *plaustra.*"

The scholarly world, which is very interested in Philotis–Tutula, does not seem to have rendered justice to her acrobatic talent. Perched in a fig tree (a tree hardly favorable to this exercise), she must brandish a torch while spreading out her cloak behind her—unless it deals with a veil and cloth (see above). Such a production is hardly justified if it deals only with concealing the flame from the view of the enemies, who moreover were so deep in sleep that the women could steal their swords.

I believe I recognize here an image familiar to the Roman iconography: the feminine personage who is carried off toward the sky in a flight of scarves and veils (*uelificatio*), and who sometimes brandishes a torch: for example, on the armor of the statue of *Prima Porta*, on the bas-relief of Carthage inspired by the *Ara Pacis* (in the Louvre Museum). Although the identifications of this figure depend on the executed scene,[12] one sees there most often a divinity of the nocturnal sky: Night, Selene, or Luna. Thus, regarding the cuirass of Augustus, Albert Grenier wrote "the sky spreads out her veil, the Sun in his chariot rushes forth preceded by Aurora who sprinkles the dew, while the Moon already half-way vanishes with her torch grown pale."[13] The two feminine figures are even so closely joined that G. K. Galinsky, identifying incorrectly the "torch bearing *uelificans*" with Venus comments: "Aurora carries Venus."[14] In fact, contrasted to the impetuous, virile image of the Sun, Aurora and the Moon have been

[12] In this way does a winged female figure, bearing a long torch, illustrate the apotheosis of the Empress Sabine on the arch of Portogallo; see Jean-Claude Richard, *Latomus* 25 (1966), 793.

[13] *Le génie romain dans la religion, la pensée et l'art* (Paris, 1925), repr. 1969, p. 371. The parallel is provided in the first verses of Horace's *Carmen Saeculare*; cf. Kressling-Heinze's edition.

[14] *Aeneas, Sicily, and Rome* (Princeton, 1969), pp. 201 ff. and fig. 138; pp. 229 ff. and fig. 162 on the bas-relief at Carthage; idem, "Sol and the Carmen Saeculare," *Latomus* 26 (1967), 620–621. Opposed to the identification of the torch bearer as the goddess Venus: R. Rebuffat, "Les divinités du jour naissant sur la cuirasse d'Auguste de Prima Porta," *Mélanges de l'École française de Rome* 73 (1961), 161–228 (the personage would be Night).

treated by the artist in the movement of flight as Siamese sisters, forming only a single silhouette.

The attributes of Philotis in the scene of the signal are therefore those that classical iconography ascribes to the Moon.[15] But this characteristic cannot be separated from the rest of the account of which it forms the essential peripety. Moreover, the account itself cannot be dealt with as independent of the ritual it claims to explain. It is the *caprificus* which establishes a clear relationship between the allegorical position of Philotis and what we know of the rite, since this tree is at the center of the July 7 ceremonies.

To be more exact, I think that the stance of the heroine, atop her perch, brandishing a torch whose light she hides from the enemy, is a lifelike representation of the partition of the lunar sphere, only half of which sheds its rays the night of the Nones. This interpretation takes into account four elements which it treats jointly: the servant, the fig tree, the screen, and the torch.

It is not a question here of promoting the existence of some "Moon cult" in ancient Rome. In the "Junonian" complex of the Nonae Caprotinae, it is both as regulator of the seasons and of feminine sexuality that the Moon plays a role, a role established in any case by the place of the festival in the calendar.[16] At the point where the myth and the rite intersect, the

---

[15] In Augustan art, the representation of the Moon as a torch bearer seems to be Hellenistic in inspiration. But the apotropaic or symbolic function of the torch in the magico–religious domain, and particularly in certain feminine cults, is in Rome, as elsewhere, a reality independent of iconographic conventionalisms. The women who form the delegation to Coriolanus carry torches (Dionysius of Halicarnassus, 8.44.1). Now, this "historical" episode serves as an *aition* for the dedication of the temple of *Fortuna muliebris* (Dionysius of Halicarnassus, 55 ff.; Livy, 2.40.12). Cf. Ovid, regarding the cult of Diana on the Aventine: "femina lucentes portat ab Vrbe faces" (*Fasti*, 3.270). See also Propertius, 2.32.9–10; Statius, *Silvae*, 3.1.56–57; and regarding these texts, the commentary of Robert Schilling, "Religion et magie à Rome," *Annuaire de l'École pratique des Hautes Études* 5th sect., 75 (1967–1968), 36–37.

[16] See Kurt Latte, *Römische Religionsgeschichte* (Munich, 1967), p. 233 n. 2. Cf. the valuable commentary of A. S. Pease's edition (3 vols., Cambridge, 1955–1958) of the *De natura deorum* on 2.68. At the Calends the "lunar" Juno is invoked under the name of *Iuno Couella*.

caprificus, the support of nocturnal light (in the myth) and the instrument of gynecological initiation (in the rite), is also the symbolic meeting point of the astronomical and sexual planes.

Disguised as dawns, the moons—their accomplices—let themselves be captured by the darkness which has no power over them and which they dissipate instead of being swallowed up by it. The chasing away of darkness comes from their apparent victory over the dawns.

Thus, certain elements of a lunar mythology, which agree with Dumézil's exegesis of the Matralia, come to light. According to this explanation, Aurora, threatened by Darkness, is in sympathy with beneficent Night, her sister, whose son (the young Sun) she coddles. The difference is that here the *ancilla* does not represent Darkness as a slave woman driven out of Matuta's temple but as kind Obscurity, the role of Darkness having devolved upon the enemy army.

The duality of the heroine's names (even if these names are relatively "modern") illustrates this role of mediator. *Philotis* is a courtesan's name, and the one who bears it is, at least in appearance, accomplice to the unrefined appetites and hostile darkness propitious to Venus.[17] *Tutula* is what her name indicates: The Tutelary, a divinized abstraction whose domestic cult includes the use of candles and lamps[18]—here a bestower of victory through the very light she diffuses.

Indeed, as often happens in Rome, the myth has been integrated into military history. Yet Livy rejects the episode (probably because Camillus plays no part in it). Such as it is, reinterpreted through patriotic propaganda, it retains its mythical elements; the Romans are not limited only to diurnal victories. Even when his ally Aurora is waning and Camillus absent, the legionnaire can count on supernatural help coming from the nighttime sky.

[17] This "divinity adored at night" is the scornful definition of Aphrodite given by Euripides' Hippolytus (106). In Plautus' *Curculio* the gibe, Venus *noctuuigila* (196), spoken to a courtesan, perhaps restores a ritual epithet.

[18] See W. Ehlers, *Real-Encyklopädie*, vol. 7, col. 1600, see *Tutela*.

This analysis[19] points out, without separating them, the paths of several interpretations, interdependent as expected in matters of lunar symbolism and efficacy. It opens up a field of research unexpected in Roman studies where admittedly the heavenly bodies—the sun, moon and stars—had not been the objects of great imaginative ferment, nor even of much ritual concern. Yet, successively, the sun, with the festivals of Mater Matuta and Angerona, and now the moon, with that of the Nonae Caprotinae, take their place among the hevaenly assistants. At the height of the classical age, Rome continued to call upon them in scenarios which, however, had lost their mythical interpretations without being replaced by any Greek substitute. Neither Helios, nor Eos, nor Selene, nor with greater reason Artemis, were associated with them. Although Mater Matuta was identified with Leucothea, the interpretation, based on a secondary trait, was rather misleading and clouded the issue. Yet we are assured that substantial mythical explanations had initially corresponded to these long-lived rites. As frequently happened in Rome, the explanation for the Nonae Caprotinae, which had turned from myth to history, even persisted in the anecdote of the slave woman atop a fig tree raising a torch hidden on one side by a screen. The mythos for the Matralia and the Angeronalia (Divalia) have been completely forgotten, or at least ignored by the formulators of history. But they are still perceptible through the rites themselves and are confirmed by corresponding Indian or Germanic myths.

The opinion of modern mythologists is not, however, entirely unjustifiable. The religious concern of the most ancient Romans did not focus on the heavenly body itself, neither on the moon nor on the sun, but rather on the light it gave. There is neither a "festival of the Sun" nor a "festival of the Moon." There are rituals intended to revitalize the diurnal light at the coming of the two solstices, that is, on the eve and at the end of its decrease. On the other hand, there is

[19] Paul Drossart continues with interesting thoughts on the double Carmentalia that surround (on January 11 and 15) the Ides, that is, in theory the first full moon of the year.

a ritual, just after the summer solstice, intended to strengthen the nocturnal light. Neither the Sun nor the Moon is a "hero," the object of the festivals, no more than Day or Night as such. During the Nonae Caprotinae, where Juno—patroness of the fertility of women—is honored, the moon in its first quarter is typified, not named. In the festivals leading to the solstices, the sun takes second place to the two feminine figures, protectresses of men and nature in these two crises. It is noteworthy that the summer solstice, or rather the summer solstice's zone of oscillation in the most ancient calendars, with its lengthy preparation, and as if in contention with darkness, does not contain any *feriae*. What we have here is an example of the utilitarian and operative—not speculative or poetic —character of religious portrayals in Rome.

As for the etiological legend of the Nonae Caprotinae, what it suggests about the mythical décor and plot makes us again regret that the infatuation of the Romans for Greek marvels did not motivate them to record their ancestral knowledge before losing it. Professor Drossart is undoubtedly right in interpreting the scene where the slave woman climbs up a fig tree and waves a torch that lights only half of the landscape as a representation of the first quarter (of the moon). I can do no more than entrust to the ethnographers the duty of trying to learn if this clever and precise setting is found elsewhere.[20] In any case, it belongs to a group of known stories, that group in which a lunar symbol is hoisted to the top of a tree. I myself have previously cited examples regarding the folklore that the Georgians attribute to Saint George, heir among other things of a Moon god.[21] The following is a variant collected from the Mingrelians:

> Saint George was a big eater who each day consumed a cow, two pounds of millet, one and a half pounds of wine. God was

[20] Emil Sieg has shown that the single wheel of the Vedic sun's chariot is luminous on only one side. Upon arriving in the west, the sun turns so that, the dark side then facing the earth, it returns to the east without being seen, *Nachrichten der Göttinger Gesellschaft der Wissenschaften* (1923), 1 (cf. 1928, p. 195).

[21] "Tityos," *Revue de l'histoire des religions* 3 (1935), 66–89.

displeased with this gluttony. One night when St. George was asleep, God took out the saint's stomach and hung it on top of a fantastically high oak tree. The next day, when the saint awoke, God asked him if he wanted to eat. But George, having understood everything, answered that he was no longer hungry. Then God allowed him to be honored at the four cardinal points "within reach of the Creator's arrow." God thrust his arrow in the four directions, and thus was marked off the area of Saint George's cult. As for the tree on which God had hung the stomach, that fearsome organ devoured it to its roots in one day.

We can also assume that the fig tree, providing both nourishment and the means of a lunar ascent and mimicry, is a vestige of a "world tree" as was the case in so many religions (Mircea Eliade, *Patterns in Comparative Religion* [1971], chapter 8; cf. chapter 4, on the moon). We can also compare numerous Indian facts cited by Odette Viénot, "Le culte de l'arbre dans l'Inde antique" (*Annales du Musée Guimet* 59, [1954]).

Finally, it is noteworthy that another etiological legend of the Nonae Caprotinae, mentioned by Plutarch after the preceding one (*Camillus*, 33.9–10), also recalls a known lunar symbolism. It is on this day that Romulus was said to have disappeared, suddenly enveloped by a cloud, or during an "eclipse of the sun." This is one of the explanations given for this disappearance (*Romulus*, 27.6):

> Some fancied the senators, having fallen upon him in the temple of Vulcan, cut his body into pieces, and took each a part away in his bosom.

No matter what opinion one holds regarding political men and meetings, this description of savagery is hardly admissible. It reminds the readers of *Isis and Osiris* of the dismemberment of Osiris' body for which, according to probably authentic Egyptian sources, Plutarch gives a precise lunar interpretation.

We are now in a position to answer the questions asked at the beginning of this appendix.

The long interval, in the *feriae statiuae*, which extends from the Matralia of June 11 to the group Poplifugia–Nonae Caprotinae of July 5 and 7, belongs to the second type. It does not indicate a break but rather an extended unity. The Nones terminate a period in which the main concern—also expressed, moreover, in various ways outside the great *feriae* (Quinquatrus Minusculae, *dies natalis* of Summanus)—was to rescue or to replace daylight. After twenty-five days, the service of the moon during the Nonae Caprotinae brings to an optimistic conclusion the lengthy, stylized uneasiness begun by the Matralia.

On the other hand, the Poplifugia and the Nonae Caprotinae together do seem to represent the two facets of this happy conclusion. The first portrays man's panic before the first quarter of the first month when night lengthens. The second celebrates the "compensation to dawn" that the moon, in the same season, guarantees to man.

Bibliographical Note

The publication of *Camillus* succeeds in a tradition that is no less important for being young. It was inaugurated in 1966 when the University of California Press published a comprehensive overview of the work of Professor Dumézil by a young anthropologist, C. Scott Littleton, who was the first of several who received their doctorates from UCLA under the de facto aegis of the Indo-European Studies program that had been instituted a few years earlier by Jaan Puhvel. Littleton's book, which was entitled *The New Comparative Mythology: An Anthropological Assessment of the Theories of Georges Dumézil* and went into a second, augmented edition in 1973, was followed in 1968 by the publication of Donald Ward's monograph, *The Divine Twins: An Indo-European Myth in Germanic Tradition*, as volume 19 of the University of California Publications series, *Folklore Studies*.

The year 1970 saw a relative explosion with the appearance in print of three separate titles comprising four volumes. California finally came out with the papers from a conference that had been held at UCLA March 17–18, 1967, in a volume edited by Jaan Puhvel under the title, *Myth and Law Among the Indo-Europeans: Studies in Indo-European Comparative Mythology*, while the University of Chicago Press, prodded no doubt by Dumézil's presence among the visiting faculty of their mother institution, issued translations of two of Dumézil's then recent books, *The Destiny of the Warrior* (translated by Alf Hiltebeitel from *Heur et malheur du guerrier: Apsects mythiques de la fonction guerrière chez les indo-européens* [Paris, 1967]) and the two-volume set, *Archaic Roman Religion, With an Appendix on the Religion of the Etruscans*, Preface by Mircea Eliade (translated by Philip Krapp from *La Religion romaine archïque, suivi d'un appendice sur la religion des Etrusques* [Paris, 1966], revised French edition, 1974).

Chicago continued to focus on translations, and two more appeared under their imprint in 1973: *From Myth to Fiction: The Saga of Hadingus* (translated by Derek Coltman from *Du mythe au roman: La Saga de Hadingus et autres essais* [Paris, 1970] and *The Destiny of a King* (translated by Alf Hiltebeitel from "Entre les dieux et les hommes: un roi," which constituted part three of *Mythe et épopée II* [Paris, 1971]. The same year California followed suit by bringing out *Gods of the Ancient Northmen*, an updated version of *Les Dieux des Germains: Essai sur la formation de la religion scandinave* (Paris, 1959), complemented by four essays on Germanic mythology which had previously appeared in other contexts. This ensemble was put together by Einar Haugen, who had farmed out the translation work to his Harvard students John Lindow, Alan Toth, Francis Charat, and George Gopen, and subsequently edited the results. A two-part introduction by C. Scott Littleton and myself serves to present the volume. Following its appearance along with its siblings, the publications trend entered a quiescent phase. The next year, 1974, saw only one title reach the light of day, when California brought out another volume of conference papers, *Myth in Indo-European Antiquity*, edited by Gerald James Larson and coedited by C. Scott Littleton and Jaan Puhvel. This collection is distinguished principally for including an essay by Dumézil, whose presence at the conference held in March, 1971 at Santa Barbara, California, marked the end of his academic sojourn in the United States.

With Dumézil's departure, his two American publishers fell into a silence that is just now being broken. Since returning to Paris, Dumézil's output has been frighteningly prodigious. Of the five major books to come from this period, *Camillus* is only the second study in English to deal entirely with problems of Roman religion. The principal part of the work is "La saison de l'Aurore," which forms the second section of *Mythe et épopée III* (Paris, 1973), and this is augmented by the first two appendices to that volume, followed by the eighth and ninth "Questions Romaines" which appeared originally at the end of *Fêtes romaines d'été et d'automne* (Paris, 1975). The selections were made conjointly by the editor and the author. It is hoped that this second wind will impel publishers here to make accessible yet more titles from the all-important corpus of Dumézil's writings, now that the way has been cleared by Dumézil's 1978 election to the Académie Française.

The English translations of Dumézil's work which have appeared are important not only because they endorse that work and make it accessible to a wider audience. These translations are also all from that part of Dumézil's corpus which Littleton has called the "phase de bilan," a program that the author began in 1966 and in which he offers a final summation of his thoughts and research on the Indo-European question. These books, then, represent Dumézil's revision, augmentation, and reconsideration of his earlier writings. In the case of each translation, Dumézil has made additional corrections to text and notes, so that the English versions are, by and large, definitive.

In 1977, in the foreword to his *Les dieux souverains des Indo-Européens*, Dumézil outlined the overall plan for his *bilan* and discussed its execution. The body of work is divided into three major groups: theological concerns, literary manifestations, and the traditions of individual Indo-European peoples.

The theological section focuses on myths and rituals containing traces of tripartition. Originally Dumézil had planned a panoramic overview, but he abandoned that project when he realized that this material was already contained in *Les dieux souverains des Indo-Européens, Archaic Roman Religion*, part two of *Mythe et épopée I*, 2d ed. (Paris, 1974), and *Gods of the Ancient Northmen*. Individual studies of each of the prongs of tripartition can be found in the aforementioned *Les dieux souverains des Indo-Européens* for sovereignty; in *Destiny of the Warrior* [and also in part one of *Mythe et épopée II*—curiously, Dumézil omits mentioning this work although it is clearly relevant] for the warrior problem; and in a yet-to-be-assembled collection of previously written articles, properly revised and commented on, for the third prong, which is diffused throughout the spectrum of concepts relating to welfare.

The literary group is complete and comprises the three-volume set of *Mythe et épopée*, to which may be added the volume *From Myth to Fiction*.

The final division is limited to dealing with the traditions of the Indo-Iranians, the Scyths, the Latins, and the Germans. In Dumézil's view, the panorama in Celtic and Greek tradition—and presumably in Baltic and Slavic as well—is too mutilated to repay the effort of a separate study for each of them. The introduction to *Les dieux souverains des Indo-Européens* deals with some of the Indo-Iranian problems, and a collection of essays is foreseen to complete that dossier. A second such collection is planned to perform a similar function for the Scyths. The Latins and Germans have already been taken care of: *Archaic Roman Religion* constitutes the basic Latin compendium, and this work is complemented by *Idées romaines* (Paris, 1969), *Fêtes romaines d'été et d'automne, suivi de dix Questions romaines*, and the section "Quinze Questions romaines" from *Mariages indo-européens* (Paris, 1979). As for the Germans, *Gods of the Ancient Northmen*—and also *From Myth to Fiction*, notably the appended essays—represent Dumézil's final utterance on the subject. If further work on the Germans is to be done, it will be carried out by the likes of Werner Betz at Munich, or possibly someone else.

While this *bilan* is certainly systematic, the natural overlapping of categories deprives it of neatness. It is a matter of some comfort to realize that most of the important works have already been translated into English or are about to be, but there remains one sizeable hole in the fabric, and its name is *Mythe et épopée*. In retrospect, it appears to have been poor publishing strategy to have tackled the translation of these volumes piecemeal, as it is now clear that eventually there can be no substitute for having the whole set in English. But as long as past policy dictates the future course, then surely the next order of business should be to make Dumézil's latest—and presumably final—word on the warrior complex available by bringing out a translation of the first part of *Mythe et épopée II*, "L'enjeu du jeu des Dieux: Un heros (Śiśupāla, Starkaðr, Herakles)." This theoretical disquisition on the heroic predicament constitutes a tightly knit monograph in its own right as it takes the argument begun in *Destiny of the Warrior* through uncharted waters and launches a new perspective on the problem. It is self-evident that without a full understanding of the tensions and contrasts at work between the earlier and later studies no further progress on the warrior question can occur.

In closing, a note of caution should be sounded. While Dumézil's work is certainly compelling, it must not be mistaken for a closed system. Further research, even in areas already covered by Dumézil, is not only desirable but necessary if the discipline that he founded is to persevere. Readers interested in a complete and current bibliography of Dumézil's writings should consult Jean-Claude Rivière et al., eds., *Georges Dumézil à la découverte des Indo-Européens* (Paris, 1979), pp. 239–271. Although considerable attention is also given to the works of other scholars who have made noteworthy contributions to the field, whether or not they were influenced by Dumézil's thought, the bibliographies found in Puhvel, *Myth and Law Among the Indo-Europeans*, pp. 247–268 and in Littleton, *New Comparative Mythology*, pp. 239–259 contain additional valuable material and in general benefit from a more judicious selection.

Index

Compositor:	Freedmen's Organization
Printer:	Braun-Brumfield, Inc.
Binder:	Braun-Brumfield, Inc.
Text:	Compugraphic Palladium
Cloth:	Holliston Roxite C
Paper:	50 lb. P&S Offset

269